The ArtScroll Series®

מסורה

Rabbi Nosson Scherman / Rabbi Meir Zlotowitz

General Editors

Times of

Published by

Mesorah Publications, ltd

Challenge

Inspiring stories of triumph over fear and adversity

by Seryl Sander

FIRST EDITION
First Impression . . . May, 1988

Published and Distributed by
MESORAH PUBLICATIONS, Ltd.
Brooklyn, New York 11223

Distributed in Israel by
MESORAH MAFITZIM / J. GROSSMAN
Rechov Harav Uziel 117
Jerusalem, Israel

Distributed in Europe by
J. LEHMANN HEBREW BOOKSELLERS
20 Cambridge Terrace
Gateshead, Tyne and Wear
England NE8 1RP

THE ARTSCROLL SERIES®
TIMES OF CHALLENGE
© Copyright 1988 by MESORAH PUBLICATIONS, Ltd.
1969 Coney Island Avenue / Brooklyn, N.Y. 11223 / (718) 339-1700

ISBN:
0-89906-556-2 (hard cover)
0-89906-557-0 (paperback)

Printed in the United States of America by Noble Book Press Corp.
Bound by Sefercraft Quality Bookbinders, Ltd., Brooklyn, N.Y.

This book is dedicated to
the memory of my dear parents

ר׳ יצחק אליעזר בן ר׳ מרדכי ע״ה

ט׳ אדר ב׳ תש״ל

מרת סעריל שײנדל בת הר״ר שמחה נתן ע״ה

כ״ז תשרי תש״מ

They eternalized the unique qualities of that special breed, known as *"tzu G-t un tzu leit."* It can rightfully be said of them, כמים הפנים לפנים לב האדם לאדם, *as a face is reflected by water, so is a human heart reflected by another* (*Mishlei* 27:19).

They were loved and respected by all who knew them. They passed on a proud European, chassidic heritage to their children, and left them and their fellow Jews a legacy of caring and sharing, as they did in their lifetime. May they be *melitzei yosher* for their children and look down favorably upon our *maasim*.

תנצב״ה

736 WEST 186TH STREET
NEW YORK. N. Y. 10033
———
RES: 927-0498
OFFICE: 923-5936

שמעון שוואב
אב"ד דק"ק
קהל עדת ישרון
נוא-יארק, נ.י.

To the Editors:

I have read the articles which you sent me and I was
overwhelmed with the outpouring of Emunoh and Bitachon
which is found on every page. This book both makes you
weep and it makes you wipe away your tears and smile.
Although I would suggest to change once in a while certain expressions, as a whole this is a powerful Mussar
Sefer which will do a great service for mature and emotionally healthy people. For some of the weaker souls
it may not always have the desired effect. To all those
who have a foundation of true Emunoh either from childhood or by adoption, you are giving a strong dose of
Chizuk to the many who are in dire need of it. The z'chus
of this labor of Chesed which you have undertaken is
immeasurable.

Simon Schwab

Rav Simon Schwab

Iyar 5748

R🜨FEH INTERNATIONAL

Reaching Out -   Furnishing Emergency Healthcare

GRAND RABBI L.Y. HOROWITZ
THE BOSTONER REBBE

RABBI MAYER A. HOROWITZ
N.E.C.C. DIRECTOR

בס״ד

Rosh Chodesh Iyar 5748

The Talmud relates many stories which are meant to emphasize
a particular point, important to Jewish life. Many times it
is by means of a story that one can get a point across, even
more so than by the direct approach. Throughout Chassidic
history we find the story used as the medium to deliver the
proper message. It is because of this that TIMES OF CHALLENGE
edited by Seryl Sander and published by ArtScroll is such
an important addition to the wonderful literature being published today. Emunah, faith; bitochon, trust; tikvah, hope; all
come across clearly in the chapters of this book, recited by
people whose experiences and behavior should serve as inspiration to us all.

  Providing help to the desperately ill and their families
is certainly a special mitzvah. Chizuk and support to them
should be the goal of all who can provide it. TIMES OF CHALLENGE
certainly does.

  May Hashem Yisborach spare us agony and pain in the zchus
of this mitzvah. May he bless all of us with the best of health,
and nachas from our loved ones.

    Sincerely yours,

    The Bostoner Rebbe

1710 BEACON STREET•BROOKLINE, MASSACHUSETTS•02146•(617) 566-9182

Foreword

by Rabbi David Grossman, C.S.W.
Director of Pastoral Service
Metropolitan Jewish Geriatric Center
Brooklyn, New York

אברכה את ה׳ בכל עת תמיד תהלתו בפי (תהלים לד:ב)

Human experience has its times of joy and sadness; its moments of victory and defeat; and its periods of accomplishment and futility. Such was the life of the immortal King of Israel, David. His life was filled with harrowing experiences, with trials and tribulations, miraculous deliverances and great achievements.

At the moment of his severest affliction, when he was forced to flee for his life from King Saul and seek refuge among the enemies of his people — upon his deliverance he proclaimed: "I shall praise Hashem at *all* times; let His praise continuously remain in my mouth" (*Tehillim* 34:2). Having been cast down from the heights of success and popularity to such depths of despair, King David did not lose his courage to weather this stormy period in his difficult life. Even though he had been despised and rejected by men, he was fortified with blissful awareness that Hashem was constantly at his side, helping him to the goal of ultimate salvation. His miraculous escape had taught him that under no circumstances should one complain against Hashem, since all His ways are infused with kindness and mercy. Realizing that man cannot comprehend the implications of every given situation in life, King David humbly accepted his lot with the knowledge that Hashem directs the world at all times for the benefit of the wise and righteous. Therefore, even in times of tragedy, he understood that there is reason to bless Hashem.

Since the path of life is strewn with difficulties and pain, King David taught us a cardinal truth of our Faith: "All the paths of Hashem are kindness and truth" (*Tehillim* 25:10). If the sufferings are decreed to atone for prior sin, then they are truth, justly deserved. However, if they come to test the sufferer in order to bring him closer to Hashem, then they are kindness, an opportunity offered by a loving and caring Hashem.

This essential topic of faith, which is one of the most fundamental aspects of Torah *hashkofah*, was seized by King David at every opportunity to expound in public gatherings. He felt obliged to announce the many acts of kindness that Hashem had performed so the masses would be inspired to trust Hashem, as the *posuk* states: "I proclaimed Your righteousness in a vast assembly" (*Tehillim* 40:10).

It is with these thoughts that we welcome the publication of this precious volume — a collection of true case histories of very trying situations in the lives of individuals and their families. It is a herald of news, a source of inspiration and guidance to us all in facing the great struggles of life. As we read these personal experiences of those who have suffered in misery and tragedy, we begin to realize how much *emunah* and *bitachon* we need to face the realities of life and thereby, be worthy of individual Divine Providence.

Happy and blessed is the man of *emunah* who wholeheartedly places his trust in the munificent compassion and kindness of Hashem, in his profound awareness that it is Hashem alone Who is the sole arbiter of man's destiny.

ברוך הגבר אשר יבטח בה' והיה ה' מבטחו (ירמיה יז:ז)

Acknowledgments

For their devotion and confidence in me, my thanks to all my friends who didn't want their names in print.

For Miriam (Rottenberg) Berger who was "always ready" and who helped with suggestions and constructive criticism. Thanks for painstakingly proof-reading and correcting the galleys. For my neighbors who helped me unwittingly in many ways. I knew I could always depend on you.

To Rabbi David Grossman, who wrote the preface, my special thanks. Your *mentchlichkeit* and eagerness to help in this and other projects will always be remembered. You helped me more than you'll ever know.

I would like to express my recognition to Rabbi Chaim Wainkrantz whose example and inspiration helped me confront all my challenges, great and small.

Thanks to all the individuals, especially Mrs. Feig and my sisters, all in the חנוך field, who took time out from their busy schedules to look over the galleys and called me with their positive feedback. Every phone call meant so much.

To all the staff at the O.D.A. Medical Center in Brooklyn, I am grateful to you all for your constant support. Access to the copying machine at all times was crucial to me in the months of preparing my manuscript.

To Mr. L. Moskowitz, Administrator of Aishel Avraham in Brooklyn and Mrs. R. Hoffman, Director of volunteers, I want to say *yasher koach*. You touched me with your appreciation of my work. You gave me carte blanche to the copy room and provided the Home's facilities and equipment whenever I requested your assistance.

For my family, without whose help and encouragement this book could not be possible — I thank you for all your understanding, patience, co-operation and support while I was pre-occupied with the publication of this book. May *Hakodosh Boruch Hu* bless your lives with *brochos* and *mazel*. May we merit the coming of *Moshiach* speedily and in our days and be reunited with our parents and grandparents.

To everyone who contributed stories and invaluable life experiences to inspire a broad reading public: I can only say that I feel privileged to know you all. My life has been enriched in the years since we've been involved together in the production of *Times of Challenge*. Some of you have become special friends. May you always feel that unique relationship with the *Ribono shel Olam*. May He shower you all with His blessings of *kol tuv*. Thank you for helping me invest the message of the *posuk* in *Tehillim* through the pages of this book, טעמו וראו כי טוב ה' אשרי הגבר יחסה בו . — "Taste and see that Hashem is good; fortunate is the man who takes refuge in Him."

Thanks to Rabbi Sheah Brander: Your graphic style and creativity makes this book so appealing.

To Rabbi Meir Zlotowitz and Rabbi Nosson Scherman, General Editors of Mesorah Publications, my respectful thanks and appreciation for your sensitivity and understanding of my project. It is a privilege to join the roster of impressive ArtScroll publications. Thank you for assisting me in my personal goal of spreading *chizuk*, comfort and inspiration to the general public.

I am indebted to Mrs. Judi Dick, for giving her talent and time in editing this unique book. A combination of her skills and depth of *hashkofoh* (outlook) enhanced the layout and final results of this book that exceeded my own expectations. May I humbly and respectfully state that you have my profoundest appreciation for what you did. This experience has perpetuated a meaningful friendship. ישלם ה' שכרם כגמולכם הטוב.

I must extend special thanks to Rabbi Avie Gold of ArtScroll who always made himself available to help with any problem, large or small. He guided me in the world of publishing and was always congenial and helpful.

For Mrs. Menucha Silver and Chavie Gluck, my thanks for your diligence and enthusiasm as you "movingly" typeset the stories, and for your graciousness under stress.

The greatest *shevach v'hodoah* to the *Ribono shel Olam* — אין אנחנו מספיקים להודות לך ה'. We still could not thank You sufficiently Hashem, our G-d — for Your infinite kindness and *siyatah d'Shmayah* in every aspect of our lives.

Many sincere thanks to the Berger family for the supplement: The Jewish Way to Suffering, the perfect ending to Times of Challenge. The message written in Mrs. Berger's o"h inimitable style is: "Keep strong, have faith in Your compassionate Father, You can do it אשריך וטוב לך. I have only one regret that I never met this illustrious lady who has been described as a queen. It is a privilege to feature this precious work in my book.

To all the above my heartfelt thanks ימלא ה' כל משאלות לבכם — May Hashem grant your every wish.

Seryl Sander
ב' סיון תשמ"ח
May 19, 1988

Cover Painting

By Sharon Lichtenthal.

הנה לא ינום ולא יישן שומר ישראל

Before going to sleep every night, I say these words in the *Shema*. Knowing that Hashem protects my soul while I sleep allows me to rest peacefully. The next morning Hashem restores my soul to my body so that I may continue to praise Him and observe His commandments.

In this painting, the golden Hebrew letters dance in space, they are timeless. The letters, both transparent and opaque, have a feel of inner and outer movement. Hashem is everywhere, knows everything and transcends time, space and form. The Guardian of Israel watches over His people and all mankind at all times and even more so in . . . times of challenge.

[Sharon Lichtenthal is an art therapist who works with cancer patients. She has become sensitized to the unique relationships that the *baal nisayon* has with his Creator. This painting is her tribute to the courageous: the cancer survivors who embrace and cherish life and those who were *niftar* with an unwavering faith. Glossy prints of her cover painting may be ordered from the artist: Sharon Lichtenthal, c/o Mrs. S. Freilich, 116 Rutledge St., Brooklyn N.Y. 11211.]

Table of Contents

❧ The Jewish Way to Suffering

❧ Poems

Introduction — Tales of Triumph

W hat does a driver do when his car goes into a sudden skid and his mind goes blank with panic?

What does a mother do when she is hit with the thunderbolt that her baby has a crippling, life-threatening illness?

Or if she learns that she herself has only months to live and that her loved ones will soon be without her?

These crisis are different, but, in a way, they and all desperate situations are similar. When the awful moment arrives, we often can't think. Our calm deserts us and our instincts take over. And instincts are often wrong; that is why this book is so inspiring, so informative, so useful and so important.

This book is about people who coped, and grew, and triumphed. Sometimes there was a happy ending and sometimes not, but even when the patient did not survive, the people who shared their stories with us emerged stronger, nobler, wiser, more caring, with overflowing reservoirs of faith and gratitude. Even they — despite aching wishes that the end could have been different — gained so much from their ordeal that they were glad to share with us the struggles and triumphs of an excruciating slice of life.

In commenting on *Akeidas Yitzchak* (the binding of Isaac upon the altar), *Chiddushei HaRim* says that Abraham could not be tested by a sudden command to put a knife to his son's throat; a person's senses can desert him at such a traumatic moment. Rather, Abraham — and all people — was being tested for how he had prepared for the challenge. Every human being can fill his internal storehouses of faith, compassion, and perspective so that his instincts are molded and honed in time for the awful moment that we pray will never come. That is the purpose of this book. We are convinced that our readers will be forewarned and forearmed, and the marvelous people who bared their innermost selves in this book have done it because they have treasures to share, and they care enough to do it.

Perhaps my own experience will be a good example.

A few years ago I was helped and deeply touched by a mother who reached out to me with extraordinary *chessed* (kindness). For Sury it was a natural gesture; I will never forget it. When she called, my husband and I were in the hospital with our year-old baby. It was the second week since his diagnosis with a malignant tumor, a cancer that can be a sentence of death. Most of my family lived out of town. We were lonely and bewildered. We were new to the trauma of serious illness. The urgency of my baby's condition permitted no time for investigating other doctors or treatment protocols. We leaned on our *Tehillim*. A *bikur cholim* volunteer knew Sury well and asked her to respond to a need, my need. Sury knew only that I had a very sick baby and that I must be as lonely and afraid as she had been when she was in my shoes. Her daugther had been diagnosed two years earlier with a different tumor, and she had completed her treatment successfully. Sury had a lot to share with me. After listening for a few minutes, I felt transformed. She reassured me about the medical center and its competent, caring staff. We were at the threshold of the next phase of my son's illness, as he was about to begin chemotherapy. Sury gave me a crash course, but with a twist. She was feeding me information that I could have easily had from my son's nurses; and they were all dedicated and loving. But this was different — because Sury was a Jewish mother, with a heart like mine, who strengthened me with her verses of *Tehillim* and her blessings. She asked if she could visit me one day soon. I eagerly awaited her visit and it was the start of a precious friendship. The months ahead were filled with new experiences and anxieties. She was always there to smooth the way with her phone calls, advice and encouragement.

Seven years have passed. *Baruch Hashem*, my son is a survivor. We are grateful to *Hashem Yisbarach* and we are ever so proud of him and our other children. He is a victor — even though he is in a wheelchair. He attends yeshivah, he is happy in the mainstream of life. When his class was about to be transferred to a different department of his yeshivah, I went to thank his principal and his rebbe for everything they had done, but they would not let me. *They* thanked *me* for the experience of having him as a student. I broke down in tears. I probably had not cried as much since those terrifying first days after his diagnosis. But now they were tears of joy. And I don't know if it could have happened without the process started by Sury, because she helped me learn a new definition of victory.

I have a tremendous gratitude to Sury and the many others that supported me in my time of need. Thanks to them it became natural for me to respond in kind, to be there for others who were treading new waters with sick children. I have witnessed the healing effects of *chizuk*, when it is offered genuinely. There is real comfort in knowing that someone else can relate to your problem. The heaviness of the heart can sometimes be too much for a soul to bear. Fear creates awful isolation. The effects of reaching out with this kind of *chessed*, of sharing experiences and feelings, can break through the needless barriers of fear. There is comfort in meeting those who have suffered and who have recovered; who have survived and resumed their lives. To envision yourself a few months or years down the road of life as you see those who have suffered and come back to a measure of themselves, this is the partial comfort. The knowledge that the road back from the *tzarah* can be scaled — that it is not impossible — is the first inkling that a measure can be acquired.

It is because of this personal experience that I, like many others, resolved to devote much of my time and energy to caring about others and sharing my experience with them. Each of us has received much more than we have given because faith and strength are contagious. It was not easy for the heroes and heroines in this book — the victors — to share their agony with others. But when we asked them to help others by telling their intimate stories, these brave people all agreed. Uniformly, their response was, "If I can help even one person, I will gladly share my experience with you."

Some of the stories in the book were written by the people involved, others are taken from taped interviews. All are the unembellished truth, though some of the names have been changed to protect the privacy of the families. Most of them are anxious to help others who need them.

The statement at the end of the *shivah* visit, המקום ינחם אתכם בתוך שאר אבלי ציון וירושלים — "The Omnipresent will comfort you among the other mourners of tzion and Jerusalem," is not a wish, or a blessing, or a hope that the bereaved will be comforted. It is a charge, and an expression of faith — "Hashem *will indeed* comfort you." Just as all those who have loved and lost before have eventually been comforted, so too, will you. The survivor says, "I can tell you. I've been there." This is the moving testimony of the cancer survivor who describes his ordeal with great pathos, who lifts us with the hope he felt when treatment was finished, and then expresses his soaring gratitude after being off treatment for five years. He tells about the relief after every check-up that makes him feel like a million dollars.

Those who died are also victors — they and their loved ones came to accept the harsh decree without diminished *bitachon* and *emunah* in Hashem. That they — as a result of their attitudes towards death and dying — enable us to better ourselves and our attitudes towards life is to their eternal credit.

We invite the reader to become acquainted with these profiles in courage as I did. Their perspective of themselves and the world around them has most assuredly changed. They have a different vision now, a greater clarity of purpose, a more finely tuned sense of what is important and how to help those who are in the throes of illness and those who have suffered. The reader is urged to master these feelings through the description of their *yesurim*, and thereby to elevate his own existence.

❀   ❀   ❀

One final caveat. This treasury of inspiration should be taken in small doses. It should be read one moving story at a time. Read one and set the book aside. Let the message of hope ferment and percolate within your soul. Then, in a day or two, read another. Each story will mean so much more to you that way.

This book contains the essence of human souls, the essence of triumph, the essence of challenge surmounted. It will thrill you and enrich you. And if it does, you will join the company of victors.

A Crisis to be Weathered

You Can Get Anywhere on Spirit

ואני תמיד עמך אחזת ביד ימיני (תהלים עג:כג)

My son became paralyzed from the waist down due to a malignant tumor at the age of thirteen months. He had a neuroblastoma that affects babies and young children. However, this is not a story of gloom; this is a story of an enchanting, invincible boy who dares anyone to become depressed about his limitations as he sways to the rhythm of Shabbos *zmiros* in his wheelchair. But more important, it is a story of *bitachon* and how I felt overwhelmed with the comfort of the *Ribono shel Olam* and His kindness.

Five weeks of lethargy and physical weakness in the lower extremities ended with x-rays and a spinal tap that spelled it out for us. It was Divinely ordained that very competent doctors could not detect my baby's problem. Hashem had covered their eyes but now it was revealed that Yanky's unusual symptoms were caused by a malignant tumor. This caused an unexpected interruption in his normal development. On that day in the winter of 1981 we were hurled unprepared into a world of neurosurgeons and specialists in my son's condition. The primary goal was to relieve pressure from Yanky's spine and prevent any further damage. The neurosurgeon explained the pattern of my son's tumor and a very humanitarian oncologist, Dr. M., described the chemotherapy program that would be designed for Yanky's ultimate cure, with help from Above. The field of chemo was a familiar one to me. I had lost my mother not long before. During those trying times I had developed a life-line, a link to my dependable *Tehillim*. I remembered being strengthened in difficult days when my mother's condition worsened. *He will not fear bad tidings, his heart is steadfast trusting in Hashem (Psalms 112:7).* I knew a big challenge awaited us: How not to become depressed and worried about my baby's life-threatening illness. I swallowed hard as I listened to a capsule outline of the next eighteen months. These would be our messengers of good will. My son was a patient in Royal Victoria Hospital, a center with an excellent reputation. We were doing our part. Now I pass my burden to You, Hashem. Your shoulders are broad enough. Relieve us of our concerns and help us, was my silent prayer.

After midnight Yanky was wheeled into the operating room for his emergency surgery. We settled down for the night. I thought of my bond with Yanky; I had overwhelming tenderness for him. He was my fourth child and he came into my life on the heels of losing my mother. Yes, I was very attached to him but what of the *Ribono shel Olam* and His love for every one of His creations? Lessons from *hashkafah* classes reminded me that His love for my child and myself knew no bounds. When Hashem endowed man with sensations and emotions, it was a mere sampling of the true feelings that we will experience in the World to Come. So even a mother's strong love for her child cannot compare with the love Hashem has for all His creations. I focused on this basic principle of *emunah* and spoke to Hashem, "Father of all children, compassionate Father, I love my child so and I implore You to send Your guardian angels to protect Him. I'm asking You because I can't help him now. But You, Hashem, You created him; You love him; and You know what's good for us. I know You also have the power to heal him. I now resign my child to Your care. Send Your protective angels to watch him and to guide the surgeon." I slept until the morning. Dr. R. informed us that the surgery was successful. Later we learned that Yanky would undergo additional surgery to remove the mass from his chest when he was sufficiently recovered.

The pediatric staff at Royal Victoria were very accommodating and his recovery was uncomplicated. A secondary tumor had done irreversible damage. Yanky was unable to feel sensation or bear weight. Hashem gave me the thoughts that strengthened me for what lay ahead. I felt it was the merit of generations past that kept me going. כי אבי ואמי עזבוני וה׳ יאספני. I no longer had my parents, but I now felt direct contact to Heaven.

The *Tehillim* became my best friend. I involved Yanky, who was just regaining his former spirit, in a *shevach vehodaah* project during his seven week hospital stay. I would come into his room in the morning and discuss his progress. "We're going to say *modeh ani*, Yanky. Guess what we'll thank Hashem for? Well, today you smiled at me. You also took your first drink of milk. You know Hashem gets our thanks for every little thing." And so the days passed. I discovered an awareness that Hashem was protecting me and my baby. We walked in the halls with Yanky's I.V. pole in tow. He was the first baby in the hospital to have a broviac (an in-dwelling catheter) installed that would facilitate procedures when he started his chemotherapy. We were introduced to elementary nursing as we cared for his broviac and filled syringes. It proved to be a blessing in disguise. He only suffered minimum trauma because most of the blood-drawing and all his chemo was done through the broviac. When he got stuck countless times (blood tests in the clinic) I comforted him and crooned to him, "It's all right to cry, *tattile*, because Hashem hears you. He's right beside you. He cares for you and He will help us." After six weeks he had sufficiently recovered for his first round of chemotherapy. It was not an easy day for me. I had recent memories of my parents' reaction to these same poisonous drugs. With Yanky's head nestled on my shoulder, I started our daily *bitachon* talk. "Do you know what *bitachon* is, my sweet child? *Bitachon* means when we can put our complete trust in Hashem. When we feel that and we can relax knowing that we are secure in His hands, that's the best feeling there is. And today is a very special day. We will tell Hashem, 'We trust You completely because You know what is good for us. And You will put the proper thoughts in the doctors' heads. They will know what doses of medicine will help in the cure.' You know, Yanky, a person like this not only trusts Hashem, he becomes relaxed and content." I found myself in a compulsive dance with Yanky and an I.V. pole as I sang *Ivdu es Hashem besimchah*. I bit my lips and tears burned in my eyes, but I sang.

Soon after, we were discharged. We would come back every month for a three-day in-patient treatment and intermittently for blood tests. I did passive exercises with Yanky. There was no return of sensation and I had to accept the fact that the tumor had rendered him paralyzed. Yanky was a real trooper and *shlepped* around the house using his upper arms and stomach muscles. He was very alert and happy.

Hashem was very good to us. Yanky tolerated the chemo well. He was on a vitamin regimen that counteracted the nausea and vomiting side-effects. He lost all his blond curly hair, including his eyebrows and eyelashes. After ten rounds the doctor reviewed his case and decided it was enough. I felt that the doctors' decision was Heaven sent. I decorated the bulletin board in his room with phrases of thanks to Hashem and explained the meaning of the words to curious medical students.

In that year we had watched the passing seasons. I used to describe the various scenes to Yanky. One cold winter day we looked at our backyard, the abandoned swing-set covered with snow, the trees barren and the air desolate. "We can't see it, but the activity of renewal is beginning beneath the cold snow. Do you see those trees? There will be buds one day, which will turn into blossoms and leaves. Now if Hashem can transform this into a living breathing sprouting spring, can't He help you?"

His older brother listened fascinated and remarked, "Mummy, when Yanky starts yeshivah, he'll know all about creation."

In the summer, I used to give him daily rides around the camp grounds on a Big Wheel. He was only eighteen months, but he loved to do what the others were doing. I folded his legs in front of him and attached a rope to the handle. I described the scenery as we made our rounds. "Look, Yanky, so many beautiful flowers and trees. Look at that hill. That's a monarch butterfly we just saw and a rare yellow one on the dahlia there. Let's stop and watch these busy ants build their home. Yanky, quick! or we'll miss the sunset. Isn't it just breathtaking?! Do you know who does all this? Do you know who's in charge here, Yanky? Of course it's Hashem. Now if He can make the birds fly, the ants crawl, the trees and flowers grow, the sun set, can't He help one little boy? Can't He make you get well?" This nourishment for my soul and for Yanky's soul kept us going.

When we came back to the city we were scheduled for a C.T. scan. The nurse had given him an injection, but the anesthetic didn't take completely. He was fussy on the table as the technicians readied the camera. I was beside him and soothed him. I called silently to Hashem to protect him, to send us good results. When the big camera was lowered on his chest I could see panic in his eyes. I sang a lullabye to the words מן המצר קראתי קה ענני קה במרחב קה over and over till the test was done. Even in the confines of the scanning machine I find You, Hashem. There is a saying, "Where is the *Aybishter*? Wherever you let Him in." The scan results were fine. We were ready for the second phase of Yanky's care: rehabilitation.

For us this was a lesson in relativity. Yanky was a survivor and we were grateful that we could talk in terms of progress. I remember overhearing two women whisper at a tea, "I wonder how she's taking it."

Many months later I spoke casually to one of them and said, "Yanky is our challenge and with help from Above we're dealing with it. He's coming along fine."

We entered the world of orthotics and braces. Dr. Shaw's goal was to make Yanky stand and try different equipment for ambulation. He was measured for braces. It was very exciting. The day that he was fitted was dramatic. We were *zocheh* to see Yanky stand before our eyes. With happy tears I clutched him close to me as I said the *"shehecheyanu"* blessing. "I want to walk to the window," Yanky said. Sweeter words were never heard. He was two and a half. He soon mastered the walker with ease and enjoyed using it outdoors. He knew how to handle curious onlookers. Someone approached his aide Kathy and questioned her about her charge's status. He turned and advised her, "Never mind, Kathy. We're going for a walk."

Yanky's haircutting deserved the fanfare it got. After a year and a half of baldness he had Shirley Temple locks. When he was four and a half we registered Yanky in *cheder*. His sweet nature developed as he grew. We were amazed that he had a special gift, a sense of humor. He was able to find joy in other's fun, even when he was limited. When he started nursery, his teacher devised different methods to "bring out his personality." She thought of a remote control car, but Yanky was already giggling, watching three boys compete for a little car. It didn't matter that he couldn't get on it and ride; others' joy made him happy. When his younger siblings took their first halting steps he cheered them on. He watched in fascination and shared the family excitement with his older sisters and brothers.

Yanky fell and broke his leg. He tolerated eight weeks in a body cast. What a trooper — in the heat of the summer. When the leg healed and he was back in his braces, he referred to the fracture and cast as the cause for his disability. "Once I had a broken leg and that's why I wear these braces. That's the way I walk now."

The fracture interrupted his physical therapy but he quickly caught up. On one of his walks with his walker, he headed for the corner store with Kathy. I was across the street and watched them.

Mr. Gross beamed at this four year old making his way prudently into the store and greeted him cheerfully, "*Shalom aleichem*, Yanky. So nice of you to come in today."

"*Aleichem shalom*, Mr. Gross, this is Kathy. Kathy this is the grocery store and this is Mr. Gross. I'm going to buy a licorice. Please put it on my mother's bill. Okay? Bye bye."

Most mothers consider the daily bus pick-up a normal event. Yanky's first pick-up by a genuine yellow bus was a grand occasion for us. The *cheder* was very accommodating and they removed one seat to allow a parking space for his wheelchair. (He had a second walker in school for ambulation.) That day was a grand occasion for us and all the neighbors who proudly watched. "One small step for man, one giant leap for mankind." I got on the bus to share the view and hugged and kissed him wishing him good luck on his first run. He was dumbstruck and had nothing to say. In *cheder* he charmed his way into the *rebbe's* heart and became an instant hit with his little friends. Both his walker and wheelchair were objects of great interest. Hashem blessed him and as he progressed in learning he was at the top of his class. He considered himself normal, with the same needs as other five year olds.

He decorated his wheelchair armrests with Royal Mounties stickers proclaiming, "When I'll grow up, I'll be a Mountie!" Brave little boy, he asked to go to the grocery for me. "Are you afraid that someone will kidnap me?" he asked, noticing my hesitancy. "Don't worry. I'll grab him and choke him and he'll run away!" I was convinced.

We reviewed basic safety rules and he promised he would ask for help from a grownup if he needed it. He returned home, triumphant, everything intact in a bag behind him on his handlebars. "Look, Mummy, I didn't even break a single egg."

I visited school one day and noticed a certain rowdy boy, and wondered if some of his friends were wild. "Oh, him? He wasn't always wild. Me and Shmuly made him wild."

One day after physical therapy we took a city bus home. It was our first ride on a specially designed bus for the handicapped. Yanky loved the special service he got from the driver. The rear ramp became a lift. I stepped on with Yanky and his wheelchair. The driver pushed a button to lift us into the bus.

Once on an outing with some friends we had occasion to use this type of bus again. As the bus backed up and parked near us, he waited patiently looking like a prince on his throne waiting for the royal treatment. A few stops later a young handicapped man got on and was positioned in front of Yanky. He turned around and greeted him, "Hi, fella!" Yanky was shy and overwhelmed, but the next question got a smile from him. "Do you know how to pop a wheelie?" (This means lifting up on the hind wheels to get up a curb) As the man left he gave Yanky a thumbs up sign. Comrades in arms.

If I had to take inventory of my family and assess how we've adjusted, I would offer an opinion by my eleven-year-old daughter. She told us about Yanky and why Hashem made him different. "He can't run and play catch or ride a bike like other boys. I think Hashem just has people in different roles for a reason. He needs certain parts acted out; so different people get the roles that are suitable for them. Special parts are reserved for special people who can do a great job. These are the most important parts in every play. Hashem chose us to be the right family to help Yanky develop and He made Yanky the star by giving him a special and beautiful part, because Hashem has confidence in Yanky and knows that he will do it right."

Yanky flourishes as he grows. When he was in grade three he no longer had door-to-door service. On a rainy day I greeted him as he raced home. With a smile a mile wide he was telling me, "Look, Mummy, I'm like everyone. I come home in the rain."

Now we just come to the clinic once a year for routine checkups. It's six years since Yanky's ordeal. What a blessing that he doesn't remember his hospital days or treatment ways. We visit the pediatric floor which was a vital part of our lives and some of his nurses are still on staff. They ooh and aah over him, exclaim how he's grown, hug him, talk to him, and he stares blankly, oblivious to this outpouring of affection.

Yanky's home therapy helped him reach a new goal — crutches. This was a new adjustment and required a great deal of perseverance and balance.

About a year into this stage of walking Yanky proved once more that you can get anywhere on spirit. The therapist was ready to let go and Yanky took off on his maiden voyage. A policeman on the beat obligingly halted traffic for his first crossing attempt. Before long he was making it before the light changed — triumph written all over his face. I practiced with him outside and many interested pedestrians looked our way. Yanky had mixed reactions to this unnecessary attention. One day he insisted that he wasn't going to take another step till a staring toddler moved out of his way.

Self-confidence personified, he's a pleasure. In *shul*, he's the ringleader. Strangers tell me about his antics and his older sister says, "This boy is so delicious! You can get addicted to him!"

One spring Yanky painted a T-shirt with a message, "I'm Mummy's *kiddush Hashem*." No looks of pity, please. We're all proud of Yanky.

Yanky was due for a new wheelchair. We got a modern stream-lined European import fifteen pounds lighter than the old model. Yanky cruised around in his new chair. It was classy looking with red upholstery and didn't give that invalid impression. The footrests on this model have metal in a criss-cross slat design. Yanky's always decorating his chair. One day he highlighted the footrests with some novel stickers: "Dangerous wires. Beware of *lashon hara*." Wherever he goes he looks like a blond prince on a throne.

One summer day I observed him outside and enjoyed the banter as he played with his friends. They were sitting on their Big Wheels and he was in his Row Car (rehabilitative car) "alive with pleasure." I watched him enjoy living.

Yanky progressed from the elementary walking to steps. He suggested to the therapist that they go upstairs on a tour of the bedrooms. Bursting with pride I watched my seven year old son walk the rooms of his home on his own two feet for the first time. We really know the theory of relativity. For us it was a horn tooting occasion and we had a small Shabbos party for his friends. On that day he told me proudly, "Mummy, I'm going to walk to the Champlain Bridge one day!"

Hashem has given us bountiful *chasadim* and *zchusim*. The joy of Yanky is difficult to articulate. The *naches* of watching this boy develop into a unique personality is rewarding in itself. The potential that he has, the ways in which he touches people in his life (as one of his Rebbes said, "It's a *sipuk nefesh* to have him in my class," are all *matnas chinam*.

May Hashem give us the wisdom and Divine guidance to raise him properly. May Hashem preserve Yanky, give him life so that he can be a true servant of Hashem and grow in the wisdom of the Torah and *Yiras Shomayim*.

❦   ❦   ❦

[Yanky is eight years old, doing very well in *cheder*. He enjoys a lively social life, is mobile and active, a real presence in his *shul* and community. The sky's the limit! — Ed.]

A Different Kind of Success Story

כי אבי ואמי עזבוני וה' יאספני (תהלים כז:י)

There have been many success stories of those who survived cancer. This is not one. This is, however, a different kind of success story. After two years, I have "successfully", but not painlessly, survived my mother's battle with cancer.

My mother suffered a very rare form of liver cancer diagnosed as hepatoma. We see only a few cases a year in the United States. After numerous blood tests, a sonogram, and a C.T. scan, Mom and I sat in the oncologist's office, awaiting the verdict. Dr. K. gently told Mom, who was a mere forty-eight years old, that he, with the help of G-d, would fight this illness. Mom left the conference room to be examined. Before Dr. K. left the room to meet her, he turned to me and said, "She has maybe five to eight weeks to live. Someone must know." I felt the blood drain from my face. I was frozen in my chair. How could this be? She had just begun to live. After my father's untimely passing, life was difficult for her. She, however, went back to school and trained to be a gemologist. She eventually started her own successful business. Her children were married with children of their own. She now had the time to do the things she wanted to do. Dr. K. was telling me now it was over. How could it be possible?

My mother and I left the office together. She was to begin chemotherapy treatments immediately. I could barely look into her eyes for fear I would cry. I ask myself now, why didn't I cry? As I search the past, I realize that she did not want me to.

We stood on the corner before reaching my car. She looked at me and said, "Don't give up. I will tell you when it's time." I drove her home. Thus began the incredible battle she fought.

Dr. K. administered the chemotherapy treatments without hope. The tumors grew rapidly. I asked him to refrain from telling her this. She was full of enthusiasm and I did not want him to dampen her spirits. She did, however, know that the pendulum could swing both ways. She had to be aware that there was a possibility the treatments would be ineffective.

The treatments were quite difficult for her. There were many side effects that were more difficult than the illness itself.

There are some in our family who believe that Mom lived an additional six months because of the treatments. There are those who believe it was the strong will that Hashem blessed her with. During those long months, she lived to see the births of two grandchildren. She managed to put all her affairs in order.

On the night of her birthday, after a wonderful family celebration together, she slipped into a coma. She died the next day. I held her hand as she drew her last breath.

❃   ❃   ❃

The *shivah* period was a time that I spent with her friends and associates. I took comfort in hearing about some aspects of her life outside of her family. Although some people were afraid to speak of her for fear it might hurt me, others tried successfully to recount stories about her. These anecdotes exemplified her true *midos*.

During this time I had to face the difficult task of telling my children their grandmother would no longer visit them. I decided that only the truth would work. I explained that she had been quite ill. They were already aware of this because I was spending time with her, away from home. I explained that although she loved us, she could no longer visit. It was time for her to return to Hashem. She would have a complete recovery there.

I finished by reminding them that after *Mashiach* comes, we will reunite with all who we loved and lost. The children's responses were interesting. They wanted to know simply, "Will *Mashiach* be coming tomorrow? What did Grandma take with her? Who will live in her house?" After these questions, they returned to their playing. Every so often they would come to me and let me know they missed her.

A few months after my mother's passing, I spoke with a telephone friend, Mrs. Freida Feig of Brooklyn. She is a member of a support group of people who take the time to call and speak with cancer patients and their family and friends. Mrs. Feig had offered many words of advice and comfort during and after my mother's illness. She also helped to put my feelings into perspective. When I felt depressed she let me know it was natural. She raised my spirits with anecdotes and quotations. She provided me with the strength to continue.

After a few months of communication, I asked Mrs. Feig if I too could participate with this wonderful undertaking. I would be grateful for the chance to be helpful. Several weeks passed and Mrs. Feig called. She would like me to call a Mrs. K. in Brooklyn. She too had been suffering from liver cancer. Would I care to call her and offer some comfort?

I was afraid to make the first call. What would I say to this woman? I am not a psychologist nor a doctor. Then I thought of Mrs. Feig. What would she do? I realized then it was most important just to listen, just as she had done for me.

Mrs. K. was also in her forties. She was angry. She felt she had always been a good person. Why did this happen to her? I quoted from *Bereishis Rabbah*: A potter does not test the vessels that are cracked. To tap even once is to break them. Solid vessels no matter how many times they are tapped, do not break. So Hashem does not test the wicked but the righteous, whom He loves.

Our first conversation flowed nicely. She was able to say things to me that were difficult for her to say to her family. I was an anonymous caller. She had a young daughter who would soon marry. Mrs. K. did not want to burden her with her ailments. I listened carefully and realized I was hearing some of the things my mother was unable to tell me. We had also been very close. I was pregnant with my youngest son. Perhaps my mother had also feared burdening me. I wondered how much she had kept inside.

Mrs. K. and I maintained our telephone relationship for quite a few months. Her condition steadily worsened. One day, she barely had the strength to talk. She gathered enough strength to ask how long my mother lived after her diagnosis. I told Mrs. K. that she lived to see her new grandchildren and then she became tired. She "held on" to see that everything was in order.

Mrs. K. also "held on." She lived to attend her daughter's wedding. Shortly after the wedding her condition rapidly deteriorated. She was comforted that her daughter was settled in her new life. She told me she was very tired. A few weeks later the call came from a friend. Mrs. K. had passed away.

The news brought sadness. I was not emotionally able to attend the funeral. I thought it best to remain anonymous to the family. Perhaps the daughter might call for comfort. I was glad that I had the chance to help this wonderful woman during her lifetime.

I found that these experiences strengthened me in two ways. First, I have become more appreciative of the time that Hashem has given me. I realize that life here is but a short visit. I make a conscious effort to utilize the time that I have without waste. Since my mother's untimely death, I ask myself daily, have I fulfilled my potential today? Did I utilize every opportunity to do a good deed?

How many of us say we have no time for volunteer work? Many of us work long hours or have large families to care for. These are not reasons. We all have access to the telephone. There are endless opportunities to do *mitzvos* by telephone. Only a few moments on the phone to an ill or elderly person could change his life.

Secondly, my experiences have strengthened my trust in Hashem and the World to Come. I no longer fear death as I did previously. I now understand that death is just another stage of the life cycle. There is a story of a chassidic *rav* who died and returned to his son in a dream. "Fear not death," he told his son. "It is as if I stepped from one room into another."

We do not have the answer as to why some of us live one hundred and twenty years while others leave the world before it seems our time. We must trust in Hashem's judgment. Only He knows what is best for us.

An Appreciation of Rabbi Goldstein

אחת שאלתי מאת ה' . . . שבתי בבית ה' כל ימי חיי (תהלים כז:ד)

ear Rebbe (you never would let us call you "Rebbe" during your lifetime) *zt'l*,
Who will teach us?!
Who will strengthen us?!

When worried with the fear of the unknown, who will tell us — "Everything is from Heaven; there are no accidents; *Hashem Yisbarach* is kind; nothing happens that is bad. The last thing Hashem created us for is just to be frightened, without purpose."

When pondering the purpose of creation, who will tell us — "Each individual person is created in G-d's image. In addition, each *Jewish* person has a special soul, this makes him unique and outstanding. He has the intelligence (the *tzelem elokim*) and the tools (the soul) to affect the entire universe, past, present, and future, by his actions. Effort is never wasted, the *mitzvah*, the results of a *mitzvah*, are eternal."

About praying, who will tell us — "We are masters of our destiny. We can control the future by prayer, a *mitzvah* that has the capability to change the universe. No prayer is unanswered."

When coping with anger, who will tell us — "Every anger is due to a personal discomfort. If a person remembers that every discomfort is a gift from *Hakadosh Baruch Hu* and results in sins being wiped away, then anger becomes impossible. How fortunate is such a person! The best thing in the world is happening to him and, at the same time, he is getting rid of sins. Wow!"

When concerned with doing *mitzvos*, who will tell us — "We look for the correct way of doing *mitzvos*. If it comes hard, it is a test; if it comes easy, it is a reward. We do a *mitzvah* because it is a *mitzvah*, and our reward is *daracheho darchei noam*. And in addition, the most delightful deeds are in the category of *hatznea leches*. Each person should have at least one *mitzvah* that no one knows about but the Ribono Shel Olam. Doing a *mitzvah* when no one sees stymies the *yetzer hara*.

When being overwhelmed at all the Torah we do not know, who will tell us — "Whatever makes you think that anybody knows enough to be able to say he knows what everything is all about. If a person believes that Hashem created the world and gave us the Torah, that person is appropriately as *frum* as anyone can be. Get used to it. You'll never know everything. But it can sure be fun trying!"

When unable to cope with thirty six hours of things to do in a twenty-four-hour day, who will tell us — Dovid Hamelech felt the same way, בהמות הייתי עמך, but in a positive fashion; Look, Hashem, I'm perfectly happy to be an animal in your service. Even if it's not exciting or rewarding right away, it will cause a very bright future, both in this world and in the World to Come."

When groping for the right way to raise our children, who will tell us — "Chinuch is not 'perfecting children' but 'teaching children to perfect themselves'; that no matter how many mistakes a parent makes, they are never fatal."

When coping with challenges, who will tell us — "No one can go uphill at a steady pace without stopping occasionally to catch his breath and get his bearings. If life were always perfect and simple, it would not be a challenge. And if you remove the challenge, man is reduced to a robot. The name of the challenge is *nisayon*."

When complaining about too many projects, who will tell us — "Spreading oneself thin sure doesn't leave much anywhere, but has anyone ever accomplished anything of real note by spreading himself only thick?"

When pondering difficulties, who will tell us — "Pain is bearable if the person knows there is a time limit to it. If he knows it won't end, even one minute becomes unbearable."

When asking the same question for the tenth time, who will say — "You have the information and the tools to think it out on your own. Stop using me as a crutch."

Rebbe, I've stopped.

Mrs. Levitin

❦　　❦　　❦

[Rabbi Goldstein was the beloved principal of Bais Yaakov, Detroit, for over twenty years. He passed away in 1984. — Ed.]

Life After Death

כי חלצת נפשי ממות . . . (תהלים קטז:ח)

My eyes are heavy, I know I need sleep. Fear holds on and does not let me. My mind wanders, I can see my husband in his hospital bed. He is ill with a very aggressive form of Hodgkin's Lymphoma. No sooner does he get his chemotherapy treatments, than the lymph nodes are back. He can't hold on, his body is breaking down. He says he is frightened. His breathing is very labored. He closes his eyes. He does not want me in his room, he wants me home with my children. This he does not say, but I see it in his eyes as he opens them.

Tonight we say our good-bye on the phone as if it were our last. I open my eyes. It is morning. I must have slept. I know I must call the hospital. My hands shake as I dial his room. Terror rips through my body as the phone rings. He answers, I am in disbelief. I tell him I will be there soon. I walk toward the hospital, I see the doctor leaving. My heart skips a beat! It's over, I'm sure! The doctor tells me that my husband had a cardiac arrest. He is being worked on in ICU. I run to the nurses' station. Swallowing the lump in my throat, I tell them who I am. They tell me to wait in a room beyond the sterile doors. They will let me know when I can come in to see my husband. As I sit in this small room alone, I can't help thinking of the past months since this illness interrupted our lives.

A doctor I do not know comes in to tell me he has suffered another cardiac arrest. The team is trying to revive him. This doctor leaves. I'm frightened and alone, and as I look up a familiar face is standing there. My husband's personal physician is there. He advises me about the possibilities of a respirator. He then leaves. I close my eyes and pray that if he must go let it be with dignity. The doctors return to tell me there is nothing more to be done, he is gone. I am numb, I want to cry but the tears don't come. My best friend walks off the elevator and holds me in her arms. I am confused. I exit the hospital this last time with a feeling of emptiness. I then come home to wait for my children and stare at the door he will never again walk through. I think I am in shock.

※　　※　　※

The scene you have just read is true. It happened to me over two years ago. It can happen to anyone with this dreadful illness, but it does not have to end your world. Let me not fool anyone, for all the fears and depressive moments that follow are real, but it is okay to have them. It is okay to take time to mourn, as a matter of fact it is very important to do so. No one can measure the amount of time it takes to mourn a loss. When you do so let it hurt as much as you can; be as angry as you desire, it's all right. Hashem understands that you are human.

If you really do take time to have these feelings and mourn, the pain will eventually subside. You will be able to pick up a *siddur* or a *Tehillim* again. The anger will settle into a corner and you will be able to get on with life. Though you may think it will never happen, it will. You can get through it with time. I know, because I've been there. I took the time. Though there were times I never believed I could make it, I did. My life has changed and I have grown from my experience. The strength my children and I found in ourselves and each other has been an extra added bonus. Though I will never forget my husband and what happened to him, I have let a new world open up for me. You can too as long as you allow it. Hashem will always be there for you, waiting to help whenever you ask.

※　　※　　※

It is two and a half years since I lost my husband. With Hashem's help we take each day at a time. *Baruch Hashem*, *yom yom*. I went back to work. My children and I have made adjustments with each other and are coping beautifully.

Catch Me If I Fall

כל עצמותי תאמרנה ה' מי כמוך . . . (תהלים לה:י)

When I speak people listen very carefully. If not, they will miss what was said. My speech is impaired because I have cerebral palsy. When people see me I appear "as one drunk." I walk about shakily supported by two metal crutches. All of my muscles are subject to involuntary spasms which cause my face to grimace and my hands to clench, for which I take medicine daily. My mobility is limited and I tire easily. I have a poor sense of balance and I have to admit that sometimes I fall, invariably causing more damage to those around than to myself. Despite all this I am married to a wonderful man and have two healthy adorable children This is my testimony to all that Hashem helps all who have trust.

My parents were holocaust survivors and I was born in Romania shortly after the end of the war. My father had prospered in the post war boom so it was decided that I should enter the world amid the comforts of home. My mother was attended by an inept midwife and a doctor who wasn't there when needed. No one knows for sure, but this could have caused my disability. Perhaps it was the lack of oxygen during birth or the jaundice which developed afterward. No one knows. I was a difficult baby, crying nightly until the age of two. My mother noticed that I did not kick my feet like other babies. Mine lay flat in the crib. My stages of development were much slower than those of other children. Only my parents understood what I was saying when I started talking in my second year. I did not crawl or creep until I was three years old.

We fled Romania when I was seven months and reached Israel about a year later. Times were hard in the new country, doctors were scarce and they didn't know how to help me. My illness had not yet been diagnosed. At age three I had to stay in a body cast for a few hours a day to straighten out my neck. I still have fond memories of my mother showing me photographs to amuse me. She used to sit on the floor with me for hours massaging and exercising my skinny legs. They were like sticks and remained so until I was a teenager. My parents were advised to leave Israel and go to a country where I could be educated. So my father left his lucrative business and we traveled to Canada. There I was placed in a nursery for disabled children and I learned English quickly. It was here that the cerebral palsy was diagnosed.

Luckily there was an excellent school for me in Toronto. The physical therapy I received there enabled me to walk at last. I wore hip to ankle braces to straighten out my legs. At the age of nine I learned to walk with crutches and a helmet which protected my head from daily falls. I shall never forget the day my mother was called to school to be shown how her daughter walked without human assistance. The therapist put me out all alone in the schoolyard and I screamed in terror. I was simply afraid to walk without someone behind me to catch me if I fell. Therapists worked on my speech, trying to slow me down and relax so I could be understood. In occupational therapy I learned how to feed and dress myself, taking pride in doing the things other people take for granted.

Learning to read opened up a whole new world for me, since I could not run and play like other children and reading was something I could do sitting down. At the end of the eighth grade I had perused almost every book in the extensive school library. A happy and friendly child, I managed to play with the neighborhood children. I could turn one end of the jump rope and recite the rhymes to the tune of the bouncing ball. My two brothers and my two cousins and I were very close and we had many good times.

Our home environment was very close and religious. Special treatment was never given to me because of my handicap. I was punished just as my brothers were when I misbehaved. This attitude is extremely important for a disabled child and has made me the happy, well-adjusted adult I am today. As I could not attend a religious school my father taught me the *aleph-bais*. Later on I went twice a week for lessons to a Hebrew teacher's house. In the seventh grade I tried to enroll in the Bais Yaakov but it wasn't destined. The English teacher said that the competition would be too much for me. My friends did promise to help me with the stairs and maybe if I had pushed the matter with much more conviction, I could have succeeded in my dream of attending a Jewish school. I tried another school, a much bigger one, but the principal wouldn't even consider me. I would hear the Bible stories every morning at the public school I attended. Then I would go to *Bnos* on Shabbos afternoon and the group leader would wonder how I knew the answers when she quizzed us about the *parshe* of the week. Luckily the *Bnos* wasn't too far away from where I lived and I could walk there with my cousin and two loyal friends. This sense of belonging to the community made me feel very good.

Every summer I went to a special camp for a few weeks. The first time I went I was seven years old and after five weeks I gained ten pounds. My mother was ecstatic as I was a skinny little thing and this was a big step forward for both of us. I loved camp and was a big favorite of the counselors because I was always giggling.

My mother had a cousin in the United States who kept urging her to bring me to New York to see a specialist in cerebral palsy and also an orthopedist. They recommended therapy and more therapy. I was also taken to *rebbes* for as many blessings as possible. And when I was twelve years old this cousin took me to the country for the summer. She was convinced that I could do much better physically and she took away one of my crutches. It wasn't an easy task because as always I was afraid of falling. But she succeeded and I walked with one crutch for twenty-four years. Even though she had four daughters she made me help with the dishes so that I should get used to working with my hands.

In the eighth grade the principal gave me an electric typewriter because my handwriting was almost illegible. When we moved to New York about two years later and I attended regular public high school, life was made much easier because I could type all my assignments. Only the students in my homeroom were disabled. I sat in a wheelchair and was pushed from class to class every hour by able-bodied students. It was really the first time that I was not in a sheltered environment and I felt great. I even surprised myself that I could surmount hurdles with a little extra effort and some common sense. The teachers accepted my handicap and called on me in class. Some of the tests I was able to take in class, but when essays were involved I used my typewriter. For an important test, such as a Regent, I was assigned a person to write my answers. This proves that disabled people can survive in the outside world but I guess it depends on the circumstances. I attended my high-school graduation with a sense of exhilaration. My bubble burst when I tried to land a job and realized that there was nothing I could realistically offer a future employer. I was advised by guidance counselors and employment offices that the best thing for me was to go to college.

College is no place for an orthodox Jewish girl, so I did not go willingly. I knew some people who attended Long Island University, so I applied there and was accepted. Fortunately the government pays for schooling for people with disabilities. I aimed for a degree in sociology so that I would become a social worker upon graduation. For the first two months I traveled from home to school with a van but that proved too difficult because there was a lot of waiting involved. A friend lived in the dormitory and as she liked living there, I decided to move in too. I lived there for four years, including one summer. I needed some assistance for daily needs, such as small buttons, zippers in the back, putting rollers in my hair and picking up kosher frozen dinners in the cafeteria. The government paid a roommate to help me. Every Friday afternoon my father would pick me up to go home for Shabbos and I would be back by Sunday evening. Living with different types of girls was interesting and enjoyable.

Since I always enjoyed reading and learning, academic life was very fulfilling. I studied hard, but was just an average student though one semester I did make the Dean's list. Again, it gave me great satisfaction to travel from class to class, but this time instead of using the wheelchair I walked with the one crutch, carrying my books in the other hand. I felt as free as a butterfly.

Armed with a B.A. in Sociology I set out to look for employment. Again, it was the same story — I needed more schooling. If I wanted to be a sociologist I had to finish graduate school because there were too many people with the same problem. Since I had no intention of continuing in school I abandoned this avenue and looked around for anyone who would be willing to hire me. I had always liked books so I tried to find work in a library. But alas that was not possible physically because the books are unusually heavy and two hands are needed to lift them. Finally, I took a bookkeeping course at a special workshop just to have something to do. But I knew I could never be a bookkeeper because the handwriting has to be precise and I happen to hate numbers.

Then I had a lucky break. The camp where I had been a camper for the past seven years had some job openings and I was hired as supervisor of four chamberpersons. Our job was to make sure that all the beds were made in adult camp and the linen was changed once a week.

This was the summer I met my husband-to-be. He had also been to this camp before, but he had worked in the kitchen and I hadn't met him because the camp was so big. This year he came to the camp for his two-week vacation because he really had no other place to go. When the two weeks were up, he gave up his job and returned to the camp, bringing his worldly belongings with him. Somehow it was *bashert* that we got to know and like each other. No one could believe how lucky I was, least of all me. Not even in my wildest dreams did I ever think I would marry. When I went to Israel to pray at the holy places, it never occurred to me to ask for a husband.

Everyone who attended my wedding was happy for me, but I was the happiest of all. I was in my white bridal gown when my mother-in-law and I first met and we liked each other immediately. Throughout our courtship my fiance assured me that his mother would like me but I never really believed him. Standing under the *chupah* was an emotional experience for me and my *chassan*. Even the guests were overwhelmed. The high spirit felt by all had people dancing till the wee hours of the morning. As my friends lifted my chair, I felt like a princess waving to my prince. For the grand finale my *chassan* and I joined in the ultimate *mitzvah tantz*. Even though I was without crutches all evening, my guests watched in disbelief when I rose to dance with Michael. I recall how my heart was full of thanks to the *Ribono shel Olam*. After a whirlwind *sheva brochos* week, we settled into a happy married life.

I was referred to N.Y.U. Medical Rehabilitation Center to learn some kitchen skills. After an evaluation the therapist concluded that the best way for me to cook was to be seated so I built a special kitchen in my rented apartment. It was a one-piece low counter, with two sinks and a stove built into it. I am a very stable person and was always content with my lot. So it was that I cooked and did the laundry with a great deal of pleasure and pride. I felt like an artist creating as I tried out new recipes. The rehab center had outfitted me with a cutting board with two stainless steel nails on which I could pinion my onions and potatoes. Thus I could peel and cut them. An electric broom which was light and easy to handle kept my floors clean.

Eight years and a new apartment later, I found we would be blessed with a child. To everyone's surprise, including myself, it was a quite normal period of time. I was able to walk around on two crutches right through. My son was born three weeks early, a little underweight, but perfect. It was a traumatic experience to look at that tiny little baby and wonder how on earth would I ever be able to take care of him. The one thing that kept going through my mind was how I would get him to school when he would have to go the first time. This depression lasted about three months, but I was frightened that it would last a lifetime. Of course I needed round-the-clock help. Thinking he was breakable I didn't even try to touch him until he was about seven months old. With great joy my husband and I watched him grow and develop into an adorable little child.

When my son was two and a half, I gave birth to a little girl. She was also born early and had to be in an isolette for about three weeks. My mother-in-law came in from another state to take care of her little granddaughter for four weeks. And she is ready to come and help at a moment's notice if I don't have a lady to help me.

❦   ❦   ❦

My son is now five and my daughter three. They both attend yeshivos and learn Torah. They are already happily assisting me in little things around the house. Both my children are self-confident and well-adjusted. Although they are aware that I am different they proudly introduce me to their friends.

My husband deserves most credit. He committed himself to an unnatural situation by choosing a disabled partner for life. His awesome selflessness was responsible for my meaningful existence. It is to him that I will be eternally grateful.

Our Cup Runneth Over

צרה ויגון אמצא, ובשם ה' אקרא . . . (תהלים קטז:ג-ד) . . .

t began with the remoteness of a trans-Atlantic telephone call, and the immediacy of the voice of our oldest son, Raphael, talking in my ear: "Mazel tov. It's a girl. There's a problem, but we're taking care of it."

Raphael and Chana were married just over a year earlier — the night after Purim, in Yerushalayim. And now, a year later, their child was born in Shaarei Tzedek Hospital. The doctors immediately discovered that she had a hole near the base of her spine, and they agreed that she should be sped by ambulance to the Beilenson Medical Center near Tel Aviv. Facts tumbled out, one after the other, mixing optimism with fatigue, hope with dejection. The operation, which is delicate neurosurgery, was performed by a Dr. Shalit, who is very highly regarded, and the success of his efforts determined how much control she would have over extremities, bladder and so on. Rav Chaim Graineman counseled them on every step of the way. The Steipler Gaon suggested that they give her a name which would be a "hook" on which to hang their *tefillos*. Raphael chose Bracha, a name which is a prayer unto itself.

We were familiar with spina bifida. Very close friends of ours had opened their home to Eli, a five year-old boy with spina bifida, who was bright, aggressive, ambitious — but severely handicappped.

We then began networking — talking to parents of spina bifida children: some wheelchair-bound, one that actually joined the dance corps in her high school ... learning about shunts that drain excess spinal fluid from the brain into the stomach, and that require occasional adjustment or replacements ... urinary tract infections, kidney problems. "Life will never be simple for your kids again," said one father of a spina bifida girl.

❦　❦　❦

Two and a half years later, during a hospital strike in Israel, one of Bracha's kidneys became infected, but her parents did not discover it until it was too late to save the kidney. They flew to America with Bracha and stayed for three months — over Purim. Here she had the best medical attention, surgery on the kidney, and several thorough check-ups. With the catheters, syringes and pads, they had a veritable clinic with them. We lived together that winter and observed up close how Bracha's physical limitations and deep-grained shyness made it difficult to get to know her. Her hands were weak, her speech slurred, yet her precious smile and large dark eyes expressed curiosity and interest at every turn. She was only too content to lie on the ground and watch the passing parade, but her parents wanted her to want more. They built a "sled" — a padded platform on wheels — on which she could pull herself around. Chana was on the floor with her, spreading a trail of raisins to lead her on, talking to her, coaxing her to follow the snacks ...

Eliezer was born two weeks after his sister's second birthday, and he and Bracha grew very attached to each other. She enjoyed his antics and he basked in her attention. She attended the Ailyn School for Disabled Children, where according to the teachers she displayed unusual ability in letter recognition, remembering *brachos*, and time relationships. But then, she had the added advantage over the others of a *Shabbos* to look forward to every week, *Rosh Chodesh* to start every month, and a full year of *Yomim Tovim*. "I can hardly wait till Purim," she told her mother after her fifth Chanukah. "I want to dress up like a *kallah* — a bride!"

She was outfitted with leg braces, and we all had high hopes that she would get off the ground and learn to swivel from foot to foot, sort of "walk" like the rest of us.

❦　❦　❦

Again it was a trans-Atlantic telephone call. This time from Moshe, our second oldest son. "Bracha is running a high fever, and they don't know what it is." She never suffered ordinary colds, flu, or the usual childhood diseases, but condition-related infections and blockages were not infrequent. She had recently had the shunt in her head replaced ... And then the doctors discovered that she had menengitis. "It might be a good idea if one of you come."

I took a Tuesday flight. (My wife, Devora, joined me there the next day.) They had added the name Alte. When we stopped for refeuling in London, I said a *kapital* of *Tehillim* after *Shacharis* for "Alte Bracha bas Chana." When I got off the plane in Lod, Moshe greeted me with the report that Alte Bracha had died that morning. Funerals for little children are not announced in Jerusalem, but nonetheless a hundred or so people were gathered at the Chevra Kadisha hut. Raphael spoke — with strength and *emunah*, I was told, but no more details. I had very much wanted to be there with my children during their wrenching, painful farewell. Instead, I walked into their apartment in Bayit Vegan — where a concrete ramp accommodated a little girl's wheelchair from the living room-porch to the street. The tall wax candle burned, and flickered on my son and daughter-in-law, sitting on the floor in mourning for their lost little girl.

Raphael and I embraced, and then I sat down on a dining room chair to share their sorrow and listen to them probe for meaning and hope for some measure of comfort.

It was like witnessing the past eight years of his life passing through the door — old friends, Ponevezher *chaveirim*, relatives, neighbors, Bracha's teachers and attendants ... With several visitors Raphael presented his situation to them and asked them to comment: "Do you remember the *Gemara* in *Kesubos*, *ches amud bais*? (Some did immediately, others shrugged.) The teacher of Raish Lakish's son lost a child; others say it was a teen-aged son. So Raish Lakish and Yehudah bar Nachmeini, his *meturgeman*, went to console the man. 'Say something regarding the child,' said Raish Lakish, and Yehudah quoted the passage, 'And Hashem saw this and turned away in disdain from anger for His sons and daughters' (*Deut*. 32, 19), and added, 'When the fathers antagonize G-d, He is angry with their sons and daughters, and they die when they are yet small.'

"Raish Lakish later objected: 'You have come to console? You are adding to his pain.'

"Yehudah answered, 'I told him as follows: You are worthy enough to carry the sin of the generation.'

"How do you understand this *Gemara*?" Raphael asked. "Is there comfort in losing a little girl for whatever transcendent reason?"

The question hung in the air like a heavy, dark cloud. I do not recall any answers that dispelled that cloud.

Rav Shlomo Zalman Auerbach, *Rosh Hayeshivah* in Kol Torah and revered *posek* in Yerushalayim, walked in the door, unaccompanied.

"Once the mourner has spoken, new *menachamim* need not wait for him to open the conversation," he said, without waiting for Raphael to "open the conversation." He continued, "The *Gemara* in *Babba Kamma* tells us that when Rav Shmuel bar Yehudah lost his daughter, the rabbis told Ula, 'Come let us go to comfort him.'

"[Ula] said to them, 'How càn I offer comfort together with [you] Babylonians? They blaspheme [against G-d]. They say, 'What could I have done?' And if they could have done something [to over rule G-d's decree of death], would they have done so?'

"The *Rama* decides in favor of Ula, that one musn't express oneself in such a manner, but the *Maharshal* decides otherwise. There is nothing wrong with expressing oneself in the manner of Rav Shmuel bar Yehudah. All he meant to say was, 'We did all that we could.' "

Reb Shlomo Zalman sat silent for a few moments permitting the message to sink in. Then he told us how the Chasam Sofer was asked by one of his sons why he always quotes his *Rebbe*, Rabbi Nosson Adler, but seldom mentions the *Hafla'ah* (Rav Pinchus Halevi Horowitz) who had been *Rav* in Frankfurt-Am-Main, where the Chasam Sofer had grown up.

Replied the Chasam Sofer, "The *Hafla'ah* was very great and I learned much from him. But Rav Nosson Adler was lacking very little from being a *malach* ... Reb Nosson had a young daughter, an exceptional girl — bright, understanding, full of *yiras Shomayim* — who passed away suddenly when only fourteen. He was heartbroken over his loss, but when the *Shabbos* during his *shivah* arrived, he removed his mourning garments, dressed for *Shabbos* and conducted himself fully as he did every week. There was no sign of *aveilus* on his face ... He was called to the Torah for *Kohein* and again for *Maftir*, as was his practice. During the middle of the *Haftorah*, I noticed a tear well up in his eye and trickle down his cheek. Without pause, he brushed the tear off his face and flicked it away — glistening like a jewel — and he continued reading."

Again Reb Shlomo Zalman paused, as he let us realize that even the greatest of men are overwhelmed by emotions, try as they might to control them ... We are not *malachim*.

With that, he arose, asked where Chana was sitting, said a few comforting words to her, recited "Hamakom . . . " to her, to Raphael, and exited.

When Rav Gedalia Eisman, formerly Mashgiach in Kol Torah, entered the room, one felt the warmth. Like Reb Shlomo Zalman Auerbach, he radiated concern, but was not weighed down by the gravity of his feelings. Survivors tend to search for meaning in the tragic untimely loss of a child, and any lesson, any insight gained, is a thread of reason in a situation that seems to defy understanding.

"Mesilas Yesharim notes that animals are content with themselves, while human beings tend to feel that they are missing something. If man is the end purpose of Creation, why should he feel as though he were lacking? This is to goad him toward perfection. Only through sensing that one is not yet all that he is meant to be — in terms of possessions, or accomplishment — will he strive to improve. Man's awareness of his mortality is a factor in this dissatisfaction with himself. Remembering one's ultimate death helps one avoid sin by creating a tension between complacency and urgency. Maharal tells us that with merely hearing the command to write the words, 'And Moshe died . . .,' Moshe Rabbeinu felt his mortality with an immediacy that permitted him to write those words as a fact."

Raphael's Rosh Hayeshivah, Rabbi Abba Berman, referred to Shlomo Hamelech's maxim, "It is good to go to a house of mourning rather than to a house of rejoicing." An element described as "good" is present in mourning, which must seem strange. But elsewhere, "good" is defined by David Hamelech: "Kirvas Elokim li tov — Closeness to G-d is good to me." If the tragedy of loss and the loneliness of death, which pervade the house of mourning, bring one closer to G-d, and the folly of this-wordly pursuits become more dramatically apparent, then these constitute the "good" that one gains from this house . . . Some good can grow from the tragic black hole of a personal loss.

Raphael recalled Rabbi Yochanan's comment that, "Children are not yesurim shel ahavah (when G-d inflicts a person with suffering out of His love)." This refers to not having children; but having a child and losing it is indeed yesurim shel ahavah (Berachos 56). Losing a child can be infinitely more painful than never having a child, asked Raphael. Where is the ahavah? He offered, receiving a child from G-d, and then having Him take the child away is an encounter with Him. It represents a relationship with Him, no matter how painful.

"This is not an original insight," Raphael added, citing the *Bais Halevi* (Rabbi Yoseif Dov Soloveitchik on the *pasuk*: שבטך ומשענתך המה ינחמוני — "Your whip and Your staff, they comfort me" (*Tehillim* 23:4). The whip inflicts punishment, and the staff offers support. Both give the sufferer comfort, for both testify that "even when I walk in the Valley of the Shadow of Death, You are with me." Whether through pain or support, both are encounters with G-d, and ultimately both can be sources of comfort.

More than one of the comforters recalled the Chofetz Chaim's comment that all the questions that one might raise in the context of the paradox of "the righteous suffer, while the wicked rejoice" can be laid to rest in awareness of *Sod Hagilgulim* — the Transmigration of the Soul.

Raphael's cousin, Shea Briezel, brought with him a treasury of *Chassidic* tales that seemed to illustrate the Chofetz Chaim's maxim:

The Baal Shem Tov was approached by a righteous couple that did not have a child until later in life. He was a charming little boy, who was unusually gifted and seemed to gravitate naturally to Jewish knowledge and devotional activities. Then, quite suddenly, he took sick and died — at age two! Why were they given such a treasure, only to lose him?

The Baal Shem Tov told them of a royal prince in a distant land, who was unusually precocious and of serious bent. The king engaged a priest from a monastic order devoted to academic pursuits to tutor the child. The tutor was actually a Jew who had converted to Catholicism because of unusual pressures that he could not withstand. Now he decided to compensate for his defection by teaching the prince the wisdom of the Torah. The boy took to Torah as if born to it, and by the time he was twelve, he decided to become Jewish. He could not muster the will power to leave his home and accept Judaism until he reached his fifteenth birthday. Then, through an intricately planned "accident" as a cover, he slipped away and joined a small Jewish village, where he converted and lived a life faithful to Torah and *mitzvos*.

"All that his soul was lacking," explained the Baal Shem Tov to the bereaved couple, "was a pure entry into this world and the two years of a genuine Jewish upbringing that he had missed after he had reached maturity. G-d searched the earth and found no more fitting a setting for this precious soul than the two of you, and your home. So you hosted this pure soul for two years, and now it is basking in the spiritual bliss of *Gan Eden*."

A close acquaintance advised them that all sorts of explanations will be offered, but nothing that is said can still the heartache, and they shouldn't expect otherwise and then be disappointed with themselves ... Reb Gedalia Eisman suggested that they take a trip after the *shloshim*. They did, joining us for a family *simchah*, staying over Pesach.

❦ ❦ ❦

Jerusalem is a city of unique customs. For instance, parents that lose a child do not accompany the body to the burial. On the morning that the *shivah* is over, however, they do visit the fresh grave. My wife and I thought the visit at this time would be too traumatic and advised Chana against it. But her "Oma" was going, and so was her father, her mother and Raphael. So Chana went too. And so did we. We got out of the car on Har Hazeisim, looking down a sweeping hillside of grave stones lying flat ... the panorama of the Old City, stretching on to the wide Jerusalem horizon. Chana, Raphael and the others made their way to "the Portions of the Infants" and found the marker indicating "Bracha bas Raphael." We stayed some ten feet to the back. We all said a few appropriate chapters of *Tehillim*, dried our eyes, and returned to the car.

Chana later said, "For a week I sat numb, not coming to grips with the reality of Bracha's passing. Now I know that Bracha is no longer with us, and I can continue."

A friend dropped by that afternoon. He remarked to me, "I really admired Chana for her moxie."

"What do you mean?"

"I've often passed her pushing Bracha in her oversized stroller, smiling for the world. But I can imagine her problems, the way that poor child dominated her day. Well, now that's over."

It wasn't the time or place to "put down" my friend, but in all honesty I thought he should know how wrong he was in his assessment of the five years Raphael and Chana had Bracha. For his part, Raphael had once commented how he felt their involvement in Bracha's travails and triumphs had brought them closer together ... Chana had confided in my wife, "When I would pass people on the street, pushing Bracha in her stroller, I could feel their pitying glances. I could almost hear their unspoken thoughts: 'Poor thing! How her parents must suffer with her.' And I would think, 'I also had felt that way when I'd pass a mother with a crippled child. But it's so far from the truth! Bracha was a delightful child. Always happy. Learning new things every day. Accomplishing new skills week by week. She enjoyed life and we enjoyed her, too. The only consolation I have is that experts say that she would become more aware of her handicaps when she turns six or seven, and then would become bitter or angry. That would have been difficult ... At least she was spared that."

❧ ❧ ❧

A cup can be called by a variety of titles, depending on what it contains. For instance, there is *Kos Hatareila* — a Cup of Bitterness and *Kos Tanchumim* — a Cup of Consolation. For us, there was a *Kos shel Bracha* — A Cup of Blessings. If others can learn from how our children dealt with a bitter, bitter chapter and found some consolation, then that is a blessing to be shared.

❧ Life Is a Mixture
by Fradel Berger

Life is a mixture
Of sunshine and rain
Laughter and teardrops
Pleasure and pain
Low tides and high tides
Mountains and plains
Triumphs and defeats
Losses and gains
But ALWAYS in ALL WAYS
Hashem is guiding and leading
And He alone knows
The things we're most needing
When he sends sorrow
Or some dreaded affliction
Be assured that it comes
With Hashem's benediction
And if we accept it
That it is for our good
We'll be showered with blessings
From Hashem above

✦§ Final Days

by Carol Schneider*

She died behind her silent words,
Her quiet thoughts could not be heard.
I found it hard to read her eyes,
She must have seen through hopeful lies.
How much she knew I could not tell,
She took her role and played it well.
And even though I surely tried,
Her deepest thoughts were kept inside.
What mystery deep within her heart,
As she prepared this world to part.
Her wisdom far beyond her years,
Could help protect her from her fears.
The things she saw I could not see,
She surely glimpsed eternity.
And so I trust that if she feared,
For her alone the mystery cleared.
Her thoughts within content to be,
As she surrendered gracefully.
but words are not the only way,
Of telling what we have to say.
A touch, a look, and words left unsaid,
We chose to take that way instead.
I held her close in time of pain,
Yet closer when her life did wane.
And I can only hope she died,
Content to have me by her side.
I have no doubt she was at peace,
The moment that her life did cease.
Her gentle spirit now at rest,
And I can say we did our best.
Though words there were not many of,
The thing we knew for sure was love.

* [Mrs. Schneider wrote this poem two years after her
ten-year-old daughter Lisa died. It first appeared in the
newsletter of the LODAT Candlelighters affiliate in Wiscon-
sin. — Ed.]

Times of Tribulation

We Will Get Better,
We Must Get Better

גם כי אלך בגיא צלמות לא אירא רע כי אתה עמדי
שבטך ומשענתך המה ינחמוני (תהלים כג:ד)

houts of, "Mazal tov! It's a girl! She's beautiful!" and she's right here near my heart and I close my eyes as the tears flow freely, because she is whole, and she is beautiful, and I thank Hashem for bringing me to this day, and for watching over her till birth, and I can't help thinking — Hashem — You've done Your job, and now You've entrusted her to me.

We name her after two grandmothers we knew and loved. Miriam and Ruth were not just names to us, but representative of the grandmothers who lived into our lifetimes, gave us beautiful times as children, and then were called from this world. I tell you all of this because you have to understand the utter joy and thankfulness I had been coming from when I suffered my loss. The tremendous joy and gratitude that I had felt upon her birth made the depth of my pain all the deeper at her death. So just as she began to grow, to fill out her small stretchies, to need a larger pamper, to smile at her Ema and turn her head at her name, she died, less than three months old, in her sleep. An unexplained sudden infant death, my beautiful baby.

In the emergency room they asked us — do you have a Rabbi we can call — and my husband and I looked at each other — because he is the Rabbi — we who had comforted others; now we were bereft. Amidst the terrible crying, the searing pain in the heart that felt like it would never go away, came the practical questions. How could we tell my parents, my husband's parents? How could we tell the children? What were we to do — we had to plan a funeral, a burial, a *shivah* and then we would pick up the pieces of our shattered lives.

So many questions tear at the person who is suffering. What did I do to deserve this? I must be a terrible person. Why did this happen to me? Can I be angry at Hashem? If I am angry at Him and I express my anger, will He only reach out to smite me some more? Why was this beautiful little soul denied a chance to live, to love, to learn? Surely she was completely pure. Then it must be a punishment to me, the errant adult.

As I return to the outer world from the inner one, I ask: How will I handle being the object of pity? How can I accept comfort when there is no comfort? I've lived a good and happy life. Can I ever be the same person I once was? Can I ever dance with a full heart at a *simchah*? Will every family photo from now on have that awful emptiness? Can I go back to the supermarket and walk down the pamper aisle without crying? Can I watch the peers of my baby as they grow from infancy to toddling to childhood to young adulthood? Can I run the risk of another child? Can I ever watch, handle, feed, someone else's baby?

What will I say when they ask how many children I have? I *have* three, but I *had* four. She existed; her life made a difference; how can I deny her? Yet can I burden an innocent questioner with my tale of sorrow? What shall we do with her clothes, her room, her untouched gifts, her little personalized picture frames and socks. Why didn't I take more pictures? Maybe it's better I have so few — maybe it's not healthy to keep looking at them and bursting into tears.

We made some decisions. We go home from the emergency room to tell the children. We tell them we love them. We tell them we *can*, we *must*, *still* be a happy family. We tell them we have suffered a terrible, irreversible loss, but no one is to blame. We all loved her so dearly and completely, and our pain is indescribeable, but we *will* get better, we must get better. We will never forget her, but neither will her life, nor her death, be the center of our lives. There will be times over the next months when Ema or Abba will cry. That happens when someone we love dies. Crying is good — it helps us let out our feelings. We'll try not to cry too much, but if you kids want to cry, that's okay too. No, you will not die, too. Most people die when they're old. Some people die younger. When you die, your soul goes up to Hashem. Your body rests in the ground, in a grave. We put a stone on a grave to express to ourselves and to the world who the loved one was and what he or she meant to us.

We're going to bury Miri here, but *al t'nai*. We're going to re-inter her in Eretz Yisrael before the *shloshim* is complete. Ema and Abba planned to be laid to rest in Eretz Yisrael after 120 years. You children will choose your own places. But Miri will never have a husband to be buried near. She only has us — and just as in life we would have tried to give her the best, in death, we will give her a fine resting place on a sunny hilltop in Eretz Yisrael, right next to where Ema, Abba, Babi, Zaidy, Grammy and Grampy bought their graves.

Another decision. Both Abba and Ema will say a *hesped* at the funeral. We will have a graveside funeral — simple — for a pure and simple soul. No one knew her as well as we — no one knew her as well as me. I speak of my love for her, of the death of potential, of not knowing what her first word would be, where her first step would take place. I speak of the way she looked at me as she paused in her nursing and I can see any mother who ever held and fed her child and experienced that simple social behavior imagine a little what such a loss is like.

The pain of the soul. The physical pain — from ending the nursing so abruptly. I cry and cry during *shivah*. Friends I have not seen for ages, reaching out as my head is filled with pictures of the baby. Talking, listening, trying to make people feel that they've comforted me, trying to reach every person who comes in with the message that their visit was appreciated, their visit served some purpose. Trying to find comfort from what people are saying. Trying to sort out the occasional stupid remarks and discount them. Wondering all the while what I will ever do when *shivah* is over.

The people, the troubles that crawled out of the woodwork. The incredible revelations of people who looked happy, looked elegant, gave charity, danced at weddings, yelled at their children. There were those among them who had also suffered, who had loved and lost, who had borne the deepest of pain. Could I too emerge from my pain and be my old self again, so that a stranger who had not known me in 1982 could meet me sometime later and not read from my countenance of what I had suffered? Could I possibly resume walking the streets of the world unblemished, without a sign of my loss, like an ordinary person? It seemed hard to contemplate, yet there walked those others, who, looking well and wonderful as they crossed the threshold of the mourners' house, spoke of the same unspeakable pains as I was feeling, but in the past tense.

For us, my husband and me, this was the beginning of a new understanding of *tzaros rabim chatzi nechamah* — because we had asked ourselves: What can that mean? Why should I be comforted by the fact that others have suffered. Why would the suffering of others make me feel any better? The answer is that seeing those who have suffered, and who have also made a recovery, resumed their lives, suvived, *this* is the *nechamah*! To see yourself a few months, years, down the road of life as you see those who have suffered and come back to a measure of themselves, this is the partial comfort. The knowledge that the road back from the loss can be scaled — it is not impossible — is the first inkling that there is a measure of comfort out there to be acquired.

Words that had meaning, words that gave comfort. The friend who had lost her beloved father a short time ago spoke of the question she found in a chassidic *sefer*. How will we recognize those we loved when we meet them after 120 years in the World to Come? If they died young, will they have grown old? If they were hurt or wounded, will they have healed? How will we know them, how will they know us if we have changed or aged? The answer is that we will know them, we will recognize them because they will be clothed and cloaked in the good deeds we do in their name. I could relate to this. I could see my baby come toward me in the World to Come draped with the *tzedakah* and *chesed* I would do in her name, we would all do in her name. I would no longer feel that half my life, or my whole life, for that matter, had been snuffed out. Now I would live for two. I would do all the good deeds and the *mitzvos* for myself, and I would also do the ones she had not lived to do.

I could appreciate the beautiful days fully, for her, as well as for me. I would dance on joyous occasions myself, but with an extra measure, for what she would have danced, had she lived. Through my life, I would give her life. There had to be *some reason* why she had lived, however briefly, why she had entered my life, and left it so abruptly, so painfully. And as much as I would sometimes feel, as a mother does, *mir far dir*, that I should have gone in her place, there was some unfathomable reason why I still lived, why I was still blessed with life. And I was going to use it, to cherish it, to live it as fully as I could.

Another friend mentioned the story reprinted in Rav Zevin's

Sipurei Chassidim, of the baby born to a loving, fine, Jewish woman, who lived two years and died suddenly. The mother went to the Rebbe who had given her the blessing for the child and he told her a strange story of a certain Jew who grew up to be an outstanding member of the community who, unfortunately, had been lost among other nations for several years during his youth. It was only through a special spark that this unique soul possessed that it was able to renounce its foreign background and return to Judaism. The story tells us that when this soul was reunited to its Maker after 120 years, Hashem felt that the soul, as wonderful as were the deeds it had achieved on earth, lacked one thing. For two years it had been nursed by a stranger. So the special beautiful soul had to return to earth, to a fine, caring Jewish mother, for two years. And this soul was her baby, the one that had lived two years and died.

I had never thought much about the transmigration of souls, but I understood that the teller of the tale was trying to tell me that mine, too, was a special home to whom a special soul had been sent for a short sojourn, a small *tikun* on its way to *Olam Haba*. The storyteller wanted us to feel special at having been chosen. And though I found it hard to believe, in my heart of hearts, I said that stories such as these are not told without reason. I was happy I had nursed the baby almost exclusively, and I found a small comfort in thinking that perhaps there was something special about my baby's soul.

Another friend sent me the story of King David and his first child with Bas-Sheva. She reminded me of David's behavior while the child was ill. He wore sackcloth, he fasted, he prayed, he spoke to no one. Finally the child died. Everyone was afraid to tell David because if he had mourned so while the child was still alive, while there was still hope, they feared for his life if he learned the child died.

David began to realize they were shielding him. He asked outright and he learned that the child had died. To everyone's shock, he removed the sackcloth, got up, got dressed, and asked for something to eat. When the servants questioned him on his bizarre behavior, he explained, "While the child was alive, I prayed, I fasted, I humbled myself; there was still hope. Now that death has won this round, אני הולך אליו והוא לא יסוב אלי — I shall go to him — he shall not return to me. And since he still lived, there was work to be done."

In the work of the poet, there are "miles to go before I sleep — miles to go before I sleep." And those miles must be covered through good deeds and good works.

It was not so easy. I knew all these things in my mind. But to have your mind overpower the source of tears, to have your mind overpower the source of pain, to have your mind force yourself to greet your public, to go to school, to *shul*, to meetings, to business as usual, that is another thing.

There were times when I said to myself it would be easier to just have a breakdown — retire to a hospital for a month or two. But in thinking it through in more lucid moments I began to take a very practical attitude. What feelings, thoughts, actions, are productive, useful? And what feelings, thoughts, actions are wasteful and unproductive? Clearly, guilt is a very damaging and unproductive feeling. I was lucky. I knew I had been a good and caring mother. I had read in all the literature that Sudden Infant Death Syndrome, or SIDS, was neither predictable nor preventable and that I had nothing to feel guilty about because nothing I could have done would have prevented my baby's death.

And yet, the question remained. What if I had checked the baby earlier? If I had found the baby before it was too late, I could have begun CPR while there was still time. Like any mother, sometimes I had let the baby cry. I could feel guilty about that too. But, I began to pull myself together and say: "Will it do me, my husband, my baby, O"H, my remaining children and family any good if I devour myself with guilt? Will it help anyone in this entire world if I end up in an institution? "Of course not. I had to do what was practical, what was valuable to the living. I had to get better. I had to discharge any negative, useless guilt feelings, and apply all my energy to being normal, being the kind of wife, mother, daughter, teacher, friend I always had been. I had to take charge of my life.

Shortly after I came to this conclusion in my heart of hearts, I came upon a wonderful essay that my husband's *Rebbe* had written some years earlier and it crystalized for me in beautiful, poetic Hebrew the exact feelings that I felt I had had. As I read it, I couldn't help feeling that my having thought of it myself cemented its meaning for me. Had someone external just told me about it, I might have said: "That's easy for *you* to say. But the *Rav's* words confirming my own thoughts gave me great strength.

In speaking of Job and the terrible *tzaros* that befell him, the essay discusses the age-old philosophical problem of צדיק ורע לו — "Why do the good suffer?" The *Rosh Yeshivah* identifies two different kinds of personalities: *Adam HaGoral*, man of fate, is tempest-tossed by bad things, by troubles. In these brutal waves he is torn, battered, as he goes whichever way the winds and storm blow him. *Adam HaYiud*, man of destiny, is different. He too is tossed and battered by troubles. But he doesn't accept his fate passively. He gathers his strength and steers himself through, above the storm, and changes his *fate* into his *destiny*; he understands that his goal must be להפך את הגורל ליעוד, to change his fate into his destiny.

Other thinkers, speak of individuals who changed their *fate* to their *destiny*, who *did something* at this point in their lives to say, "I must give meaning to this event by changing my life in some way." Some do it by becoming active in organizations or support groups for the victims of their particular problem — some do it by giving lots of charity, or doing research on the medical problem that affected them; or by writing a book, or by changing jobs, or realigning priorities — but each is characterized by a firm conviction — to change the fate into destiny. Somehow this event was not a scourge, but a crisis to be weathered, a turning point to be cherished, an opportunity to do something that would otherwise never have been done.

It was not clear to me at that moment precisely what I would do, but I think that from then on, I took charge of my life. I would go back to work. I would try to have another baby as soon as Hashem would give me the gift — not to replace, but to fill my empty arms, to respond to death with life. And I would share. I would have, unfortunately, over the next five years, many chances to give strength to families who lost babies. People would call and lead my husband and me to bereaved families. I would listen, I would talk. I would call, I would be there, I would share. I would help them understand that their feelings were so normal. I would say aloud for them what they were afraid to say aloud, lest it be considered crazy or "out of sight" by the blessedly uninitiated.

I could tell them about how we decided what to write on her tombstone — words that would help us say when we visited the grave — "Yes — that is what she was. This is how we felt about her."

מרים רות בת יצחק צבי ורחל
ילדה חמודה
נשמה טהורה
אהבה רבה אהבנוה
נקטפה בנשיקה י"ז טבת תשמ"ב

We wrote מרים רות בת יצחק צבי ורחל, both father and mother, because we both felt the need to be joined with her memory through the stone. I would tell them how I put away the crib after *shivah*, how I packed the boxes of beautiful unworn gifts and wrote on them, "with *mazel*" as a mother who had lost a child to SIDS thirty years ago told me she did. I would tell them how I looked at her picture and cried, not wanting to torture myself, but somehow needing to.

I could tell them what others had told me in their turn — that the statement made at the end of the *shivah* call, המקום ינחם אתכם בתוך שאר אבלי ציון וירושלים, was not a wish, or a blessing, or a hope that the bereaved will be comforted, but a charge, and a statement of irrefutable fact — "Hashem *will indeed* comfort you." Just as all those who have loved and lost before have eventually been comforted, so, too, will you. It has to be that way.

"I can tell you. I've been there. But you have to help yourself." הבא לטהר מסעין אותו — "He who comes to be cleansed, the Almighty helps him." We have the concept of *hishtadlus*. We have to try. We are in charge of our lives, of our destiny. We have to spare no effort to put our minds in control of our emotions — יגעת ומצאת, תאמין. If you desire it, it won't be just a fable — it will be real. If we will it, it can happen. And I believe in the power of the mind, of the intellect, to assess the situation and say — what is the best response? What is the response that will be most noble, most practical, most helpful to myself, to my family, to those I love and live for?

Once we decide upon that response, every fiber of our being has to go into implementing it. Even when I wake up in the morning and feel like going back to sleep for two weeks, I have to rise, dress, look my best, do my work, meet my public, get through that day. We are helped by talking things through with whatever network of support we have built for ourselves — a husband, a wife, a parent, dear friends, a trusted rabbi, doctor or therapist.

I was very blessed. I had a strong marriage, supportive parents and in-laws and good friends who helped to smooth the way. My prayers were answered, and my determination to respond to death with life fulfilled. Before our baby's *yahrzeit*, I had a beautiful little son. It was a tension-filled time. There was so much riding on this child emotionally for both my husband and me.

We named him very significantly, we felt, Moshe Hillel, for the memory of our Miriam Rus O"H. Moshe — because Miriam watched over her little brother Moshe in the bulrushes, and our

Miriam would watch over Moshe from *shomayim* — and Hillel for our own *Hallel*, our rejoicing, and because his *bris* was on Chanukah and the complete *Hallel* is said each day, and also because we light candles each night in a pattern that is *mosif v'holech* — our light and our joy is multiplied progressively, as was the *p'sak* of Bais Hillel — .ח׳ נרות והלכה כבית הלל

We chose to have the baby put on an infant monitoring program which meant that whenever he was asleep, he would be attached by electrodes to a small machine, a monitor, that watched his breathing and heartrate, and would send an alarm if anything was irregular. For me, this was not a reflection of any lack of faith, or *emunah*, but an affirmation that I believed with a full heart that this child would make it, but I also felt that it was my responsibility as a parent to do the best I could. Just as I would always buckle my children's seatbelts no matter how short a distance I rode, I would always attach the monitor because I had to do my part — to use all the technology available to be a partner with *Hakadosh Baruch Hu* to protect my baby and try to guarantee him life through my *hishtadlus*.

Every aspect of the baby's birth became a *déjà vu* experience for me. I relived in my mind bringing home the baby that we lost, her first feeding, her first trip to the doctor. The first three months were the most difficult; my joy in him was tempered by the memory of my joy in Miriam and how that joy was doomed to be cut short so abruptly. And yet, the awe and wonderment and the profound gratitude for the great miracle of his birth was even greater.

When we heard during his naming at his *bris*, קיים את הילד הזה לאביו ולאמו, and the blessing זה הקטן גדול יהיה, I cried very real tears, knowing that these prayers were not just words, but true supplications for life and longevity. But, the baby survived, his parents survived, and he brought a tremendous amount of joy into our lives. He did not *replace*, but helped to *restore*. To this very day we find him to be a special little boy with a *lev tov*.

The story doesn't end here. We were blessed with a little girl, whom we named Shira Nomi — also for Miriam Rus — because Miriam went out and sang *shira*, and we also wished to exult in our new baby girl, to sing *shira*; and Nomi — for her love and devotion to Rus. We had another little girl less than two years later, and I feel that these children have enriched our lives immeasurably. Our three older children still speak of the baby we lost and they have made her name familiar to the younger ones — integrating Miri's memory comfortably into the fabric of our family life.

Over the years we have given *tzedakah l'iluyi nishmas* Miriam Rus, my husband and I have delivered public *shiurim* and dedicated them and other learning to Miriam Rus and to the memory of other *kedoshim*. Our friends at the *shul* dedicated the *shtender* in the new *bais medrash* to the baby's memory. Although at first tears came to my eyes each time I saw the beautifully embroidered letters, לזכר נשמת הילדה מרים רות ע״ה בת הרב יצחק צבי ורחל, I now can look at it, and feel that it is an expression of the love and empathy our friends felt for us. And an indication of our involvement in *talmud Torah* for her, as I said earlier, an attempt to live *for her* as well, to do the good she did not live to do, and give meaning to her short life through deeds and study done for her sake.

Though the chapter is concluded, the story is not over, because the human mind is such that we continue to live with our memories. I am no longer cut to the quick by the thought of Miri, or the magnitude of what I lost, but I experience twinges of pain at different moments in life — on ט׳ באב when we mourn the destruction of both Temples and the millions of children killed in those and subsequent holocausts — at the time of a family *simchah*, when people ask how many children I have, when I pray Rosh Hashanah and Yom Kippur and say מי יחיה ומי ימות and remember how I prayed on the High Holy Days I was pregnant with Miri, little knowing that by *Shabbos Bereishis* I would have a perfect baby and by י״ז טבת she would have died.

But I have lived with all this. I also have a stronger recognition than ever before of how much I am blessed. I don't think of what bad I must have done to deserve a *tzarah* such as this, but I gear my daily soul searching to being the best kind of person I can be. I don't believe that *cheshbon hanefesh* should be geared to searching for the particular sins that might doom us to particular punishments. Our Sages tell us שכר מצוה בהאי עלמא ליכא — that rewards for *mitzvos* and punishments for sins are all settled in the World to Come. In this world we have to live a good and ethical life for its own sake. There is not a day that goes by that I do not say בלב שלם ובכוונה יתרה the prayer מודה אני לפניך — thank You Hashem for each day that dawns afresh in a beautiful world.

I have stronger intimations of my own mortality now than I had then; I am aware of what death is. I have seen it. I am still frightened of it, because of the great pain it causes the survivors. But I am less frightened at the prospect of my own death. I want to live long and fully, of course, but I am more sure that something awaits me after I have "crossed the bar." The death of my child has strengthened my belief that there is a World to Come. With our limited vision or narrow perception, we find it hard to imagine a world beyond our own world. But they exist, "Yes, I believe that there is a World to Come," the song goes.

So with what then, do I conclude? I have been struck, but I have survived. Losing a child is one of the most terrible and painful things that can happen to a person. And yet, the person who lives through this can still go to visit Eretz Yisrael and speak to family after family who lost grown children, tall, beautiful sons whose potential had already begun to see fruition, and say: "I can put my own tragedy in perspective. Far greater *tzadikkim* than I have experienced *yesurim*, and the Talmud does speak about something called יסורים של אהבה."

Though the initial pain of my loss seemed to be unbearable, I have borne it. Though the loss itself was irreversible, I have, thank G-d, three subsequent children who have been a source of enormous joy and who make life very full. Mine was not the kind of tragedy you continue to live with every waking hour. For this I am deeply grateful. I have walked away, and I have not been smitten again and again, G-d forbid. My life, my soul, my self, my family, my relationships with people, my relationship with the Almighty, have all been enriched by Miri's life.

To answer the question I asked myself at the outset, "Could I ever again be the person I was before the tragedy?" I have to say, "Yes, I am the same person I once was, and yet, I am not. I can, once again, be happy with a full heart, as I never thought I would be able to be. But I have a different kind of vision now than I had then, a greater clarity of purpose, a more finely tuned sense of what is important, of how to help those who have suffered." There is much yet to say, but I'll stop here, and continue the conversation another time.

❦ ❦ ❦

[It is six years since Miriam Rus passed away. Mrs. Rookie Billet leads a fulfilled life, enjoys her family and career. She teaches Jewish studies and does guidance at the primary and secondary level. She gives lectures and *shiurim* and assists her husband with his rabbinical involvement. — Ed.]

Bitachon: The Greatest Cure

לג:לד (תהלים בעודי לאלקי אזמרה בחיי לה' אשירה)

leven years ago my friends were speculating as to how long I would survive. A chronic pain in my throat, a lumpy sensation that never seemed to go away, was diagnosed as malignant lymphoma.

Upon hearing my grim diagnosis, I was numb with fear. In agony I cried to Hashem from the depths of my soul. He answered me with a cloudburst of His blessings. *Baruch Hashem*, I made it. I survived. My message is one of hope and encouragement.

I have always been an observant Jewess, a legacy from my mother, who imbued all her children with awareness of the Almighty. She taught us to place our faith and trust in Him. Where I grew up, I had never had the opportunity for formal yeshivah training. Thus, I never really acquired the skills to examine my relationship with Hashem.

I was already praying three times a day, keeping Shabbos and *kashrus*. I studied some *chumash* every day, and devoured as many books as I could get on Torah topics. I attended all the lectures I could manage. Getting this scary disease catapulted me into a crash course. I no longer had time to take the slow route.

Just before becoming sick, I had started attending courses in *chassidus*. They were wonderful! In retrospect, I see how these classes were G-d's way of preparing the emotional curative for the physical nightmare which was to follow. They opened up for me a whole new way of understanding Judaism. After I became ill, I prayed with more fervor than ever before. I composed many of my own short prayers to Hashem, and referred to them several times a day. Sometimes it was a simple "Dear G-d," or "Please, G-d," or "Help me, G-d." Other times the prayers took the form of more lengthy discussions with the One Above. There was much examination of my life thus far — my deeds, where I was holding. There were commitments on my part to undertake additional *mitzvos* and to correct what I perceived had to be corrected. I quickly saw that the more trust I put in Him, the greater were my spiritual rewards. As my earthly being trembled on the brink of death, my soul soared to the heavens. Hashem, in His infinite wisdom, used what without Him would have been one of life's ugliest blows to open my eyes to life's fullness and beauty.

❦ ❦ ❦

I had visited doctors for several years with pains in my throat. Shortly after moving to Miami, the undiagnosed condition grew dramatically worse. Breathing became difficult. I began to lose my voice. The doctor I consulted put me on antibiotics. My condition didn't improve. I awoke one morning with the feeling of something pushing up and out of my throat. This time I would not be put off as in the past by the doctor's officious secretary. My fear gave me the courage to insist on seeing the doctor that same day.

The doctor took one look at my throat, dashed out, and came back with his associate. They scheduled me for a biopsy in a small local hospital almost immediately. They told me nothing. But the urgency with which they acted gave me an idea of the seriousness of my condition. I was frozen with fear.

That visit was *erev Shabbos Teshuvah*, the eve of the Sabbath of Repentance. Again I can see how Hashem was there for me. He granted me the holiest Shabbos of the year in which to devote myself entirely to fervent prayer on my own behalf that I survive what was to come.

Not feeling comfortable with my local doctor's handling of my case, after Shabbos I called my sister to ask her to make an appointment for me with an eminent surgeon she knew in New York. On the following day, Yom Kippur, my awareness of the seriousness of my condition intensified the awesomeness of the day. I spent the day in *shul* literally praying for my life.

The day after Yom Kippur my family and I flew to New York. I kept my appointment with the doctor in New York City. As he peered down my throat, I saw his eyelids flutter for just a second. That gesture confirmed my darkest fears.

"No wonder you feel like you're choking," he said. "You've got a growth filling your whole throat and neck area."

Scary as it was, I felt relieved. After the many doctors I'd seen to complain about pains in my throat, I'd finally found an expert who confirmed that there was something seriously wrong. This thing was not in my head, as the doctors who prescribed tranquilizers had inferred. I was not crazy. I really was ill. Hopefully, now I could get on with some treatment.

As the Succos holiday approached, it gave me an additional opportunity to prepare myself spiritually for whatever lay ahead. I took every opportunity to enter the *succah* — to say a blessing, to sit quietly, to think about what I had to face, and to turn to Hashem for His support.

The pathology report after my surgery revealed lymphoma. The prognosis sounded like a death sentence. What followed was a long, harrowing journey towards the distant possibility of life. For more than six weeks, weakened by surgery and the ravages of serious illness, my world was reduced to the New York City bus route between our hotel and the hospital where I received daily radiation treatment. The bus trips were arduous; eating the simplest meal was a painful ordeal. Overshadowing every moment was the agony of living with a disease so devastating that many people never mention its name.

Many times I felt I couldn't go on. I lived for the weekend, when my husband and I would go to Boro Park to spend Shabbos with our dear friends. Their loving concern gave me the strength to make it through another week. Their second daughter would wait for me to arrive each *erev Shabbos* to wash and dry my hair. This was a special kindness that I'll never forget. I could never have gone through the physical effort of washing my hair myself. That simple act of kindness gave me insight into the Torah directive to help clean the patient and the sickroom when we visit the sick. I learned firsthand how much helping a patient become clean — and *feel* clean — contributes to the patient's recovery.

At last I returned to my home in Miami with a clean bill of health. I began follow-up care with local doctors. I was constantly assured that I looked well. And yet my body refused to accept this. A year and a half passed, and I still wasn't feeling any stronger.

I lived through a nightmare of listening to doctor after doctor announce, after a brief examination, "You certainly look well, and everything seems okay." Not one of them ever really heard me or stopped to explore what I was telling them about my body. I could sense them fitting me into a middle-aged-woman syndrome: the doctors' real message to me was, "All your aches and pains are in your head." My complaints were brushed aside.

Eventually I experienced kidney blockage. After extensive scans and tests I learned that the lymphoma was back, more virulent than ever. It was in an advanced third stage.

I felt as if I'd been hit over the head with a sledge hammer. I had suffered so much already. How could I possibly go through all that again?

With trembling fingers I dialed the Bostoner Rebbe's number and told him that my doctor wanted me to begin aggressive chemotherapy immediately.

There was a pause when I finished telling him my story. Then the Rebbe said, "Sorah, I want you to come to Boston. You and Seymore can stay in our home, and I'll arrange an appointment with Dr. F. at the Dana Farber Cancer Center."

What a burden this was off my shoulders! His concern lifted me out of my desperation. That he would take over my case and invite us to stay in his own home brought relief beyond measure. I didn't know then the extent to which the Rebbe is world renowned for his work with critically ill patients, taking them into his New England Chassidic Center and setting them up with the top doctors in Boston.

Seymore and I flew to Boston. Dr. F. confirmed the earlier diagnosis. He told me that 70% of patients survived a year and half. Still, he was confident that with a new treatment plan plus experimental high-dose methatrexate my chances were good.

"Dr. F." I responded, fervently, "with the help of G-d, I'll write pages in your medical records each year until I'm 120."

I truly believed that, with G-d's help, I would survive. I knew that *bitachon*, my absolute trust in Hashem, was the most important thing. I saw Hashem as the key in directing the outcome of my disease. No matter what doctors and statistics might predict as my prognosis, I held fast to what the Bostoner Rebbe had told me. "We don't believe in statistics," he said. "Prayers — your own prayers, your children's prayers — all these are important in addition to the best medical treatment."

I knew that ultimately all was in Hashem's hands, so I looked to the Torah for my direction. We are told to find the best doctors available. Thanks to the Rebbe, I was in the hands of the best doctors. On the advice of a young friend, I went on a medicinal macrobiotic diet. I was getting some of the best nutritional support to be had. I worked to repair the emotional aspects of my life. And I went on an extensive spiritual odyssey.

I stayed at the Rebbe's home for three months. The spiritual and emotional support I received from the Rebbe and Rebbitzin, the congregants, and all the very sick patients and their families staying at his Chassidic Center were as much a part of my recovery as all the medical treatment I received. Everyone around me, family and friends and strangers, cared about my welfare and wanted me to make it. I was wrapped in a cocoon of love. This gave me the impetus to really get on my own case, to get out there and fight for my life.

After three months I was able to return to Miami to continue my treatments with my local doctor, under the supervision of the doctors in Boston. I endured eight more months of chemotherapy. It was physically and emotionally devastating. At times the pain was excruciating. And yet it was the most uplifting time of my life. I felt connected to Hashem in every aspect of my being.

My awareness of His workings in the world increased a hundredfold. I was sick — very sick — but I was soaring. Hashem opened the heavens for me. My life was a garden of miracles. There were the big ones, when I would look at a calendar and wonder, "Will I survive another week to the next chemo treatment?" — and then feel myself carried through it. Or when I didn't think I could bear the pain any longer — and it would let up. There were hundreds of little ones that at any other time I might have missed. Suddenly my eyes were opened. I was seeing in a way I'd never seen before. I might be carrying a bundle, and just as I felt I had no more strength to go on someone would appear to help me. Or when I was feeling low and lonely the phone would ring, with just the right person on the other end to lift my spirits.

As my relationship with Hashem deepened, I connected to other people on a more spiritual level. It was terrific for me to hear what people I hardly knew were doing for me. There were those who said numerous prayers for my recovery; others were saying *tehillim* and giving charity in my merit.

My family was wonderful. My husband took over the management of the entire household. He did things he never dreamed he could handle. My older son, Yehuda Leib, who was then at yeshivah, brought home *sefarim* for me to read. His selection was made to order for the state I was in. My younger son Jeff showed a sensitivity beyond his years in his consideration and support. Momma was there in the same comforting way she had been there for me from earliest childhood. My brother Moshe called me each morning to read some *Tehillim* to start the day on a spiritual high, and I know it was no accident that the particular phrase he would select each morning was just right for me on that day. My sister Ray left her large family in Nashville to come spend precious time with me, and my sister Shelly was full of comfort, always finding the right words to soothe me. The list is endless, and what I received from each one of them is immeasurable.

I had always enjoyed being a giver. One of the things Hashem taught me through this dread disease was how to be a taker. I guess that was another thing I had to learn. The smallest of tasks was often more than I could manage. As a result, I had to ask and ask. I learned what it was like to be on the receiving end. Friends would call to cook for me, to invite my family and me for Shabbos. Those people who gave of themselves to me were so warm and generous they made the lesson of taking easy.

In my classes I had learned concepts such as: The manner in which you ask Hashem for His blessings is the way He gives back to you. If your 'asking' Hashem is with *simchah* — joy — then Hashem gives you what to be happy about . . . All that Hashem gives is for our good . . . Hashem gives only what we can bear . . .

All these thoughts and messages lifted me straight up to the heavens, because I saw each lesson working in my own life. I understood that everything works for the positive in our lives. I changed from a pessimistic, "down" person (where my health was concerned) to an optimist facing each day with new reserves of joy. More and more I was grateful to Hashem. Each day Hashem gave me more for which to be grateful.

As I sought the best the medical field had to offer, I also sought blessings from all the *Rebbes* with whom I could visit or correspond. In retrospect, I think these blessings were a key factor in my survival.

When a *Rebbe* gave me a *brachah* and a *segulah*, I was so unbelievably euphoric that I am sure that that was a turning point in my recovery. I believe the joy I experienced as a result of the *brachos* was a powerful healing factor.

The *bitachon* I developed was beyond my wildest dreams. I didn't really know what putting trust in G-d was all about until I had to deal with my illness and its possible consequences. I am eternally grateful to Hashem for allowing me to come to a profound awareness of a much deeper relationship with Him as a result of this dread disease.

Almost a dozen years have passed since my first surgery. With the return of health and vigor I became involved once more in the material things of this world, but my life had been changed forever. If I am not always there now, I can still recall the unbelievable spiritual heights I reached during my illness. The quality of my life is so enhanced that all I can say, with much humility, is thank You, Hashem, thank You.

❧   ❧   ❧

What follows are excerpts from the last chapter of *Second Opinions*, a self-help book for cancer patients that I have written. It is based on my own experience, and also the experiences of scores of people I have assisted professionally as a marital and family psychotherapist specializing in counseling cancer patients. It is a practical guide covering what a patient needs to know to increase the odds of surviving cancer: What to ask. Where to ask. How to ask. And how to cope with the emotional ravages of the disease. In my opinion, *bitachon* is the patient's strongest weapon.

✑ Faith

This chapter is for my sister in spirit, Carolyn. Together we soared to spiritual heights which, before the dread spectre of cancer challenged our very existence, we had scarcely dreamed of. Carolyn's cancer eventually did cause her death. But it never conquered her. She was a giant of spiritual strength. To the end her every moment was a celebration of life. And I, who through the mercy of G-d have come through the clouds of doubt and pain and despair to the brilliant clear skies of a life made endlessly richer by my experiences, cannot close this book without a closer examination of the motive force which guided and uplifted me. That force is faith.

Until recently spirituality had no place in serious medical texts. The term "faith healing" has for many a bogus ring. And yet, in spite of skepticism from the medical profession, the phenomenon has stubbornly persisted. Terminally ill patients whose doctors have given up on them, who have nothing going for them but determined faith, suddenly go into remission. Because of these perplexing cases, some doctors are taking another look at the role of faith in healing.

In my own case, I know that without faith I would not have made it. As I think this book makes clear, I don't advocate a mindless, airy, wishful thinking. I certainly would never counsel a person with a diagnosis of cancer to turn his back on medicine and just have faith that things will turn out all right in the end. But I do plead that, as you enlist the "big guns" in all other areas — the best medical, emotional, nutritional, and physical resources available to help you fight for your life — you also go for the "top gun" spiritually. If I did not include this chapter in my book I would be leaving out the most important lesson in my experience, and a key factor in my recovery.

All my life I considered myself a devout Jewess. And yet when my malignancy was confirmed I found myself thrown into a turbulent sea of fear. How could I begin to cope with this enemy camped in the cells of my own body, threatening my very life? Terrified, I turned to G-d. I threw myself almost exclusively into the study and practice of my religion. I prayed. I read. I studied. I attended classes on the Torah, encouraged by the young chassidic women in my neighborhood, who would call me up faithfully on the night of the classes to see if I was up to attending. They would pick me up in their cars, helping me down the stairs, making sure that I was comfortably seated. They were grand. Their simple, uncomplicated good will kept me going when I might otherwise have given up. I was deeply grateful.

It wasn't easy. What was required was no less than a thorough and often painful examination of my life, past and present: What I'd been, where I was at, where I was going, what I needed to do. But gradually, as I developed a keener sense of what was happening to me in a spiritual context, my attitude towards my illness changed.

I cried, I laughed. I connected to a Higher Source, and I was euphoric. What began in fear blossomed into ecstatic, delirious happiness. From its beginnings as a random straw to clutch at in hurricane-strength winds, my faith became a powerful force for survival. Armed with this faith, I was able to turn my attention to the nitty-gritty details upon which my survival depended. I could do the necessary research, ask the right questions, find the best doctors. I had the strength to unearth the best nutritional and dietary recommendations to nurture my body. I could assume a positive, hopeful, happy attitude.

Faith is real. It is the underpinning of daily life. A catastrophic event such as a serious illness initiates an examination of what it is, essentially, that makes us tick. Ignoring the question of faith can be fatal. We all know of cases where doctors have given a patient excellent odds for survival, and yet that patient died. Fear takes over to such an extent that the patient simply gives up. Or the patient, unable to sustain a belief in making it, opts for an extravagant final fling and then, predictably, goes into a swift decline.

On the other hand, countless others with hopeless prognoses recover and go on to lead productive lives. And many times all that these lucky ones have going for them is faith. Essentially what faith seems to do is to connect you to the survivor within. I see it as that spark of G-dliness we call the soul. It is a powerful source of life-giving energy.

❦   ❦   ❦

Not everyone who has faith will overcome cancer, though studies indicate that these patients tend to survive longer. Some will inevitably die of their disease. But the quality of their lives, up to the final moments, is transformed and enhanced by the power of faith.

As an example of this I'd like to return to the case of Deborah, the young woman with severely metastasized lung cancer of whom Dr. D., evaluating her prior treatment plan after examining her history and condition, said, "My dear, they're using a soldier when you need a whole army."

Deborah was very young, only thirty-one. By the time she got to Dr. D. she was a veteran of the war on cancer. She'd been through the whole tour for five years — botched diagnoses and treatments, shattered hopes, grim prognoses. And yet all the time I knew Deborah she never once questioned, "Why me?" She was never bitter. Her energies were devoted to finding G-d, to understanding Him and basking in His glory. During her final months, far from cutting down on her many activities, she added to them.

When I was leaving on a visit to Israel, Deborah gave me a prayer to put in the Western Wall at Jerusalem. This spot, the site of the two holy Temples which were destroyed, is sacred to all Jews. We believe that a prayer placed in the cracks of this historic edifice finds its way to the Almighty.

Deborah had written:

> To the One Above,
>
> Please, G-d, let me be tolerant of all those around me who love me, with all the suffering I'm going through. Also, help me to overcome my illness. May my hope in You give me the strength and courage to go on. Please restore me to health. May G-d bless all those people who have been praying for me, who have given me the strength to go on.

Reading this, knowing how critical Deborah's condition was, my entire being cried out for her. At a time when most people would be screaming at the top of their lungs for help for themselves, she asked for blessings for those who had prayed for her. That was the quality of her faith. She survived far longer than her doctors thought possible, and even in her final hours was relating to the people around her, really living.

Over and over again, among the patients I counsel, I find the same results. The more we develop our faith, the more we enhance our chances for survival, and the more elevated in spirit we become. Spiritual elevation, once experienced, never leaves us. It can always be tapped.

In my case, faith became my modus operandi, the place I was coming from. It was a place of beauty, a place of strength, and my deepest source of comfort.

❋　　❋　　❋

Carolyn, whom I spoke of at the beginning of this chapter, transcended her condition through absolute faith in G-d. She was a young mother of three, with lymphoma. I knew her during the last three or four months of her life. Although I was never to learn much about her life prior to her illness — her work, her entertainments, her social life — our relationship was intimate. We related on a spiritual level. When her spirits flagged, she would look to me for a spiritual fix. Often an innocent remark made by another person in our presence would remind us of our experiences soaring the spiritual heights, and Carolyn would glance at me with the shadow of a smile playing on her lips, as if to say, "We know, don't we, Sorah! We've taken the trip upstairs many a time!"

At one point I had to leave Miami for New York and Boston. We agreed that I would telephone every few nights to see if Carolyn needed someone to talk to. On a Thursday evening, the night before our Sabbath, I called and Carolyn answered with, "What have you got to tell me?" I could tell immediately that she was feeling low.

I related an experience I'd had with a friend the day before. Eileen's twenty-year-old, who had Down's syndrome, was in Intensive Care. She doted on this child, and had not left her side in ten days. It was now necessary that she leave for a few hours, and she was distraught about the effect her absence would have on her daughter.

"Laurie doesn't understand what's happening here," Eileen told me. "She doesn't know how to handle it. How can I leave her when she leans on me so much?"

My reply was, "Eileen, tell Laurie how much you love her and hate to leave her. Explain that you must go away for just a few hours. Tell her she is not alone. G-d is with her. She can talk to Him."

On hearing this story over the telephone, Carolyn said, "Thanks. You just made my Sabbath." Then she hung up.

Not long after this, as the Jewish High Holidays approached, Carolyn lay critically ill in a hospital up north. At the request of her family I called her from Miami and urged her to let her husband, who was with her, remain with her through the holidays.

She answered firmly, "Bob's place is at home, praying in the synagogue with our boys beside him. I don't need him here. I'm fine."

"Then won't you let your mother-in-law, or your niece, or someone from the family share the holidays with you?" I persisted. "They don't want to think of you being there all alone."

In a sure, resilient voice that rang with confidence and joy, she replied, "I am not alone."

Carolyn's physical condition was beyond repair. By all logic she should have been writhing in agony. But with faith she was able to transform her last days into a euphoric experience. Her husband flew with her sons up to see her. Shortly afterwards she slipped into a coma. A few days later, on the eve of the holidays, this magnificent soul returned to its Source.

❧   ❧   ❧

There is an unmistakable glow about people who are spiritually elevated. The high I feel when I'm connected to G-d is beyond what I think any addict might experience. And joy isn't dependent on anything outside myself.

The experience of tapping into the spiritual reserve within you, which I call connecting with G-d, makes you feel like a giant. When you are feeling that connection you are invulnerable. Nothing — literally nothing — can hurt you. Catastrophic illness has a way of making us do some soul-searching. Suddenly it becomes important to find meaning in our existence. It is very common for terminal patients who have not previously been interested in spirituality to search for G-d.

I urge you to open up to the possibility that there is something beyond everyday reality. You might be surprised to discover a long-buried spark of hope. Cling to it. That hope is the expression of the survivor inside you. It's the ultimate weapon in your arsenal.

In his classic profile of cancer patients, Dr. Lawrence LeShan makes this point. He says, "Among those stricken by the disease, the people who are most capable of recovery are the men and women who can discover a new wellspring of hope, whatever their past disappointments, a true recognition of their needs, and of their worth as human beings."

When we are not in touch with the survivor in ourselves, we are likely to fall prey to another strong voice inside of us, the destroyer. This is the voice of negativity, which drags us down into a pit of depression, telling us there's no hope. It goes on and on like a broken record, saying, "What's the use? You're going to die. You might as well just give up." As soon as I hear that voice I turn to my "Please, G-d" tapes. The mind cannot hold both outlooks, the positive and the negative, at the same time. I make an active choice for the positive.

Having had the experience of connecting with the survivor, I can use the memory of that experience again and again to reconnect. I can still recall how very close to death I sometimes felt during the long months of chemotherapy. I was a prisoner of my body, trapped in a half-dead container that the medical profession was trying to salvage. I would lie on the couch wondering, "Will I even live through these treatments? Can I possibly survive such a murderous ordeal?

Weak as I was, I found that by doing deep relaxation techniques and a type of religious meditation, I was always able to reconnect. And no matter what my condition, I would feel at one with myself, with my Creator, with the whole world.

That experience has endured. My life is immeasurably enriched. And this has come about in part because I had cancer. The pain, the suffering, the fear spurred me on to discover the unending joy of connecting with G-d. I came to a deeper understanding of the stressful aspects of my life, and realized that I could exercise my G-d-given freedom of choice to change them. Perhaps the conditions causing the stress could not be changed, but I could learn to cope with them. As I corrected my priorities in life I could see them for the tiny, unimportant details they were.

Having cancer gave me the opportunity to correct a lifetime of unhealthy habits. I learned how my personality fit the cancer profile, rendering me vulnerable to severe illness. While heredity and environment and who knows what other factors certainly contributed their share, my unhealthy habits and repressed, hyperactive personality were bound to take their toll eventually. Cancer gave me the motivation I needed to reform.

Because of these changes, my relationships with my family, my loved ones, my close friends, have improved tremendously. I'm learning how to communicate openly, how to ask for help, how to take graciously as well as to give. And I am able to open up even more. It's a chain reaction, a continual unfolding of the beauty of life, a beauty I could never wholly appreciate until that life was mortally threatened. The ways of the L-rd are indeed mysterious.

This has not been an easy chapter to write. I wanted to share my own experience, and yet it has not been my intention to preach religion to my readers. But, as I fought to survive, faith was the strongest weapon in my arsenal.

I'd like to end by saying, with gratitude and deep humility, "Thank You, G-d, for letting me come this far."

    ❦   ❦   ❦

[Mrs. Sessile Winograd is a psychotherapist, who does marital and family counseling. It is nine years since she completed chemo for her disease. — Ed.]

The Bitter with the Sweet

וִיבְטְחוּ בְךָ יוֹדְעֵי שְׁמֶךָ כִּי לֹא עָזַבְתָּ דוֹרְשֶׁיךָ ה' (תהלים ט:יא)

As my son nears his third birthday, I sit here pondering the past three years. The happy times, the sad times, the bitter with the sweet. A little boy who is beautiful, clever, and witty, yet he can sit independently for only short periods of time. He can pull himself up to standing but he cannot walk. He can talk a blue streak to beat any kid his age — yet he's handicapped.

His life had a complicated beginning. There were many problems. Little did I imagine when they were finally over that they were really just beginning. He was about three weeks old and just beginning to digest about 10 cc's of liquid orally and it was time for us to say *Hallel* on his miraculous progress, when we got the shocking report.

The doctor patiently explained that our beautiful little baby suffered an intracranial hemorrhage. That means that there was bleeding from a burst blood vessel into his brain. It did not help to hear that about fifty percent of premature babies have this problem. She quietly explained that this could result in any untold types of brain damage, although she could not be sure of the nature or severity of the damage at this point. The only way to know is to wait and see! Wait and see indeed! What do you mean wait and see — what do you mean don't think about it for the next few months! What do you mean it probably won't be obvious for at least six months!

Staggering out of her office, stumbling blindly towards the elevators, I kept thinking: another retarded child, another sick child, we could not handle it the first time, what will we do now? And we won't even know right away — and by the time we find out, who knows? Or worse yet, maybe he won't make it and we will lose another child and there will be another irreparable hole.

But even as I was approaching the car to go home, I had already made a decision. We will treat him as if he was 100% normal until otherwise indicated. I did not even tell my husband immediately. There was time to be the bearer of unhappy tidings later, if necessary. Yet I watched over him with an eagle's eye — observing every move and judging — normal or abnormal. And in spite of it all he seemed to flourish. Although he was teeny, he was adorable. He seemed more alert every day and my spirits began to soar.

When we finally brought him home from the hospital at six weeks we were both elated and nervous. It would be another two weeks before his *bris*.

Almost immediately I decided something was not right. Being an old hand at babies I realized that although he did seem alert and in tune to what's happening around him, his body did not conform to mine when I held him — he didn't cuddle up like a tiny baby does, rather he arched his back and always seemed to be wanting to know what's going on behind him. I realized that my fears were somewhat founded when everyone started to ask, "What does he see up there?" He was always looking up at the ceiling even when held in a vertical position. I also started noticing little tremors in his legs, and thus began my saga of *farenfering* — telling everyone — it's nothing, he's just "neurologically immature," and other excuses of my own concoction.

But the day of reckoning came and my pediatrician told me "I don't like his reflexes." Once again it was patiently explained to me, as I tried to keep from fainting, that this is a sign of major problems. Major problems? How could it be? Look how well he looks. I had finally allowed myself to breathe a little more easily. He looked normal enough although I had only his intelligent eyes and smile to go by. But it was not to be — I made an appointment to see a pediatric neurological developmental specialist and it quickly became clear to me that she was not very happy with the neurological development of this child. A course of therapy was outlined and immediately begun, as it was explained to me that in this heretofore unnamed condition the children become worse very quickly and therapy is needed to ward off the stiffening of the muscles.

Now I was on a new merry-go-round — juggling family, therapy schedules with trips regularly into Manhattan, plus the normal routine of a new baby.

And every day included new milestones — good ones and bad ones. His smile was dazzling but he didn't move around much. He quickly became famous as a little charmer, yet all the coaxing wouldn't stop him from looking toward the ceiling. And still, even when we asked, no one would say, "Yes, your son has cerebral palsy." And if I said directly, "Is this called C.P.?" They would say, "Well C.P. is such a large umbrella and so many things come under it . . ." So when the day came that I heard a professional say, "All the children here have C.P." I wanted to protest and say, "Mine doesn't!" — except that he does.

He has grown up to be the ruler of the house as he sends his fifteen-year-old sister to study, and as he tells his twelve-year-old brother, "Be quiet and go to sleep!" He picks up the phone, "I want to make a call," and quietly quotes his phone number perfectly accurately.

I used to say I won't be satisfied that he's normal until I'll hear him learn a *blatt gemara*, but as I hear him say the *aleph-beis* by himself or I hear him making the correct *brachos* on food, I think I am content that he's normal.

There are times when I worry that we overreact to his unbelievable cleverness. But then I click back to reality and I remember how close he came to not being capable of anything at all. And suddenly the ecstasy seems justified.

Yet on Shabbos when he cries bitterly that he wants to go to *shul*, and after it is explained that he can't walk he says, "So I'll hold Tatty's hand," it takes the patience of a saint to stay in control. And sometimes you can't stay in control and you just sit and cry together.

Although we know a day will come soon that he will begin to walk, we also know that in an accepted fashion he will never walk normally. There is a long haul ahead — physically, emotionally and spiritually.

As the day of his third birthday approaches it seems altogether fitting that it should be Rosh Chodesh and we should be joined by *Klal Yisrael* saying *Hallel* on this special day.

But What Should I Say?

הדריכני באמתך ולמדני . . . (תהלים כה:ה)

I t happens more often than most people realize. Suddenly you hear that a friend of yours has come home from the hospital with empty arms and an ache in her heart. You quickly call your neighbor to discuss the news. Instinctively you tell her that you ought to do something. "But, what should we say?" she asks you and so, both of you end up doing nothing. It's not that you are unfeeling, simply that it's easier to pretend that nothing happened.

I too, feeling helpless, used to wonder and do nothing. No longer. I have learned the hard way that there are many things that a friend can do to help and comfort someone who has suffered a loss. Obviously, I can only tell you what was helpful for me in my time of need, but I believe much of this is universal.

1. What should I say?

Nothing that you say will really help, the **important** thing is to **listen**. Many people who are desperate to talk are afraid that no one wants to hear. Tell your friend, "I was so sorry to hear your news! How are you feeling?" Don't ask her in the middle of Shop-Rite, or while your kids are climbing over you. If, when you ask, it is obvious that you are unable to listen to the true answer, your friend will begin to be convinced that you really don't want to hear about her heartache. Ask her in a time, place, and tone of voice that show that you really want to listen and share her pain. If necessary ask, "Do you want to talk about it?" Don't pry if she really would rather not discuss it, but I firmly believe that talking about what happened helps.

2. But I really don't know her that well!

If you know her well enough to talk about her, you probably know her well enough to talk *to* her. Call her up to tell her that you were sorry to hear the news, and ask her how she feels. One of my closest friends in Lakewood moved from acquaintance to friend because when I told her what happened, she cried with me and then came over the next morning to visit me and give me *chizuk*.

3. But I'm afraid that I will start crying and make her more depressed.

It is unlikely that your tears will cause her to become any more depressed than she already is. As a matter of fact, I drew much closer to my sisters-in-law when they too cried for the pain of my husband and myself. They showed me that they really cared for me and this was very comforting. We weren't alone.

A few other do's and don'ts.

(1) Don't assume that she will be depressed or in bed forever. Most people resume a semblance of normal life within a week. On the other hand, don't assume that because she is behaving normally, she is no longer mourning. It doesn't hurt to ask how she's feeling every few weeks. Realize that she will *never* completely forget what happened.

(2) Don't tell her that her doctor was no good, or she *shouldn't* have done this or *should* have done that. Everyone feels guilty after a loss and there is no reason to make it worse. On the other hand, if you do have some practical advice for the *future*, do mention it in the form of some information that she is free to use if she wants to.

(3) Don't tell her that she is only having *tzaros* because she is such a big *tzadekess*. Most people don't feel themselves on a level to merit such suffering. She also might feel that she would be better off not being a *tzadekess*.

(4) Don't hide your children whenever you see her. She is aware

that you have children and knows she has to face them. On the other hand, don't ask her to babysit for your infant unless she sincerely volunteers. And don't complain to her about your children or tell her that she is better off this way.

(5) Do inform her close friends, those who can give *chizuk*. Also inform anyone, who is likely to make a blunder which will be painful for both of them. As far as any other discussion of the subject, check the laws pertaining to gossip before proceeding.

(6) Do tell her that you are praying for her. You may mention any *segulos* that you know of but be aware that (a) some people don't have faith in *segulos* and (b) if she does, she probably heard them already.

(7) Do encourage your husband to give her husband *chizuk*. Often husbands are ignored at these times even though they too are suffering, in addition to the extra burdens they must handle to help their wives.

(8) Do pamper her as you would any new mother. She certainly wants and deserves some special attention. Of course, don't make a fuss in public.

(9) Do share similar experiences if they end on a hopeful note. Many people really want information and *chizuk* from those who have lived through it.

(10) Above all, acknowledge what happened, encourage her to talk and continue treating her like a valuable friend. Remember, that it's never too late to show that you care.

P.S. THANKS FOR LISTENING.

❦   ❦   ❦

[This article originally appeared in *HaKesher*. The author, Mrs. P., lives in Lakewood, N.J. — Ed.]

The Last Yom Kippur

ה' שמעה בקולי . . . (תהלים קל:ב)

s the *chazan* said these words, Hadassah squeezed my hand tightly and burst into tears. But as soon as *Unisaneh Tokef* was over she regained her composure and continued praying, full of joy and trust.

This took place the last Yom Kippur of her life. Hadassah had just regained her ability to read for brief periods at a time. Although weak and suffering unimaginable pain, she insisted on praying in the Telshe Yeshivah which was so close and dear to her heart. A room across from the study hall was prepared for her with a bed, a nurse, and her medications. However, Hadassah insisted on remaining upstairs in the women's *shul* most of the day. I had the great privilege of spending the holiest of holy days, Yom Kippur, praying and talking with her. Talking on Yom Kippur? When Hadassah rested for brief periods on her bed we talked, but her talk was not mere words. Each word she uttered was a lesson for life in faith, trust, holiness, and purity.

Hadassah kept apologizing for taking me away from my praying. However, I reassured her that being with her, watching her behavior, and hearing her speak, brought me to greater levels of repentance than even praying can. "Thank you", she said. "I will never forget the kindness you are doing, sitting with me on Yom Kippur and helping me *daven*." Her recognition of good was an inspiration for others to follow in her footsteps. She was grateful for each minute thing one did for her.

It is said that a great person knows when it is his last day of judgment in this world. Throughout Yom Kippur, I had a feeling that she was trying to tell me that this was to be her last Yom Kippur. The only time she shed tears was during *Unisaneh Tokef*. The rest of the day Hadassah was full of joy. Happy in such a situation? Yes, she was happy that she was alive; happy that she was able to read by herself from the *machzor*; happy that she could spend Yom Kippur praying with a congregation in the yeshivah; happy that she could hear her father *daven n'eilah*; happy that she could wish each and every person who came over to her after *n'eilah* a good year. How well she knew what each person needed and how sincere and warm her blessings were. She had room in her heart for everyone else.

While lying down for a brief rest period, Hadassah suddenly jumped up. I sat her down and insisted that she gather strength for *n'eilah*. "Please don't tell me I have to rest, when I know that this Yom Kippur is a very important Yom Kippur for me," she replied. When I pleaded with her that her mother would be upset if she returned to *shul* right away (she was always so careful in honoring her mother and father), she answered more strongly than was her usual manner. "I know *why* I have to pray, and no one can tell me to rest now. Believe me, this is not the time to rest." As she spoke these words, there was a certain holiness in the room, an intangible feeling that these words were not spoken by an ordinary young woman, but by one on a higher level, by one who knows more than the rest of us . . . Thus I relented.

During these brief periods of rest, she asked me to keep the door of the room open so she could hear the yeshivah boys from across the hall pray. As she was dozing off, she murmured, "The angels are singing." Then with a smile she fell into a slumber.

When she awoke she asked the nurse to help her fix her wig. She thanked her many times. When the nurse left the room briefly to get something, Hadassah turned to me and said, "She must feel like a fifth wheel since I don't need her as I am spending most of the day upstairs praying. Let her feel that I needed her for something." This young woman who already heard angels singing, who was already in "higher worlds" had the presence of mind and heart on the Day of Judgment to spend time and effort on a trivial chore to make another human feel needed and important.

As I prayed with her throughout Yom Kippur I felt that with each prayer she was closer and closer to the Creator. It was not only the way she said each word, but also the *hashraas haShechinah* that was evident on her face.

At the conclusion of *n'eilah* she squeezed my hand so hard that I felt a taste of the currents of uplifting and holiness that only she could experience transmitted to me. It is a moment I will always cherish.

After the blowing of the *shofar* she turned to me and said, "Next Yom Kippur I will אי"ה be truly happy."

My reply was, "Yes, you will אי"ה have a complete recovery."

She answered me, "No, that is not what I mean at all. I mean true happiness."

The look she gave me when she uttered these words was one an ordinary person can not describe. It was one that made me feel a bit uneasy. However, seeing her clap to the singing and dancing of the "Next year in Yerushalayim", I immediately joined her.

This *ba'alas aliyah* sensed that this was her last Yom Kippur. She tried to fulfill her purpose in this world in every way, and when it was time to accept Hashem's decree she did so with love and joy.

הדסה ע"ה הלכה למנוחות
ואותנו השאירה לאנחות

✑ Friendship
by Fradel Berger

Friendship is a priceless gift
That can't be bought or sold
But its value is far greater
Than a mountain made of gold
For gold is cold and lifeless
It can neither see nor hear
And in the time of trouble
It is powerless to cheer
It has no ears to listen
No heart to understand
It cannot bring you comfort
Or reach out a helping hand
So when you ask Hashem for a gift
Be thankful if He sends
Not diamonds pearls or riches
but the love of real true friends

Happiness Nipped in the Bud

השלך על ה' יהבך והוא יכלכלך . . . (תהלים נה:כג)

I was delirious with happiness the day my daughter was born. I had two sweet boys and now a special sister would join the family — special because I was to name her for my mother who had passed away six months before. Overwhelmed with happiness and gratitude to Hashem, I gazed at this special being. However, all this was short lived and in fact, my perfect happiness was nipped in the bud when a pediatric resident informed me that there was something terribly wrong with my new daughter. He was brief and to the point. The baby had a purple mark on her back, there was an opening in the spine and she would need immediate surgery. I remember being aware that this was a traumatic incident, but I was too weak to comprehend what I was being told. My doctor was very curt and insensitive. He said, "It's just a tragedy and it has nothing to do with me." All of a sudden the room emptied, except for the janitor.

I was alone with my misery until my husband came. He had already been told about the baby's birth defect and was falling apart. I cried and cried until my pediatrician arrived fifteen minutes later. She had a tendency to over-react and explained my baby's problem with tears in her eyes. When she told me that she'd be paralyzed, I cried hysterically. She couldn't guarantee her mental condition at that time. I felt I was collapsing under the weight of the news. How would I cope with a baby who had such severe handicaps?

The baby was transferred for surgery immediately. She also had a shunt put in, to prevent fluid buildup in the brain, routine for children with this condition. After a few days, I met with the baby's surgeon. The condition was called spina bifida and no one was to blame; it was simply an accident of nature. Her lesion was very high: T12 and he was not sure of the extent of her paralysis. She wouldn't feel any sensation from her mid-chest down.

I was in absolute misery. My family and friends tried to bolster me, "Hashem only gives challenges to those who can handle it." Oh, really, I thought to myself, how would you like to trade with me. At that time, I felt very firmly that I didn't want to handle it nor grow to accept it. I glossed over her disability, saying that therapy would do wonders for her and she would be able to walk well one day. This was mainly to reassure myself. I remember the visit of my mother's sister. She was not blessed with children and through her pain, she tried to comfort me. "All my life I asked for the opportunity to raise and nurture a special child who could develop into a unique person and now Hashem has given you the opportunity." At that time her words were not very effective but as the years passed we were able to see many fine qualities in Chaya.

In the first few month's of Chaya's life, she developed as normally as my other children aside from the paralysis. There were many visits to doctors. She began home therapy and stimulation at a very young age until she was two. Then we went to a pre-school program at a rehabilitation center. She refused to co-operate when she was this age and it was an exhausting experience. The traveling was a hassle and I was relieved when we finally started home therapy. When she was two years old, I noticed the atrophy of the lower half of her body. Whenever I bathed her after that, it was a source of unhappiness. It was obvious that she wasn't perfect like my other children. I would cry "על אלה אני בוכיה" and wonder התחיינה העצמות האלה — would these legs ever be rejuvenated? My husband often took over the bathing when he realized that this aspect of her care was difficult for me. Eventually I resigned myself and said, "This is the way it is going to be."

None of my "comforters" could persuade me that if Hashem gave me this test, there was a higher purpose and that eventually I would accept it. Only one friend whose child had also been born with spina bifida had some constructive advice. I called her the next day. She was very empathetic and understood my depression fully. She gave me a lot of practical advice and I was relieved to hear that one could cope. It didn't seem all that frightening. We kept in touch often throughout the therapy experience, I was always grateful to mothers who reached out to me. I felt very insecure, like a fledgling trying out her wings.

When we went for walks I couldn't help comparing other babies in carriages. As long as Chaya was the right age for wheeling, it was not so hard to deal with; things were still beneath the surface. However, when she was three we got an oversized rehabilitation stroller. I wanted to tell everyone that she was already doing nicely in a parapodium (a one piece support system that enables a child to jump while strapped in securely) and that soon she would be introduced to a walker. Other nights I wanted to hide from the curious eyes that caved in around me. Some nights I woke up shaking. The eyes had turned into vultures! I dreaded going out with that big carriage and was relieved when neighbors' children asked if they could take Chaya to the store.

One summer when she was two years old and still immobile, she played in a twin-size playpen or lay on the grass. She couldn't turn over as the six month old babies were doing. I remember my ambivalent feelings. We adored her but she was not developing like the other children. But on days when she was irresistible, I could sing a song of *dayanu*. She surprised us with complete sentences and was a real source of entertainment. My family's easy adjustment to our "special child" kept me in check and I was able to count my blessings.

When Chaya was three, a healthy baby boy joined our family. Yossi was one of those gifts from Hashem, a care-free baby. Feedings and clean diapers kept him content. His big brothers and Chaya accepted him instantly. When Yossi started walking naturally at thirteen months, both Chaya and I had a hard time. My feelings of resentment and sadness for Chaya's limitation surfaced. I realized that I hadn't come to grips with her handicap. Chaya openly showed her feelings by pushing him down as he walked haltingly. Another reality set in when Yossi was trained at two and a half and Chaya, aged five, still had not outgrown her pampers. This was very disheartening to me and was constantly reinforced when I saw teenagers and adults, sitting in wheelchairs, all incontinent. Would our Chaya look like that as a young adult?

At six Chaya was progressing very well in home therapy. However, she balked when her therapist wanted to work on independent dressing and to learn how to put on her own braces. She also disliked exercising immensely. Sometimes she was so angry that therapy time was one big temper tantrum. It was a real test in self-control not to interfere. She majored in walking and when she got her crutches it was a great step to independence. She worked her way to five blocks and did a wonderful swing-through gait with just a little support. I asked her to pick up light grocery items for me and included a treat as incentive. When one of the neighbors spotted Chaya coming home with her package back-pack style, she asked if next time Chaya would pick up a newspaper for her at the corner. Chaya was on cloud nine. Everyone was full of praise for her kindness.

At four and a half, Chaya was ready to start pre-school. We encountered many disappointments and unhealthy attitudes by principals and staff. They were not eager to extend themselves and we were rejected by three schools. When we were finally accepted, the principal insisted that I stay home and be on call in case of an "emergency". They were afraid of the unknown, but there were never any mishaps.

One teacher suggested that I buy a battery-operated toy that would engage the other children in play so that they could become accustomed to Chaya. She ignored my claims that Chaya was naturally playful and refused to let me explain Chaya's "different way" of walking. She was in favor of the "ostrich syndrome" — "If you don't say anything, they won't notice anything different about her." Won't notice long leg braces and crutches indeed!

When we came to school in the morning (bringing her every day was part of the deal), Morah Sheila forgot to say, "Good morning," as she stared at Chaya with an unabashed "poor girl" expression. B"H this ill-fated kindergarten experience came to an end and Chaya's self-image was not affected.

The following years required my involvement with different staff members — endless arrangements to accommodate her needs. It was remembering to tip the handyman for bringing her to lunch, the bus drivers and attendants for helping her up and down.

Chaya proved herself in her early childhood education and was soon everyone's best friend. When she was in third grade she had a prize teacher who welcomed the challenge of teaching a child with a handicap. At year's end I thanked her warmly. She had brought out the best in Chaya, to which she answered that it was a *sipuk nefesh* for her and she gained a lot from the year. On those days my heart sang *Bsiyata Dishmaya*. There were other teachers who were over-protective and limited her walking, actually hindering her progress.

Even though she was naturally clever and sociable there was a lot of loneliness for Chaya. When the pavement in the yard was slippery she was grounded and many times I caught her with a dejected look on her face watching other girls play ball and rope. These were harsh realities for both of us.

When she was seven we went through a very rough time with Chaya. She had a serious skin breakdown and she required surgery. She was hospitalized for seven weeks and she was only allowed on her stomach all this time as well as the three week home recuperation. We rented a hospital bed for her. It was an unfortunate setback in her progress. She was very achy and uncomfortable. My family was very supportive and relieved me when necessary. She was very pleasant with them, but when it was my shift, she tested my patience many times. There was plenty of time to talk and sometimes Chaya would express her own frustration and resentment. She shocked me one day with this assessment of her condition. "I'll bet I know why I have this problem. It's all because of the tight corset and braces. I wouldn't need any of that if I could walk. It's all your fault, because you never taught me to walk the way you did Motty, Benyomin and Yossi." She began sobbing. Speechless, I hugged her and tried to soothe her, actually feeling helpless to help her. She wasn't permitted to sit while her incision was healing and even weeks later, the doctor advised us that her lesion was very sensitive and we would have to put the braces away for a while. He advised us to get a wheelchair, for her convenience. I couldn't accept the fact that Chaya would have to be in a wheelchair, however temporary; the wheelchair meant only one thing to me — she would be an invalid. We overlooked the expense and bought her an Amiga (a motorized scooter). She mastered it quickly, and enjoyed it. The doctor warned us that she was prone to more breakdowns of this type. It seems she was highly sensitive and, in fact, she had two more that required surgeries.

One winter I slipped carrying packages and damaged my shoulder. Chaya was four at the time. My shoulder was slow to mend and the only way I could function for my family and care for Chaya was to hire part-time help. I was very limited and continued with the help for four years. Chaya was very attached to me and resented strangers assuming her personal care. She fought the housekeepers and often drained me with her lack of co-operation. They would get angry, in turn, and threaten to quit. I knew I couldn't manage on my own but I was rapidly losing patience with Chaya. My difficulties were magnified at this time with my own limitation and I felt very burdened and tied down with Chaya. Not only did I feel incapable of living up to it; at times I wasn't sure I wanted it. Yet there was nowhere to run. My husband was over-protective and I felt we never had a break since Chaya was born. I also realized that my personality was changing, I was mellowing and too young for these changes. My sense of humor was not as keen as it once was, my patience was shorter and I overreacted to mild health conditions in my children. I was never a mother hen, but now I was desperate that everyone stay healthy. If one of the boys started coughing, I thought of pneumonia.

I pursued many leads about the newest in bracing and visited many orthotists (brace and corset fitters). She used a parapodium till she was three, afterward she was fitted for long-leg braces and was training to walk with a walker. I still can't imagine why people felt so free and easy to make suggestions. "Maybe if she wore shorter braces, she could walk better." or "My aunt in London claims that their specialists are tops." Did they really think I was uncaring about Chaya's progress and welfare? They made me feel so inadequate and guilty.

I practiced walking with Chaya whenever possible after school. For me they were proud moments, but the insensitivity of some caused minor heartbreaks. Why do people assume that a handicapped person also has a problem with his hearing? There was little recognition for Chaya as a thinking, feeling and hearing little person. We were subject to a lot of unsolicited advice about different crutches, etc. One person who was obviously floored said, "I don't know what I'd do if my child were handicapped. It takes a very special person to take care of a child like that. I know I could never handle it." Chaya's expression was doleful confusion. All our attempts to make her feel "normal" could be undone by a tactless, ignorant public. I still get angry when I hear high praise because indeed, I do "handle it." I am anything but heroic, but this is what we are expected to show to a virtual stranger.

We also need to show acceptance of our children's handicap. I had a real grieving period for the perfect daughter that she wasn't. Yet I was expected to accept. As the years roll by, I discover that I am no closer to acceptance than I was the day I was told of her disability. There were times that I experienced real depression and a feeling of helplessness. I would ask myself, "Don't I love my child?" The answer of course, is a resounding YES! But I am saddened by what has happened to Chaya, to her brothers and our lives. And we can never accept it — we have to adjust to it. Acceptance suggests passivity, and we have never been passive about Chaya's care. We cannot be passive in our daily lives, not in dealing with the myriad departments, agencies, doctors and schools involved with her care. I also get tired of educating the world, one person at a time. My husband and I have left no stone unturned in pursuing the best possible physical therapy and specialists in the rehabilitation field.

On one of our out-of-town trips to a center for her braces evaluation, my husband questioned the orthotist about the progress of other children with Chaya's condition. He tended to be unusually soft where she was concerned and a little unrealistic at first about her walking capability. The orthotist assured us, "One day your daughter will walk better than you and I, with the help of a computer." Research in liberating handicapped people from braces and wheelchairs is being conducted in Chicago, as well as in Ireland. Hashem is the Giver of knowledge and when He wills it a miracle will occur which will seem like a natural human accomplishment.

We also visited a well-known hospital for extensive urological testing. Chaya was exhausted and we prepared for the night at our motel. There was no bed for her, so she slept with me. I said the *Shema* with her and then she asked to hear my *Shema*.

Every night after *Shema* I add my private prayer and thanks for the day. This way I can reflect on the day that has passed and I become vividly aware that Hashem has blessed me one more day with His overwhelming kindness. This keeps my imagination and worries in check and I stop crossing all those impossible future bridges. " ... and thank You Hashem for the success of this day. Everything went well, thanks to You. And just as You helped me today, so I turn to You, and ask You for Your bounty of goodness for tomorrow. And thank You for Chaya. She is so sweet and good. Keep her and protect her always and make us all worthy of Your blessing." I turned to Chaya and I could tell that she liked my *Shema*.

We were once looking at a magazine for "challenged people". There was an article about a new concept in independent housing for the handicapped: barrier-free housing. The apartments and homes were equipped with ramps and kitchens and bathrooms were designed for accessibility and convenience. I suggested to Chaya that we talk to our assemblyman about sponsoring this housing concept for our community. "Imagine," I said, "when you get married you could have the ideal apartment without steps and other obstacles." (She still disliked practicing steps at this time.) To this she announced "When I get married, I won't need a ramp. I'll be able to walk and get up and down steps."

"Oh?" I said, for lack of anything better. I was dumbfounded.

We discussed this for a few minutes and she finally retreated from her overly-optimistic dream. I've never been a believer in false hope; however, I've always encouraged her practice properly, so that she'll progress to independence one day. When we saw an expert walker with crutches, she was thrilled to see that such superior walking was a possibility. She finally relented and said, "I'll do such good walking by then, I won't need the ramp, because steps will be easy for me."

Everything is in G-d's hands and still thoughts of Chaya's future nag me. I often wonder about her chances of success and fulfillment as she grows up. Now Chaya is thirteen years old and living in a happy, sheltered school and home enviroment. Will independence and marriage be in store for her? When I am in touch with young women and mothers who reassure me that the obstacles are not insurmountable, I feel better. One young mother with spina bifida had two children and was managing well, even driving a car with hand controls and a roof compartment for her wheelchair.

My main concern is that she always have sensitive, understanding people around her. I know I won't always be there to assist her when she falls. I can only pray to Hashem, the Eternal Watchman Who never slumbers or sleeps and ask Him to bring the redemption that will relieve everyone's pain.

ᴇ§ A Friend   by Fradel Berger

A good friend is like sunshine in the morning
The comfort in the ordinary days
Not the kind intrusive or demanding
Just there to share your life in quiet ways

Ready with a smile or friendly greeting
A little chat or some sweet surprises
For therein lies the joy of daily living
A good friend helping when the need arises

Attitudes

The phrase "positive attitude" has been bandied about by so many people in varied situations that it has come to mean almost anything to anyone. Therefore, to derive benefit from this discussion, we need to clarify how we intend to use this phrase.

Let us begin with some definitions of what positive attitude is *not*.

1. Positive attitude is *not* an excuse to remain oblivious to all situations.

2. Positive attitude is *not* a mindset that everything is great and that there are no problems.

3. Positive attitude is *not* an excuse to be unprepared.

4. Positive attitude is *not* a euphoric, unrealistic, rose-colored view of the world.

Positive attitude is the ability to develop a mindset to manage our thoughts.

We can choose:

To see opportunities where we now see problems.

To see growth where we now see stagnation.

To see the big picture where we now see only fragments. Yet to know that even big projects are accomplished one step at a time.

To see the future where we now see only the present.

To see the solution where we now see hopelessness, discouragement, or failure.

To believe wholeheartedly that every problem we face is a challenge the Almighty knows we can meet.

To see each day as a new exciting opportunity.

To approach each area of life with a healthy curiosity.

To realize that people need you; there are lives to be brightened, problems to be solved

A situation may be caused by factors outside our sphere of influence, but we can control our *attitude* toward each and every situation in life.

A man in the hospital is terminally ill. Someone knocks on his door and asks, "Hello, how are you, Mr. Smith?" He answers, "I am fine . . . but my body is not well!"

What he is really saying is, "Although I have no control over the sickness of my body, nevertheless, my spirit, my thoughts, mood, and my personality *are* under my control. Therefore, although my *body* is not well . . . *I am fine."*

We all know people who are physically limited or even disabled, yet live so vibrantly and do not view themselves in any sense as ill. And conversely we all know people who might be sick but surely not terribly ill, who go through life timidly, making their illness a central part of their lives.

[Excerpted from LifeLines / Techniques in Nurturing Personal Growth, by Avi Shulman]

Whenever anyone asks me why I get such satisfaction out of working with disabled people [I reply]:

You don't get fine china by putting clay in the sun. You have to put the clay through the white heat of the kiln if you want to make porcelain. Heat breaks some porcelain. Life breaks some people. Disability breaks some people.

But once the clay goes through the white hot fire and comes out whole, it can never be clay again; and once a person overcomes a disability through his own courage, determination and hard work, he has a depth of spirit you and I know little about.

Howard Rusk

There Are No Accidents

Your Family is a Carousel —
It Revolves around You

אפילו חרב חדה מונחת על צוארו של אדם,
על ימנע עצמו מן הרחמים (מסכת ברכות י:יא)

was at the height of my happiness. I was newly married and expecting my first child when I learned that I had kidney problems. At first, it was difficult to make peace with the idea. It was during this time that I found that Hashem has messengers everywhere to help show us the way. Due to side effects of medication, I had great difficulty with my balance and mobility, which resulted in arriving late for an appointment. I became increasingly frustrated and when I finally got into a cab for the ride home, I burst into tears. The driver was very compassionate and inquired about my misery. Then he taught me an unforgettable lesson: "No matter what comes your way, always remember to smile."

He continued, "At first, a smile is only an outward thing but eventually it will emanate from the heart and become all-encompassing. Your whole family, is like a carousel. It revolves around you. If you smile, it brings out the best in everyone."

This dramatically changed my outlook regarding everything. The message was clear — one must always be joyful.

There were days when I had every reason to cry, not that this lessened my trust and faith in Hashem, nor did I have complaints to

Hashem. Even on very rough days when I wonder if I will pull through, and someone asks, "How are you?" I smile and say, "I'm just fine." Hashem has done wonders with me many, many times. I have pulled through when the doctors had long abandoned hope. I underwent two kidneys transplants with transfusions twice weekly. I had seven major surgeries in eight years. Nothing ever deterred me. I never remember wanting to give up.

Holding on to one particular *mitzvah* that I made my very own has given me great encouragement. That *mitzvah* is Shabbos. I have always considered it special to put on something new in honor of Shabbos. Even the nurses in the hospital always noticed how I treated tradition with such importance. I have felt this was my merit for Hashem helping me. In times of challenge, one must hold onto something specific. In my case it was sanctifying Shabbos as a conscious thing. It has brought me inner peace. I have shown my friends that nothing was too difficult for me; I never failed to bake *challos*. I always use my nicest tablecloth, set the table with my nicest silverware, etc. The beautiful table setting is an appropriate honor for the Shabbos queen who visits with us.

Usually a challenge is very hard on a family. It is helpful to share it with others. In my case, with a young husband, I tried to the best of my ability not to make him feel that I was handicapped, different. I managed to do my housework, go places, and do everything joyfully. I have made many friends and try to keep them. I feel it's wrong to bottle up your emotions when experiencing challenge. Let friends share your sufferings as well as your joys. Of course, in order to receive, one must also learn to give. I recall a friend slipping a note under my door during the night telling me of the birth of her baby. What a difference the next day was; it was full of happiness! Another important thing to keep in mind is the fact that Hashem is Omnipotent. Nothing is impossible for Him.

❧   ❧   ❧

One year after receiving my second transplant, my ureter had to be reimplanted. It was almost like having a kidney transplant procedure. Three months later to our great astonishment, I discovered I was going to be blessed with another child. It was like a dream, a constant prayer answered. My doctor was very apprehensive and negative about the situation. "Negative?" I thought, "Not around *me*." I found another doctor. He was much more understanding. Although he was very rigorous about my care, he was positive. I did not have one problem. It was a time of such heights of spirit. I was talking to Hashem all day, in my own way, thanking Him for this great gift to come. I did not contract *even one* infection, something that had plagued me all the years.

Yoely was born to the joy and rejoicing of all. He was obviously G-d's wonder. I firmly believe He gave us this child to show the whole world that nothing is impossible. We were all on cloud nine. Everything was just so wonderful.

Three months later my urinary-tract infections came back. I was in the hospital frequently and separated from my baby. It was a terrible, terrible downfall for me. One Friday morning I got a call from my doctor that I had to be admitted. I was totally unprepared.

I'm very fortunate that I don't collapse in the face of crisis, and wonder how I will manage everything. Hashem has *always* given me the strength to counteract it. I didn't dissolve thinking, "Oh! How am I going to manage this," and, "Oh! I'm going to start crying when I have to leave my baby," and, "Oh! how hard all this is!" I just automatically go to the phone, as though I have a general, a commander. I'm a soldier and I just got this order and I must obey. Whether I like it or not, I now have a mission to carry out, and I'm ready to do what I have to do.

I was admitted to the hospital, lit Shabbos candles, and *then* I broke down. I felt that terrific longing for my baby. This was the first time I was separated from him so abruptly. It was very trying. After I was discharged I went to my parents' home to recuperate. One morning as I was cuddling my Yoely, I looked out the window and watched a mother bird sit on her nest, and as always I said my quiet request to Hashem. "Look, Hashem, at this little bird, how she sits on her nest and nobody disturbs her. She is not admitted to hospitals and is not separated from her babies. Please, please, let me also stay in my nest, my little bird also needs me."

Things never returned to normal. I had frequent hospital stays. One of the doctors on the nephrology team said that he thinks my kidney will never be normal again. When the doctor left, I started to cry very bitterly. Someone came for me with a stretcher. I was scheduled for a test. As we waited for the elevator in the hallway, I was crying uncontrollably. A gentile woman walked by and asked very gently why I was so upset. I told her how the doctor had crushed me and I was afraid my grip on faith was not so strong. She told me her kidneys were failing and the doctors in Puerto Rico had given up on her saying she would have to have both kidneys removed and go on dialysis. She contacted the doctors in New York Hospital and underwent surgery. Both her kidneys were working fine. Now she said to me, "Before I left to come here I spoke to G-d and said, 'G-d, if you need me more than my five-year-old child needs me, take me; but if You think my child needs me more, please make me get well for him.' " I believed that Hashem sent this woman to speak to me. If a non-Jewish woman could tell me this, then where am I? I just picked myself up from deep despair.

❦   ❦   ❦

This time it was a slow regression. I slowly lost my capabilities. I managed to stay out of the hospital because they couldn't do anything for me at this point. As I got sicker, I began to feel progressively worse emotionally. End-stage kidney disease affects the bone structure, the whole system gets affected when the blood stream is unclean. I was always in pain. It was a very trying time for me. Yoely was two years old at this time and this state of being unwell continued until he was three. He was a very active child and was taking advantage of me all the time. He knew how vulnerable I was and how easy it was to overwhelm me. I told Hashem, "You gave me this child. Please give me the strength I need to take care of him." This was my constant prayer. I don't do formal praying. All day I speak to Hashem, "Please Hashem give me the strength that I need!"

At one point when I was toilet training Yoely, it was extremely difficult. My husband found me one day, dissolved in tears and he told me, "Listen, you're going to have to strengthen yourself, otherwise we're going to have to give Yoely away. He can't be abused because you haven't got the strength." That broke me even more, and I said, "Hashem, please, You can't do this to me. Please help me once more, just once more." This is what I say every time: "Just once more and then I say, now, just once more and again, I say, just once more . . ." That's what a Father is for — we can come back to Him again and again with our requests. Finally Yoely was trained and he started *cheder*. He was three and adjusted very well.

The doctors wanted to remove my kidney and put me on dialysis. They ruled out a third transplant because I had seven major surgeries and there were many invasions into my body. There was a lot of scar tissue. It was very distressing. I would go to my window, watch the changing seasons, look at a bare tree and tell Hashem, "I know it's going to start blooming again." Then I would look at the spring buds on trees and flowers. "If you can renew nature, please do it for me too. I need a new healthy kidney! Where is my help going to come from?"

The doctors said there was no hope. I called medical centers all over the country, as far away as England. They all agreed that my doctors were doing everything that was possible for me. They offered no help. The thought of going on dialysis was an absolute nightmare. It means being enslaved to a machine three times a week, regardless of inclement weather, regardless of any plans I have. This cannot be considered a quality life by any means. It just means living on a day-to-day basis. A person requires constant blood transfusions, and is weak, constantly functioning on a very low level.

❦   ❦   ❦

My sister had gall-bladder surgery three weeks after giving birth to her first baby. I went to visit her in the hospital and I met her surgeon. I was shocked when he told me that she was being discharged three days after surgery. He wanted to know why I reacted the way I did. I very briefly told him my history. "I don't know if I can help you," he told me, "but there's no reason that you should be suffering the way you are. Call me at my office and I'll have some information for you." I called him the next day. He told me to get in touch with Dr. N. in the Cleveland Clinic. Clinic, I thought. The word clinic to New Yorkers means inferior care. I was so desperate I called them and asked excitedly, "Is this the clinic? Is this a big place? Is this a small place?" I was assured that this was a world-renowned place and I had never even heard of it.

I was not in danger at this point because my kidney was working well enough to sustain me right off the edge of dialysis, but no one could foretell how long it would continue this way. No one could predict on which day my kidney would call, Stop. I was sitting on a time bomb at this point. I was constantly taking antibiotics and constantly getting reinfected. After many weeks I got an appointment in Cleveland. I flew down with my husband.

As we were returning from Cleveland waiting for our flight at the airport, a man noticed that we were strangers to the city and immediately offered his help. "My name is Mr. E.; what can I do for you?" We had just been thinking where we could stay on our return to Cleveland for my medical evaluation. Would we find a Jewish home? I didn't know a soul there and here was this man confronting us with the very same question. "Hashem," I was shouting in my heart, "You are making this twisted puzzle fall into place. Praise be to Hashem."

I simply said, "Yes, Mr. E, I'll be coming back next week. Can I please have your number so I can get in touch with you if I need help or someone to talk to."

Well, this was only the beginning. The next day I got a call. "Hello, is this Rivka?" "Yes," I said. "Well, my name is Ellen J. I'm from Cleveland. I heard from Mr. E. that you'll be coming here to be treated at the Cleveland Clinic. Can I please pick you up at the airport." I was dumbfounded. "Yes," I said, "and how can I thank you enough." "Thanks? No! You are giving us this great honor we have to thank you." This was the start of a whole chain of calls to my home, from all these wonderful people who didn't even know me. They continuously called to offer me all sorts of help. It is a golden page of incredible *chesed* for all the people in Cleveland who we had the *zchus* to befriend.

I came home right before Yoely's first haircut full of optimism. Dr. N. did not foresee the complications that my other doctors were talking about. My help came straight from Heaven! My husband discussed Dr. N.'s approach (that was totally opposite from that of top doctors in the country) with the *Rav*. I just went into it completely blind, I didn't speak to any patients, my feeling was that if anyone offered to help me, even if he was on the street and claimed he had a sure-fire cure, I would believe him. I was that desperate.

I was getting blood transfusions on a weekly basis. I was totally down. Going from the kitchen to the dining room was unspeakable exhaustion and an indescribable effort. Walking up a flight of stairs was a major ordeal and I had to weigh all the pros and cons before I decided I really needed to do something. In those days I was very down, but somehow Hashem gave me the strength to call upon help. This has been an exclusive gift from Hashem, all my wonderful friends and family. Even if the driver of my car had a good word for me it was enough to refresh me.

❊   ❊   ❊

At this time, when I had practically zero strength I became involved with gardening. I couldn't climb a flight of stairs, let alone bend down to plant a few seeds. Anyone would've thought I was out of my mind. This was a few months before my transplant. Before Pesach I began planting these little seeds. During Pesach I noticed something sprouting. It inspired such feelings in me that I needed to express them to Hashem. "All I did was plant a few seeds in the soil, into dirt. Then I watered it and You can make it grow, turn it into little leaves, first two, then four, then six. You can transform a dry little seed into a miracle. The seed is so tiny and minuscule that I never imagined it would develop into anything. Can't You make my salvation sprout in the same way?"

After Pesach I flew to Cleveland with one of my brothers to have him evaluated. He was found to be a one-hundred-percent match. A month later he was rejected as a donor because he had an unrelated problem. It felt like an attack and I didn't know how I could handle this. Whenever I got terribly upset at these disappointments my husband was always there to bolster me. He would take me into Yoely's room when he was sleeping and tell me gently, "Look at our Yoely. If Hashem gave us this child, there's no way that He won't provide the solution for you. If this doesn't work out, then something else will. Don't give up."

Afterwards, a sister said she would try and after a two-day evaluation and a lot of trauma from very rigorous invasive tests we were told that her kidney was a one-hundred-percent match. A few weeks later she was also rejected as a potential donor. It was always one step forward and two steps backwards.

Then my youngest sister approached me and offered herself. All this time I was becoming more drained by the flying, both emotionally and physically. She was rejected because she was just a half match. By now I thought for sure this was it. I would call every few weeks to see if they had any donor from a cadaver for me.

Finally a sister whom I had never considered turned out to be the one that was ultimately found right. There was a lot of intrafamily politics surrounding this. People challenged the fact that a perfectly healthy young wife and mother was facing a very risky procedure. Even though she was only a fifty-percent match she was declared a suitable donor for me. My other two kidneys failed in the end because of a reflux complication due to the scar tissue from surgeries not permitting the urine to flow as it should — it was not the kidney failure at all. Things really started to move from this point on. This was the end of May. I was scheduled for June 17.

We arrived in Cleveland. We were prepared for the transplant and were in a holding area before going into the operating rooms. I was holding Chana's hand. She was sobbing, not because she didn't want to go through it, but because she was faced with an unknown situation. I was ready and eager, anxious that it should work. "Be strong" I told her. "We're going in smiling. This is not the time to be afraid." I said, "You're doing a great *mitzvah* and you're going to be strong." Hashem gave me such strength at that time and somehow she went into the operating room very happy. She's thirteen years younger than I am.

When I awoke in the recovery room, I began examining my pipes and the equipment I was connected to and I couldn't be happier — the red urine draining from a freshly cut site was a beautiful thing for me to see. I asked the nurse cautiously, "Tell me, is my kidney working?" And she told me it was wonderful. My creatinine (normal kidney blood-function level) level had reached an almost normal level immediately, a number that I hadn't heard in years. It's like a housewife who attacks a house that is topsy turvy. She rolls up her sleeves and goes to it and in no time at all she has brought order into a messy house.

Things were going wonderfully. It was as if I was in a spell, begging Hashem to just let it continue this way till 120 years. After one week we were discharged to go home. After a few days my strength improved and with my chemistry levels normal, I was able to perform as they predicted.

The first thing I did when I got home was to throw down my pocketbook, walk down a flight of stairs to visit my garden. All the time I was away I inquired about my garden. Before surgery there were just blossoms and now, two weeks later, I saw tomatoes and peppers. "*Ribono shel Olam*, I'm so thankful." I related so much to the garden. I was keenly aware of the miracles of creation. I don't know how I managed to plant those seeds, I don't know what motivated me. One day a neighbor of mine was helping me transplant little plants. It was a very hot day and the sun had practically scorched the plants. She was very skeptical that anything would ever grow, but I only had one prayer to Hashem, "Please show her that You can make this grow, even though it's so obviously wilted." I was depending on a miracle and I needed to see all this happening. This was before my transplant. Later, after I came home from the hospital and when she saw my garden she had to admit, "Rivka, anything is possible." My tomatoes were so tall, I had tomatoes that were two-and-a-half pounds each.

❈   ❈   ❈

The rest of the story is happiness. I am now seven months post-surgery and everything is going well. Once a week I have to go in for my blood test and every time they draw the blood I still feel that same feeling, "Please, Hashem, make it be good. Make it be good. Let this *Kiddush Hashem* be a continuous thing, let it always be here." It goes to show that when a person holds steadfast onto his trust and faith, even when all the doors are closed, Hashem will open a window.

There were times when I had to face the thought that my help might never come; still Hashem has always helped me again and again and yet again. He helped me gather myself from the floor. "Help me Hashem so that people can see that You are Almighty. Show everyone that everything is possible, You can do anything." My chances were so slim, I was running out of siblings, but You, Hashem, made this miracle possible.

I tell my story to everyone who is depressed, who is in dire straits. I tell them, "Look at me, I'm a living example that anything can happen. I've been down so many times." I felt like screaming to all the people about the miracles that were done to me, about Hashem's loving-kindness, about His greatness. If anyone were to ask me for advice about how to handle the rough times, my answer would be, "Make friends, get support from wherever possible. Never live in the dark. People are out there, everyone has a good word, I've been able to benefit from strangers." And for all the challenges, I can only thank Hashem.

I often think what sort of a person I would've been if I hadn't had these problems. I probably would've been busy with the mundane things of life. I was given these tests when I was very young, before I could analyze or shape my perspective about life, but I know for certain that I have definitely, positively benefited by every one of my challenges. I also say, "Please, Hashem, don't try me anymore. The gratification of seeing Your help is so great that someone who hasn't been down before cannot understand the feeling of being picked up again."

I tell those people who are experiencing difficulties to focus on some pastime or hobby, be it embroidery, sewing or gardening — don't dwell on your problem, try to focus on energy-conserving pasttimes and leave the rest to Hashem. When I had zero energy I could still fill my time productively and happily with my smocking and other little things that gave me no end of gratification. I could still be creative with my limited ability and this gave me the strength to continue. This was my therapy. I constantly saw the fruits of my labor.

My family and friends were always supportive and good for me. It's been marvelous. Whenever I hear of someone who needs help, I make myself available to speak to them, to support them, to show them I'm a live example of Hashem's kindness. He helped me and He can help you likewise. He can help over and over again.

My father-in-law told me a story about a man who came to a great *tzaddik*, the Shinover Rav (the Sanzer's Rav's son). His wife was very sick with an incurable illness. She had tuberculosis, which was fatal in those days. The Rav picked up his hands to Heaven and cried, "How can it be that You can create new lungs and can't heal the old ones?" She never experienced any more problems from that day forth.

I tell Hashem, "We don't have that power of the extremely righteous — but the one thing we have is You, You are as potent and all powerful today as the first day of Creation and I know You can help me. I know You can fix me, or replace my failed kidney, just send it somehow. I don't have to provide You with solutions; I ask only one thing of You: Please do it quickly, before I am totally wiped out." He has taken my prayers and transformed them into the miracle He has done with me.

❀   ❀   ❀

[Effervescent Rivka is a great asset to her community. Those who attend a smocking course in her home receive the bonus of her healthy outlook on life. She is feeling terrific and is constantly aware of Hashem's infinite blessings. — Ed.]

It Hurts so Much

"**A**ni ma'amin b'emunah shelaymah shehaborei yisbarach shmo hu boirei umanhig lechol habrios . . .*" Since I was a young girl I had been saying Maimonides' Thirteen Principles of Faith daily. Six years ago on an April afternoon I discovered the difference between lip service to these words and applying them to a difficult test. On that day I experienced a tragedy that shook my world. My oldest, Chaney, burst into the kitchen ashen, yelling, "Mommy, Sheva had an accident! She was getting Shmuel's ball and it wasn't even in the middle of the road. But he must've been a drunken driver! Oh, Mommy, quick! She can't move her arms or legs!" Before Hatzoloh came it was over . . . Sheva, only four years and two months old, victim of a senseless accident.

Memory flashes of Sheva and a conversation passed in my mind as I sat speechless with a neighbor waiting for the confirmation call from the emergency room. What *hashgachah pratis.* Just that week we had bought a new tape and Sheva's favorite song was *Gam Zu Letovah.* She asked to hear it over and over again. She wanted to know the meaning of the words and when I found ten minutes of quiet after supper, I sat with her and Chaney. I told them the story of Nochum *Ish Gam Zu* and how he always interpreted whatever happened as being good. She was spellbound.

I knew the meaning of the words, didn't I? A month before there was a similar tragedy when an eleven-year-old boy was hit by a school bus. I remember being totally shaken and remarked to my husband, "That has to be the absolute tragedy. I can't imagine how those parents can bear their loss!"

My husband's homecoming jarred me back to the present. He had already spoken to the doctors. I could read his face like a book. Our little lamb was no longer ours. I'm not sure how these words passed my lips. "She was a *matnas chinam* and a *mashkon*. But now Hashem wants her back." I felt the need to calm my husband and six children, but that night was a sleepless one. The shock I couldn't show my family gripped me all night. I was sure I would wake up in the morning and she would be there.

On the first day of *shivah* I experienced a feeling of grief that is indescribable. I wavered between the knowledge that there was an accounting and a Divine decree to her unfortunate death and guilt feelings that had I prayed properly and taken upon myself a *tikun* on Rosh Hashanah, I might have been instrumental in annulling the decree. Yes, I knew it was a privilege to be tested, I chastised myself. Why didn't I get the message when they were tapping on my window? Why did I have to wait for this strong banging? It hurt so intensely. I was afraid I was breaking . . .

The rest of the *shivah* was not especially memorable. I remember some insensitive, but well-meaning visitors. They reassured me, "You don't really know it now, but one day you'll understand that this is a privilege. Hashem only tries the righteous and takes a sacrifice from very special people." Did they expect me to rejoice? I didn't find any of this comforting at the time and after a while I became nervous. I never considered myself worthy to stand on a pedestal. I'm very human. I know my shortcomings. I also knew that this was a confusing time for me and I needed time to work out my feelings. One woman described the scene in heaven, so rosy. Sometimes I was relieved when night came and we could be alone. The *sefer Derech Hashem* got me aligned with proper *hashkafos*. It gave me a better understanding. I wasn't at all the worthy woman that people would've liked to perceive me. It clarified the issues of reward and punishment and existence in this world and leaving the world. I ultimately found comfort and a healthy perspective from the pages and the explanations of man's suffering and purpose in life.

The week after the *shivah* I was newly plagued with emotions and a different type of regret. If only Sheva had passed away of a terminal illness and I had been given the chance to nurse her and comfort her, but to be torn away like this and deny me my maternal instincts? This gave me no rest . . . One night I dreamed I saw Sheva, her face beautiful as she was in life. However she was severely crippled. I held her and I felt a strong spastic grip. When I awoke I realized that had she survived she would've been paralyzed forever. ה' נתן וה' לקח — "G-d gave and G-d took." I once asked my husband about the double wording in this verse from Iyov. He explained, "Hashem is compassionate. Just as He gives with compassion, so He takes with compassion." It helped. Many times when I lose control and sob relentlessly, I'll remember this and I will think, "As far as Sheva is concerned she is at peace. What could I offer her here that she doesn't have up there? Life is so complex. Does anyone know how one's child will overcome challenges in his life?" Then I conclude that I am crying because of self-pity. I am crying purely because I miss her.

When I sat down with the children at mealtimes her chair was painfully empty. I couldn't bear it. But I looked at it this way. My husband and I built a home. We had six wonderful children.

I tried my best to cope but when I needed a few private minutes to myself of crying time, I would leave the children attended by my husband or my oldest daughter Chaney and go up to my bedroom. I tried never to cry in front of the children. I dried my eyes and carried on again. I felt I couldn't break my children or my home life. When I went out, I took pains to be well groomed and kept a strong cheerful front. Even though I felt a lot of pain I viewed myself as a beacon to those who were close to me. The children always talked about her naturally, "Is it Succos now for Sheva?" "Who bought her new clothes and new shoes for Pesach?" "The *rebbe* gives stars for good behavior. I told all my friends to be good and do *mitzvos*. Then *Mashiach* will come and we'll see Sheva again."

For a few weeks that continued after the *shloshim*, I noticed a very disturbing pattern. I was organized into a schedule of sorts all week and coping, but the minute I lit the candles I felt a gloom overcome me. Instead of welcoming the Shabbos happily I sank into despair. I found I was too alone with my thoughts and Shabbos was depressing. This finally ended when I took conscious control of myself and refused to be controlled by undesirable forces that pervade gloom and despair.

During the first year after her death I was paralyzed with a feeling of helplessness and fear. I had healthy children. Dare I let them out of the house unsupervised? I became panicky. I felt I was going crazy until one day I told myself, "Yes, now you know you have zero control. You have absolutely no control over your children, yourself or any circumstances for that matter." Then like a flash it came to me, "*Ani ma'amin shehu borei umanhig . . .* ".

I used to wonder why I was deprived of molding my child and raising her to become a complete person and then give her back to Hashem when the time was due, or what we perceive as "the right time." My husband has a good shoulder and we discussed Avraham and the sacrifice of Isaac. He would comfort me that I was really trying to accept our tragedy. Even though we didn't actually sacrifice Sheva, it was as though she was offered, just as our patriarch Avraham was ready to do. He helped me reconcile my ambivalent thoughts. True, Sheva's loss has created a big gap in our family and we are all pained by it but think about the pain of the *Shechinah*, since Hashem lost His glory and does not dwell among His precious children. True, Sheva is not here physically, I can't raise her or clothe her, but by accepting this with love for Hashem, it is as though I have her eternally. I feel that if I can't come to terms with it, I could lose her forever. Now I have a keen awareness of how badly we need the final redemption. I know that people have different levels of acceptance and these *hashkafos* have helped me. There is a very fine line in how one accepts such tragedies, I feel fortunate that I am at this point.

My behavior and pursuits have changed a lot over the years. I consciously behave in a way that she would feel proud of. The fact that she was my child and I'm her parent is sometimes an influencing factor. I don't mean it in a controlling way; however, I think twice before a decision. I feel more intensively. I want her to feel proud of me and I feel it makes me a better person. For example, in the past I would always delegate *chesed* involvements to others. Now I find the time to do them myself and I feel very fulfilled. I think of Sheva every day, naturally. However, the *yahrzeit* week is still difficult and I'm grateful that it doesn't carry on into the rest of the year. Today I can be happy at *simchos* but I haven't been able to laugh the way I used to. I'm definitely a more serious person.

So . . . We Love Her Anyway

אני מאמין . . . והוא לבדו
עשה ועושה ויעשה לכל המעשים (י״ג עיקרים)

Life takes on a special excitement when something unknown is expected, such as the arrival of a newborn baby. Will it be a girl or boy? What will be the color of the hair, eyes, complexion? ... The humdrum daily routine activities become punctuated with a thrill. We seldom stop to think about the tremendous miracle of a life that is in the midst of creation, starting only from a single cell. The intricate cycles that are involved in the making of a human being of perfection are beyond the scope of human comprehension. (Only Hashem with His divine power can bestow on us such a gift.) Yet we do expect a perfect little infant, ignoring the thousands of mishaps that may befall that single cell. Hashem has installed a computer in each of us that monitors growth.

But there comes a time when it is the indisputable will of Hashem to alter the normal pattern of growth and to direct that computer to assume a different pattern, deviating from the so-called development. Man is ignorant, powerless and not consulted.

I was in my early twenties, happy and content with three normal healthy and beautiful children who added to my pride and joy. The fourth one was expected. It was Friday night; I decided to chance going to the hospital myself and leave my husband with the other children so as not to stir up a panic by my parents. The baby was born within twenty minutes. Terrific! I thought to myself. It was a girl! Perfect! Beautiful — I had one girl and two boys; now the family was balanced. One couldn't ask for more.

Since the delivery took place in an unprepared room the baby was immediately whisked to the appropriate adjacent room and I was able to hear the ongoing conversations but I saw nothing. A pediatrician was summoned immediately. Unsuspecting, I was waiting to see the newborn infant and expecting the routine procedure upon delivery. No such thing happened. After hearing a lot of murmuring in that room next to mine I was told that the baby was being sent to the intensive care unit. Why? A minor problem — poor sucking ability. Being a natural optimist I dismissed that step as trivial. I was taken to a private room, made comfortable and tucked in for the night. Sweet dreams followed. My husband will name the little one in *shul* the next day. A *simchah*! A joy!

The next day, Shabbos passed as usual in the hospital, but I began to be annoyed by the fact that nobody commented on my baby. Finally in the afternoon I could bear it no longer and demanded to see her in the I.C.U. I was allowed to walk down with a nurse and was shown the infant. Intravenous tubes were stuck into a vein in her head; a very scary sight indeed. I also noticed that she looked quite different from my other children. But I still made nothing of it. The intravenous tubes are only temporary and a child can look different. I dismissed my worries.

Sunday the baby was finally brought into my room for nursing. I had a chance to scrutinize my infant, which I did. When the nurse came to pick Sheindele up I blurted out that the child looks funny to me. (I was sure I was wrong, and the nurse would say, "Nonsense!") The nurse was in a particular hurry and said she knows no details and her job was only to take and bring infants from and to their mothers. But presently another nurse arrived with a syringe and needle in her hand prepared to give me an injection. I asked, "What for?"

"To calm your nerves."

"My nerves are fine. But there is something fishy around here."

"I don't know . . . I only work in the nursery."

Meanwhile I found out that my husband had called in the services of a private pediatrician. The suspense was growing. I found the number of the pediatrician, called him and demanded to know the blunt truth.

He said it nicely, like a diplomat, "The child has certain Mongoloid features that were clinically observed and not yet laboratory tested. But chances are that the clinical diagnosis is correct."

That was the bombshell. The world was toppling on me. I hurried with shaky feet to my room and let loose. Immediately I uttered precious words that I shall not forget for the rest of my life. 'ברוך ה אשר לא ישא פנים ולא יקח שחד — "Blessed is Hashem, Who does not favor anyone and does not accept bribes."

I was popular, outgoing and socially accepted. I always felt that I was admired and respected more than I deserve and finally Hashem was giving me something I deserved. *Hashem is not influenced by popular opinion.* On the other hand I soothed myself with the words of King Solomon. את אשר יאהב ה' יוכיח וכאב את בן ירצה — "The one that Hashem loves He rebukes and like a son to his father he is accepted."

Nevertheless, I was human. I cried for several days — with the *Tehillim* and without. I ran from the hospital. (The baby stayed because of a minor blood condition that cleared up very quickly.) I had headaches from shedding so many tears, but I felt inner strength coming. I asked Hashem to help me and I felt a surge of understanding. I knew in my heart that I would start working on programs for the retarded. This feeling came to me immediately but I felt I ought to give myself time to recuperate. A person is not an angel and should allow himself to yield to certain human emotions. But those emotions should be brain controlled and the brain should derive its juice from sources of the Torah.

The next step, of course, was to face society and first in this series was the family. My husband and I decided to come out with the truth to everyone regardless of how painful that might be. Luckily there was one brother-in-law who was a very straightforward person. He offered to tackle my husband's side of the family. I dealt with my family by myself. When the truth is revealed, you eliminate fifty percent of the burden. When you have to hide something, the pressure of constantly acting drives one insane. Besides, what is the purpose of secrecy? You are not responsible for creation. We are ב"ה dealing with a Creator Who is Omnipotent. He can make a perfect human being if He wants to.

From my own experience and from observing others, I have discovered that there are three categories in tackling similar problems. There are those who cannot make peace of mind with anything so harshly extraordinary. These people reject the child immediately, thus never giving it a chance to adjust to a warm family setting nurtured by motherly love. Such parents give up their children either to homes or for foster care. We are not in a position to condemn.

At the other extreme there are people who visualize the education of their children to the utmost, attempting to make them as close to normal as possible. During this process they usually extend themselves to an impossible goal and very often at the expense of the other children in the family who need parents nonetheless. This is also a form of non-acceptance, a thrust for the unattainable. Even if it is, to a limited extent, feasible, what is lost in the process may make it unworthwhile, because the other children may reject the child for taking away the time and attention that parents would normally direct to their needs.

A third group tries to follow a balanced middle-of-the-road approach. They handle the retarded child just as they would a normal member of their family. This is the path towards reaping many rewards. (Our experience is only with Down's children, therefore our advice is directed to those parents.) Remember, what you are doing is the ultimate kindness because you are not expecting reciprocation as with your other children.

When Hashem bade Moshe to go to Pharaoh and say, "Let my people go," Moshe in his modesty said, "How can I go since I have a speech defect?" and Hashem answered, "Who makes people blind and deaf? ... It is only I, Hashem," and with a purpose. Rashi comments that Hashem deliberately wanted Moshe to have a speech defect, so the people should not say, "Oh, Moshe was a wonderful orator and he convinced Pharaoh to yield." Hashem wanted it to be crystal clear that it was only His will that took the Jews out of Egypt. The same applies here. Hashem created us all, and each and every one has a purpose. There isn't the slightest phenomena in the universe that happened by mistake or accident, most assuredly a human being. Besides, we earthly beings must realize that in proportion to Hashem in His infinite wisdom our *normalcy* is nil. What minute difference to Hashem is forty or fifty points lower on an I.Q. test? What *does* make a difference to Hashem and to our souls is the quality of our character. How able are we to realize that we came here to serve Him, and that broad aspect includes helping one another; helping people who Hashem creates with the need to be helped.

My husband and I worked as a team. It was only with his

encouragement that we could handle ourselves and the problem realistically.

My mother remained the one problem. She was pitifully ill at the time with osteoporosis and bed-ridden. We were waiting for this *simchah* to liven her up and now this ... For two weeks she didn't see the baby because she couldn't come to me (I lived around the corner). My father came to visit me when I came home from the hospital. With tears in my eyes I told him the truth. There is no ingredient in the world like truth. He started to comfort me with the words of our sages. He told me that often there are souls that are pure but must re-embark to this world because of a certain reason and in order for them not to be blemished they are born in such a manner. These souls are of the highest caliber. These words were like balm on a wounded soul. Still, he didn't tell my mother.

After two weeks I felt physically and mentally capable of taking my child to visit my mother. The picture is vivid in my mind. My mother picked the baby up and crooned to her. After a while she asked me, "What is wrong with the child?"

My answer was, "Whatever you see is true."

But these words were said with such a self-confident tone that it saved the hour. One thing is clear. Mothers pity their daughters more than they are upset about the grandchild. Therefore if they sense that the daughter is strong, has made peace with the situation, and is ready to take it with a smile, a mother is automatically soothed. You can't imagine what a loving relationship developed later between Baabe and Sheindele. They loved each other. As a matter of fact when my mother passed away, for months afterwards Sheindele was pulling me daily to go to Baabe as soon as she stepped off the school bus.

I got used to saying, "My baby is retarded," to my friends. I wanted all of them to know in advance so that I could walk my baby on the street without the urge to hide. I called one very close friend from the hospital and tearfully told her. I'll never forget her wonderful advice: "Take it day by day." I've been living with these words ever since. Inevitably when such a thing happens to you, your thoughts wander to the far-off future when all your children will marry, but this child will remain a burden forever. Hence the most practical and sound advice, "Take it day by day." Now the child is only a baby, handle those problems and enjoy those moments. You will cross your bridges when you get to them. Who has guaranteed your life for the next fifty years? So why start worrying?

When Sheindele was less than a month old we went to the country. She was taken outside just like any other baby. You'd be surprised how this attitude immediately rubs off on the people around us. If you treat your child with equanimity, you can expect a similar effect from society.

Most burdensome to parents is the job of transmitting the bare truth to siblings. Let it be stressed, the *bare truth*: again, there is no substitute for genuine truth. You must understand that beating around the bush with children is never the right decision. Just be honest and be prepared to answer questions with wisdom, instilling in your children the real faith and trust. There is only a thin line between real and false. Real faith means I believe with complete faith that Hashem is Omnipotent and it is in His hands to alter any kind of situation. But He specifically ordained this child to me and willed this challenge to our family. It is not the desire of Hashem to alter nature; therefore it is imperative to accept this phenomenon with love.

On the other hand I have unfortunately seen many a false faith where the stricken holds on to illusions of unfathomable changes and thinks one must believe that everything will turn out great in the end. *Everything will turn out great in the end anyway*, and on a loftier level everything is *now* great. One must seek out his innermost strength to gain both love and fear of Hashem from every situation, to uplift his soul for which he has been created.

Being honest with children and the resulting *naches* will prove its rightness. When Sheindele was yet very small we were discussing retardation in our family. I also had *chizuk* meetings in my home for parents with similar situations for there is no consolation like knowing that one is not alone on earth with one's trials. My seven-year-old daughter was allowed to participate and inevitably came up with the question, "What does retarded mean?" Very plainly I explained to her that retardation means a slow growth, mostly mentally. After some thinking she uttered these precious words, "So, we love her anyway." Those words need no elaboration.

Very recently my five year old, who is always observant asked, "If Sheindele cannot talk well, how will she be able to get married?"

Again, I resorted to honesty. "Sheindele will not get married if she cannot speak well."

And so we embarked on a voyage of acceptance and a strong commitment to enlighten the chassidic Jewish community on mental retardation and its aftermath. Ignorance is the barrier to acceptance.

When Sheindele was just a few months old I began worrying about education. One person came to mind when I thought about educating the mentally retarded in a regular Orthodox school setting, Chani Weiss, director of the Bedford-Harrison Day Care Center. With her encouragement I later contacted the head of the Satmar Congregation. It pays to immortalize his words, "It is very good that you called us because we need you more than you need us. The rebbe has told us numerous times to open a class for special children, but we never had parental cooperation."

The next day I was contacted by Rabbi Hertz Frankel, principal of Bais Rochel School who began the pioneering of a class for mentally retarded in a yeshivah setting. Today the school serves thirty-two special children with a full educational program. There is also an infant program in Kiryas Yoel, Monroe, in the regular school building (which Sheindele now attends). The cooperation of the entire staff and student body is so enthusiastic that it is hard to believe that it is only a few years since mental retardation in the *chassidic* community reached a level of understanding and acceptance. Mainstreaming is now a reality, not a word in magazine articles.

Sheindele is now as well adjusted to family and friends as one can hope for. Academically, there is much to be desired, but that was never our primary concern. Socially she is well adapted and that is the most important factor. Sheindele has friends on the block. We are not ashamed to take her to family affairs and she behaves very well. Personally, the two factors seem to go hand in hand. If the child is exposed she will behave (in most cases; of course there are much more severe situations). Sheindele goes to the grocery and buys up to two items at once. The family loves her, there is no rejection. She *loves* the family, feels wanted and secure. What the future will bring nobody knows. Why worry? We've come a long way, with G-d's help, and with His help we will continue on.

∾§ Sheindele: Up-Date

Sheindele is now thirteen-and-a-half years old, phenomenal in her social ability but lacking much academically. She is only able to write her first name. We're not at all concerned about that because we gave it no emphasis from the beginning. The most important part is that she is able to attend all social functions with grace, she has friends, is well behaved and she is happy.

Sheindele is now attending a special class in Shaarei Chemloh. That is the name of the classes for special education in the regular building of Bais Rochel in Kiryas Yoel. It was founded by the very outstanding father of a retarded son. The one feature that towers above all others (and there are many) is the fact that the classrooms are integrated in the so-called "normal" school, resulting in the children mingling and some mainstreaming. Watching the scene in the playground at recess and lunch hour can bring tears to one's eyes. One sees both types of students at play. Some children are being pushed by able-bodied friends, several retarded children take their turn at rope. I do not think there is any school or yeshivah comparable to it in the entire world; yet this is the way it should be.

Sheindele has many friends and at Purim she receives the most baskets. The Big Sister Program instituted in the school carries over to children from Shaarei Chemloh who are picked up every evening for reinforcement of school activities. This is also a wonderful break for parents. On Shabbos Sheindele and other children are taken out — a wonderful respite for burdened parents. I have never imposed Sheindele on my other children or expect them to take her wherever they go because inevitably this will result in resentment from siblings. It is much better to have outside people volunteer. They are never as emotionally attached. I believe one must ask for help and never refuse a sincere offer. I recently made a public announcement, "Who would like to take Sheindele to the play in Monsey?" and of course there was an enthusiastic response.

Sheindele has a wonderful relationship with her ten siblings and is very much concerned about each and every one of them. Every night she counts heads and demands an explanation for the missing ones. When my oldest daughter recently married it took a while until she digested the fact that Sheva Chana has a different apartment. This wasn't much different from my own reaction.

When it comes to respecting her, both my husband and I request compliance from the rest of the family. She gets her seat at the Shabbos table before her sisters, as she is now the oldest girl at home. There is no resentment towards her because they are not excessively burdened with her.

We make a point of dressing Sheindele very neatly and appropriately. We take pains with her accessories. I will extend myself, even financially, to achieve a good-looking appearance for her because it makes a world of difference. Any mother loves her child no matter how she looks; however, the public notices a retarded child's appearance. At my daughter's wedding she wore the most beautiful dress. She was the only one in the family in an off-white dress. She looked absolutely smashing, dancing, and was really part of it. She attended every *sheva brachos* when her sisters went. Sometimes families will place a retarded child when there's a family occasion, but that's not at all the case with Sheindele. She's always up front. Someone remarked, "You made a fine match even though you have Sheindele!" Up to that moment I did not realize I was handicapped. Maybe society is handicapped if they regard us this way but I am not! We do not owe an apology to the world for harboring a retarded individual! This is a very important lesson.

Most people confronted with a retarded child worry about their other children, the siblings. These two episodes will totally allay your fears about sibling apprehensiveness.

The first took place when my oldest daughter was in the ninth grade. The First-Aid teacher gave the class an assignment. It was a study of various episodes that require emergency attention. My daughter's assignment was puncture wounds. To the admiration of the teacher as well as the class she delivered a self-written essay about taunting a retarded person and the *puncture wound* that results in the person's heart. For days the teacher was raving about the fact that so young a child could deliver so poignant a message and without shame or fear. The *chizuk* she got from home definitely came across: Just recently my fifth-grade daughter, without any qualms, read this sentence to her class, "I have a disabled sister." Yes! We are proud of the fact.

Another time, in the eleventh grade class of Bais Rochel, the Current Events teacher read an article entitled "My Brother that Brought Sunshine," written by the sister of a Down's Syndrome boy who brightened his family's life, and the tragedy and emptiness of his passing. At the recess period one girl went downstairs to the special class in the regular building (Hooray!), scooped up her little Down's brother, and brought him into the classroom. For the fifteen-minute duration of the break sister and friends were marveling over the bright antics of the little cherub. Three cheers for education and a hundred cheers for the mainstreaming that is a reality in the Bais Rochel building of Kiryas Yoel!

Our daughter is not considered a high-functioning child. Her aptitude is at a three-to-four-year age level, but socially she is so well adapted that she's practically on the same level as her peers. She's able to make elementary blessings but will never be able to read from a *siddur*. Yet she is in the fourth grade every day and pretends to pray from a *siddur*. She phonetically chants and imitates all the motions very convincingly.

At home she is able to help me in many ways (that is, if she wants to). She can wipe the dishes, clear the table, unpack an order and put everything in its proper place. She goes to the grocery almost daily and buys up to three items without a list. With a list she can handle more. She takes the town mini-bus independently to school on days when there is no transportation. She flags it down, pays her fare and relaxes for the ride to school. But her favorite chore is helping with the baby. She can give him a bottle, change his pamper and get him ready for bed, all the while cooing to him gently and lovingly. I permit her to take the baby out in the carriage. She goes through all the preliminaries by herself (putting on his sweater set, etc.). Since this is a large household the baby cycle keeps repeating itself so I don't think she will be out of work for a while. The main ingredient though is a large dose of love. This is the most unifying factor. The entire family loves Sheindele and she loves all of us. The community is wonderful, always helpful and ready to reach out. Together we can do the ultimate *chesed* of treating a retarded child *just like a person*.

My Special Rainbow
Brief Beauty — Enduring Memories

כל דעביד רחמנא לטב עביד (מסכת ברכות ס:ב)

I remember very well when we got the report; we were in Dr. F.'s office. He was very understanding and supportive, but not very encouraging. "The news I have is not good," he said in a broken voice and with tears in his eyes, "Your child has AML, the worst leukemia possible. The only route is chemotherapy and then a bone marrow transplant."

The decision was made to admit Leah'le immediately to our local hospital under Dr. F.'s care. He was Director of Pediatric Hematology and Oncology.

Entering the hospital building, many thoughts entered my troubled mind ... "I hope I don't meet anyone I know ... " Suddenly a familiar voice assaulted me. "Esther, what are you doing here?" It was my close friend Miriam. Now our secret was out in the open!

As I look back on the chain of events that followed, I realize that this was the best thing that could have happened. A family going through a crisis needs the support of family and friends, and ours were very supportive. Here are just a few examples:
— Meals for each day were arranged by our local N'shei ladies, so that I could spend all my time in the hospital with my sick child.
— Pesach preparations were a major concern. Girls from our

local high school volunteered their time to help clean, do laundry and take care of the children after school.

— Bills not covered by our insurance plan were paid by a fund set up expressly for this purpose.

— Prayers were offered in our child's behalf by many individuals and groups.

— Blood donors came from within our own community. Our friends together with the neighborhood Bikur Cholim organized a blood drive, and convinced their husbands and relatives to donate. Outside blood donations were never needed, even when daily transfusions were necessary! Once, Leah'le called a donor, a personal friend of the family whose name appeared on the bag of blood, and personally thanked him. How touched he was!

Our family included our parents and in-laws, both elderly. My in-laws helped as much as possible taking turns sitting with Leah'le, so that I could go home and feed my six-month-old infant, or to see my children off to school and wait for the homemaker provided by a local social-service agency. Shabbos, too, they helped by eating in shifts in order to allow us to spend some time with our children at home — to help maintain a family structure. It was a hard time for all! But, Hashem, in His boundless mercy, sent His messengers to ease our burden.

On the pediatric floor, we were greeted by a very sympathetic and caring staff of professionals. The intern and resident directly responsible for our child's care came to take the admitting history. They were Orthodox Jews and very involved with their patients. Their manner and personality eased our burden. After explaining the course of treatment to be followed, their words of encouragement were strengthening to us.

We decided that it would be most beneficial to us and our child to have as positive a relationship with the staff as possible. To be as polite and co-operative as we could ... Whenever there were problems we made our voices heard, but without antagonizing anyone.

Chemotherapy was started shortly after admission. We saw Leah'le change from an active, beautiful child to a sick, bald, emaciated skeleton. It was truly heartbreaking. The powerful drugs made her sick and nauseous and damaged her gastro-intestinal tract.

She was unable to eat and was sustained only by TPN-intravenous feeding. Despite all this her faith in Hashem never diminished. We prayed repeatedly. My husband went to his *Rebbe's tzion* and cried his eyes out. I sat at my child's bedside and constantly recited *Tehillim*. We were confident that we would be favorably answered.

❧ ❧ ❧

The Fast of Esther marked a turning point. Leah'le went into a first remission! No blast cells were found in her marrow. Chemo was successful . . . Next stop (in a few weeks) a large metropolitan cancer center for a bone-marrow transplant!

Oh, what excitement! On the day that the Jews had defeated their hated enemy Amalek — we had scored a victory against a hated and feared disease. What a joyous Purim! The hospital staff was intoxicated with joy. Especially Dr. F. who was running around the floor squirting everyone with water-filled syringes (a trick our daughter put to use later on).

On Purim, three young ladies in costume came to cheer us up. They offered to stay with Leah'le a few nights a week so we could spend time at home with our children, and also catch up on much needed sleep. This was the first time we were able to spend Shabbos as a family in more than three weeks.

Arrangements for the Purim feast were made by some well-meaning relatives without consulting us. They reasoned that it would be better to send the children to a cousin's home — "to have a real Yom Tov," leaving us alone. It was a great mistake. We were lonely and depressed. We should have been together as a family. When one assists a person or family in such circumstances — the form of assistance must be carefully evaluated to be certain that it is indeed a help.

❧ ❧ ❧

All this while our child was suffering terribly. Her blast cells were gone, she was in remission; but, her condition kept deteriorating. She was losing more and more weight, unable to eat, too weak to even sit. Her pain was so severe at times even morphine didn't work. Evenings my husband stayed in her room but only catnapped, always fearful of an impending crisis.

Some people, in their zeal to help us, caused much anguish. They called our parents to insist that we transfer Leah'le to a different hospital that they considered better. Others came to our house one evening, claiming to be sent by a prominent Rabbi, to try to "make us see the light." They meant well, but their focus was inappropriate. Their message seemed to imply that we were incapable of making decisions affecting our child's treatment. Nothing could be farther from the truth! We were intelligent enough to assess the treatment our child was given. The nursing care was quite good. We had a world-renowned specialist on the case. Family considerations, namely the emotional well-being of ourselves and our other children were better served by having our child in a local hospital.

We protested this intrusion upon our privacy. Our protests went unheeded. Besides wasting our valuable time, which could have been better spent either at home or with our child, we had to listen to their well-meaning, emotionally charged rhetoric. In addition, Drs. F. and R. were constantly harassed. It was implied that they were murderers by keeping our child in their hospital. One "friend" had the foolish insensitivity to call and say, "Should your child die in our local hospital, you'd never be able to forgive yourself . . ." How ridiculous! G-d's presence fills the entire world. He sends the Angel of Healing to all the sick, regardless of which hospital the patient is at! We are definitely supposed to make an effort through natural means; however, to insist in this fashion is tantamount to a denial of G-d's watching over everyone and everything, even if one's intentions are noble. We suffered this indignity for about six weeks, until Leah'le's planned transfer.

There is a great lesson to be learned from this: To help someone in dire need is a great *mitzvah*. Every *mitzvah* has a set manner in which it is to be performed. A kindness done in a manner that causes anguish to the recipient is not a kindness. When lending a hand we must be diligent. Always ask: "What can I do for you? How can I help?" Never dictate.

☙ ☙ ☙

Unbeknown to our well-intentioned-but-meddling friends, plans were formulated for Leah'le's transfer. She would be taken by ambulance accompanied by one of her physicians.

That morning, my friend came at 7:30, despite her family obligations and ill health, to bring us the money necessary to pay for a private ambulance. What an example of true *Yiddishe chesed*!

Dr. R. accompanied us in the ambulance. We enjoyed his company and really needed his support. We had just left a small hospital and staff to whom we had grown accustomed and were headed to a large unknown institution. We were truly frightened. Dr. R. didn't leave us until Leah'le was settled, although his responsibility was over as soon as we entered that grand hospital building. When he did leave, he took me home in a taxi and refused to let me pay.

After the initial battery of tests, Leah'le was finally settled into a spacious double occupancy corner room. The staff turned out to be very caring. Chemo was given to retain the remission we had just achieved and to prepare for a bone marrow transplant when the time would be ripe.

Miraculously within a month's time our child was beginning to look and act like a normal five year old. Her hair was growing back. Only a close look would reveal an intravenous line protruding from under her robe and hooked into an Ivak pump.

At about this time Leah'le was encouraged to start mingling socially by going to the playroom. The playroom was enormous. Almost every conceivable toy on every age level could be found there. A special section for arts and crafts was set up on one side of the room. A large selection of games and a library was situated at the other.

Art, woodworking and ceramics were just a few of the daily activities. Leah'le was thrilled. Being unusually creative, she partook in each of these activities. Oh, what beautiful projects! A tic-tac-toe game carved from wood, painted wood pencil and pad holder, paperweights made of glass with a felt backing, to name just a few. My very favorite is a wood-beaded necklace that she made as a gift for me.

In addition, evening activities were encouraged. As I was sitting near Leah'le at the weekly Bingo game, she excitedly shouted, "Bingo, I won!" When called upon to choose a prize, she selected a teddy bear and said, "I won this present for my baby brother" (then seven and a half months old). I was shocked and asked, "Are you sure you don't want a game or toy to play with instead?" She answered, "I have many toys here in the playroom — the children at home have very few toys — this is for the baby." She always thought of others.

Baking cookies was another favorite activity. Every child was given a slab of dough, a rolling pin and cookie cutters. The cookie shapes were placed on a cookie sheet and baked. The children would then enjoy their culinary arts — that is, all *except our daughter* — she knew these cookies weren't kosher. She devised a way to enjoy the baking but not indulge in the eating by distributing them to the non-Jewish nursing staff. Once she brought back a batch of freshly baked cookies and offered them to her Hispanic roommate's mother saying, "I baked these for your daughter. When she wakes up please give them to her." Little did Leah'le know that her roommate was in a coma! The poor mother was moved to tears at this kind gesture.

Play therapy plays a major role in the patient's curriculum. There a child has an opportunity to act out his individual feelings on various issues affecting his daily hospital life. The therapy is accomplished in such ways as injecting needles into dolls; all major courses of treatment are explained to the children in this manner. Through the knowledge gained in play therapy, Leah'le, gained a sense of fulfillment to have control over her health care, since she had no control over her illness.

❧ ❧ ❧

As the month of Nissan approached, we realized that Pesach was just around the corner. Our major concern of cleaning for Pesach became a reality. The N'shei ladies mobilized a group of high-school girls to come daily to help clean. Their diligence and devotion was unbelievable. Miraculously, everything was done in time.

We spent *Yom Tov* together with our children. I slept with the children in the Bikur Cholim apartment while my husband stayed with Leah'le. My husband prayed out loud at her bedside to give her a little flavor of *Yom Tov*. He then made her a mini-*seder*. She asked the "four questions," drank some wine, and nibbled on a small piece of *matzoh*. This was one of the first things she was able to keep down since the beginning of chemo. Even though Leah'le had been absent from school due to her illness, she remembered the entire story of Pesach from the previous school year. We were truly amazed.

After leaving Leah'le's bedside, my husband conducted a *seder* for us. We were even honored to have a guest at our *seder* table — a man whose wife was admitted to the hospital right before *Yom Tov*.

As for food — I cooked at home before *Yom Tov* and stored everything in disposable aluminum-foil containers to be heated up when needed. I served on paper plates and used plastic flatware. It was wonderful having a guest. It gave us the feeling of normalcy.

On the first day of Pesach, the children went to visit their sister in the hospital. It was very touching to see the children embrace Leah'le. I walked away so that they shouldn't notice me crying.

Immediately, after the first two days of Pesach, we brought the children home. My husband and I took turns sleeping in the hospital. For the second days, we decided to stay in the Bikur Cholim apartment by ourselves.

Leah'le, when well, was a vivacious child. Now that she was feeling a little stronger, she became very lively and mischievous once again. She took some syringes and filled them with water. Then, hiding them behind her back and wheeling her IV pump with her other hand, got a nurse's attention and squirted at her. They giggled at all her pranks, frankly relieved that she was well enough to do these things.

❧   ❧   ❧

Once Pesach was over and Leah'le was steadily getting stronger on IV feedings, the doctors started pondering whether or not to transplant. As the doctors saw it, there were two sides to the coin. Yes, our child's only chance for long-term survival was through a bone marrow transplant. However the doctors, knowing their patient, were afraid that her lack of cooperation (when taking medications), carelessness with toys thrown on the floor and potentially dangerous germs could jeopardize her health. Since a transplant patient's immune system has been completely suppressed, she has no resistance and a minor thing can turn into a life-threatening situation.

During this time we were impatient with our doctors and were increasingly anxious about the indecisiveness to begin transplant procedures immediately. We felt that we were sitting on a time bomb and were afraid that with every passing day she would G-d forbid slip out of remission. Thus we would lose out on the bone marrow transplant and the only chance to give her life.

At this point my husband called Dr. F. with whom he'd spent countless hours on the telephone since we left his hospital. His reaction: "I am speechless! Where did they get the right to withhold lifesaving methods from a patient?" We finally received word from the transplant team that they wanted to meet with us. We understood that Dr. F. contacted the team and made his views known.

Our first step was finding an HLA match; a sibling or close blood relation whose blood is genetically identical (not just the same blood type) to Leah'le's. The whole family went to the out-patient department of our hospital, constantly praying that a match be found. When the nurse asked "Who would like to be first?" Simie, then seven years old, jumped up without any hesitation, "Me!" We had previously explained to our children that Leah'le had a blood disease, with bad cells destroying the good ones. Therefore, we were going to take this blood test to determine who would help their sister live by donating some healthy marrow. The hospital also furnished literature and coloring books explaining the disease and treatment. Yes, our children did have sibling rivalry as all normal children occasionally do, but their love for one another was immeasurable.

A short time later, to us it seemed like an eternity, we were informed that Simie was a perfect match to be the bone marrow donor. Oh, how happy she was! She was just ecstatic! She, and only she, was given the opportunity to save her sister's life!

Leah'le's doctors decided that it would be beneficial for her to spend some time at home with her family prior to transplant and to intermittently come in for maintenance chemo. My husband and I were very concerned. As much as we wanted Leah'le home, we couldn't understand how this could be accomplished — she still wasn't eating. We were also concerned that since her resistance was very low she would pick up an infection from one of her siblings and her health would be further jeopardized. She was sent home just the same.

Leah'le was still very weak, so my husband helped her up the stairs. After she was settled around the table with the other children, she pulled out a can of soda that she brought especially for this purpose — to share with her siblings. She knew she looked different (she was almost completely bald and extremely skinny) and wanted to be accepted. Before entering the house I asked her whether she wanted to wear a hat or scarf on her head to conceal her baldness and she refused. The children were aware of the fact that her baldness was due to the strong medications she was taking. At first they stared at her for a moment. When she produced the can of soda and announced that she brought it especially for them to share, she broke the ice. What foresight from a five year old!

Simie catered to her sister's every request. Nothing was too hard for her. Oh what genuine love she displayed — she was thrilled to have her sister home! I acted as nurse: Changing the dressing on the broviac catheter and flushing out the line, as well as injecting medications.

As we had feared, eating was the biggest problem. Leah'le wanted to eat and asked for her favorite foods to be prepared. We dutifully accommodated her. She tried eating but couldn't swallow or keep anything down. It was really heartbreaking.

The next day, I was sitting outside with Leah'le and the baby. Leah'le was wearing an all-weather coat with a hood, mainly for the purpose of concealing her bald head. Several of her friends passed. Seeing her all skin and bones and not comprehending the situation, they asked, "Can she talk?" "Yes," I answered, "Why don't you try and find out for yourselves?" They did and found that their friend's warm personality had not changed; it was only her exterior appearance that had been altered due to her illness.

After consulting again with the doctors on the following day about Leah'le's condition (weakened), it was decided to have her re-admitted to the hospital — it was very difficult — but we had no choice, she wasn't eating or drinking and was getting weaker by the minute. We now had a setback; she was too weak for the transplant. She had lost too much weight.

Oh, how upset we were! In addition to the anxiety from the constant threat of relapse before the transplant could be performed, we were also confronted with family pressures. My in-laws claimed that we should spend additional time with our other children. The nurses insisted that we were needed in the hospital. We finally decided to call upon the volunteer girls who stayed with Leah'le in our local hospital. We took turns with them for weekends and occasionally on week nights — we just had to unwind. They were really a great help to us and the entire staff — cheering up and helping all patients, Jew and non-Jew alike. What a *kiddush Hashem*!

❊　　❊　　❊

It was finally transplant time. A consent form had already been signed for the procedure to be performed. Leah'le was given a private room that had been disinfected especially for this purpose. All new toys were provided for her — since the old ones may have had germs. A private duty nurse was assigned to her (one of the conditions stipulated for transplant). Caps, gown, head covers and slippers were donned before entering her room. And of course, strict hand-washing procedures were enforced.

When Leah'le was taken down for radiation therapy as a prerequisite for the transplant, I went along and waited in the control room. I would watch Leah'le inside the heavily insulated room through a TV monitor, reading to her (through a microphone) the stories of our great Sages, many of which she knew by heart.

When she returned to her room she received her dose of chemo to further destroy any remaining bone marrow. All of the person's marrow is destroyed, leaving him without any resistance against infection. He is then injected with the donor's marrow, which will ultimately grow in him to produce healthy blood cells.

The first few days following radiation therapy were uneventful. Things were going as planned. We were looking forward to the actual transplant of the bone marrow.

Simie recalls her experiences of pre-transplant procedures. She took off a day from school to go to the hospital blood bank to donate a pint of blood for herself. After donating the marrow for her sister's transplant she will get the blood that she donated back, enabling her bone marrow to rejuvenate itself more quickly.

While at the hospital that day, she also had a chance to visit Leah'le in the social worker's office, as she had been doing every Tuesday morning for about two months. These sessions were necessary to help both donor and recipient deal with the idea of transplant.

She recalls taking vitamins and iron (especially prescribed by the bone marrow transplant doctors) for about a month before and after transplant. "They tasted horrible." she interjects. Their purpose was to build up her blood supply. But most prominent in her mind is the giving of marrow. She went into the hospital on Monday morning for a routine admission procedure. The plan was to give the marrow on the next day, Tuesday, and be discharged on Wednesday morning. However, things did not go as planned. Due to many emergency surgeries on Tuesday, this procedure was pushed off. "I was very upset." she recalls. "I was given a shot to relax me. They even started an IV. I said *Tehillim* and asked Hashem that I should have enough marrow to save my sister's life and then they postponed surgery."

The very next morning Simie was taken down to surgery, while Leah'le waited anxiously in her isolation room. The procedure took about one and a half hours. Under general anesthesia three hundred pricks were made into her hips to extract enough marrow for the transplant. She remembers the huge bandage and the achy feeling thereafter. "But it got better within a week. The thing that bothered me most at the time was the fact that I fasted for two days — once the false alarm and once to give the marrow."

Now this precious marrow was headed for Leah'le. All went well in the beginning; however, the following week complications began setting in. Infection after infection. She filled up with fluid, her abdomen became distended. It was obvious her condition was deteriorating. Pneumonia had set in. Antibiotics were administered.

❈　　❈　　❈

Wednesday morning, a week after transplant, I bought her a present from her Pre-1A teacher, a tape recorder and some tapes. She lay in bed listening to them. I remember her praying that morning with unusually great fervor and *bitachon*: I had previously taught her the meaning of her prayers. Her prayers brought tears to my eyes. אני מאמין באמונה שלמה בביאת המשיח ואף על פי שיתמהמה עם כל זה אחכה לו בכל יום שיבוא... It was obvious to me that she knew that we were headed for dark times, but she had faith in Hashem.

The very next day, Thursday, things were even gloomier: Heart failure had set in. After an echocardiagram, the doctor told us to pray. They were taking Leah'le to a special-care unit. At this point Leah'le was drifting in and out of consciousness. I couldn't compose myself any longer — I couldn't hold back my tears. I just knew our beloved child was going to die. I had trust in Hashem, and I knew that everything He was doing was best for us; but I had a premonition that things wouldn't be good.

My husband tried to calm me. "Esther," he said, "they don't send a patient to die in the Intensive Care Unit. A patient who is beyond hope is put into a separate side room and allowed to expire peacefully." The head nurse and many of the floor nurses gathered to comfort me. Upon hearing this conversation, they were all too choked up with tears to speak. The head nurse simply nodded her head in agreement, amazed at my husband's perception. In fact, both the doctors and nurses thought she'd pull through — they even saved her room for her and made her bed ...

As nightfall set in, Leah'le was completely unconscious — catheters and tubes were inserted to monitor her and sustain life. My husband participated in these procedures. He lovingly crouched by her bed for an hour and a half while doctors were trying to insert catheters, since it was impossible to anesthetize her. A fantastic team of super devoted professionals worked with boundless energy to save our beloved child! Her team of devoted nurses from the pediatric floor came down to check on her condition and kept us informed. How caring!

During the late evening we were advised by the staff to go home and rest. Our daughter's condition was status quo, should they need us they would call.

No sooner did we get into the doorway of our house, than my mother-in-law told us that the hospital called ... some forms had to be signed. We rushed back (knowing in our hearts that this was just a pretense), reciting *Tehillim* out loud while driving.

We reached the hospital. When we entered the waiting area, we were informed that CPR had already been attempted twice successfully. We sat and said *Tehillim* with all our might. If we dozed, the pediatric nurses who came down to inquire about Leah'le's condition left a note saying they were there and what was happening. The nurses stayed with us after their shift ended. How could they go home? Their prize patient was fighting for her life — they waited — what devotion!

Friday finally dawned. It was about 6 a.m. Morning prayers had to be said. My husband prayed aloud with great devotion. A few minutes thereafter, Dr. B., head of the transplant team, came out with tears in his eyes and in a broken voice uttered, "She's gone!"

The entire nursing staff and transplant team gathered around to comfort us. We found out that just about the time that my husband recited *Shema* her pure soul returned to its Maker.

Many people react to grief with anger and take it out on the doctors. The doctors in the special care unit weren't the ones that killed Leah'le. They tried all night to save her life. So it would be highly inappropriate to show anger towards them. My husband thanked them. A social worker later told my husband that this had been good medicine for the doctors. He boosted their morale and this helped them deal with their pain.

While I remained in the lounge, crying hysterically, comforted by the pediatric nurses, my husband, keeping all his grief inward, took care of the arrangements. He called our parents to tell them the heartbreaking news. He then called Rabbi and Mrs. G., friends of ours, who in turn made chain calls. My husband recalls, "I was really sorry to hit them with such news at 7:45 a.m. Mrs. G. answered the telephone and went to pieces. This made me feel really bad. She contacted her husband, who helped with the funeral arrangements as well as paying for the expenses. I then spoke to the funeral director who said he'd come as soon as possible, knowing that it was *erev Shabbos* and that we wanted the funeral that same afternoon. The doctor also provided the death certificate so there would be no waiting.

❀ ❀ ❀

My husband recalls, "I went down to be *shomer* with Leah'le until the funeral director showed up. It was a very queer feeling ... It was an indescribably hard thing to do. I was emotionally ready to go into the special care unit and help the doctors insert catheters, as I did the night before ... but not to have to prepare for a funeral."

It says in *Tachnun* that when Hashem is angry, He still has mercy. The fact that Leah'le passed away that morning and there was time to arrange for a funeral for the same day was an act of mercy. Had she died close to Shabbos we would have had to remain in the hospital. This would have been too excruciating to bear.

What a tremendous burden rested on our shoulders — going home.

As we drove into the driveway, my in-laws rushed out to greet us. My mother-in-law embraced me and we cried on each other's shoulders for a few moments. My husband called Simie aside and told her the tragic news. She was aware of her sister's deteriorating condition, but there was still a glimmer of hope that her sister would recuperate. She was grief stricken and rushed to a close friend down the block to share her anguish. We gave her the choice of whether or not to go to the funeral. She decided that it would be too difficult to bear. To this day she feels she made the right decision.

❀ ❀ ❀

Despite the fact that Leah'le passed away during the summer, she had a very large funeral. Friends and family came from far and wide. Her doctors and nurses stood outside. They all came to pay their final respects to a "very special little girl" whom they all loved.

The week of *shivah* was observed at our house. Our children were home with us. Our family and friends came to share our grief and to comfort us. Dr. F. came to express his sympathies and to reassure us,

"Transplant was the only route." Many other doctors and nurses, both from our local hospital and also from the larger cancer center came. They wanted to show how much they cared!

During *shivah* countless people came and told us that we were *tzaddikim* and had the merit to have a child who passed away. They explained that this challenge is only given to special people who are able to withstand the test. Truthfully, we could have done without this unique privilege. What we can say though, is this: We are thankful to Hashem that we were worthy to have such a special child who wouldn't budge from her ideals at any cost. Through her actions she was also able to draw others near to Judaism — among them two nurses at the cancer hospital!

My husband recalls, "During *shivah* I felt the whole sequence of events were unreal. I was out of touch with reality. I was totally disoriented. I knew it was true but I couldn't believe it really happened. I dealt with the reality by making funeral arrangements and by calling friends to arrange for a *minyan* in our house. My father offered to say *Kaddish* in the memory of his beloved grand-daughter. I knew he wanted to do something, so I agreed."

Even though Leah'le didn't live, we feel that the prayers and the work of the community were not in vain. It was a community tragedy. Everyone shared our pain. Never did our child, my husband or myself question Hashem's wisdom. It was very painful to lose her, but whether or not we understand Hashem's actions, Hashem is always right. Hashem does what is best for us!

After losing a close relative, especially a child, it is normal to experience guilt. "I should have done this or that ... " or "Had I known, I would have . . ." However, one must learn to deal with these and other feelings related to the loss of a loved one. The best way not to feel guilty is to believe you're innocent. This is best accomplished by seeking professional help — going immediately helps to prevent problems in the future. Unfortunately, there is a stigma attached to going for therapy. Many assume if someone goes for therapy, they must be mentally ill. This is utter nonsense. It is no different than going to any other health professional! There is a *mitzvah* in the Torah: ונשמרתם מאד לנפשותיכם, — "You should watch over your health" — physical or emotional well being.

❀   ❀   ❀

Today, at home there is a wholesome atmosphere. Our children (even those who weren't yet born at that time) know they once had another sister. We have pictures of Leah'le out in the open, not hidden or pushed away in a drawer; yet, pictures of her aren't plastered all over the walls. The children discuss their "other sister" comfortably, but not constantly. They cherish her toys (presents that she received during her hospital stay) — but they do play with them — lovingly. They all know these are their sister's toys.

The pain we experienced with our child's death was enormous — a normal reaction. However, death, mourning and grief should not be taboo subjects. We explained to our children, each on their own level, what had happened. We were as honest as we knew how. We didn't make up fairy tales.

The usual pattern of day-by-day living goes on, with the emphasis that Hashem is the Master of the Universe — Hashem rules the world and is just in His decrees.

৵§ Faith   *by Fradel Berger*

When you look out at your garden
On a wintry day
You see it in its death-like sleep
All desolate and grey
It is hard to think that just below
That frosted terrain
All the flowers are waiting
To come up and out again

You find it hard to believe that they are there
The earth looks cold and lifeless
And the trees are stark and bare
The mind says no it cannot be
But faith says it is so
For faith can see the hidden glory
Underneath the snow

Sometimes when you look out at the world
Your heart despairs
It is hard to see Hashem Who really cares
But just as we can see the spring
Beneath the winter's path
We can see Hashem's loving
Kindness over all!!

A Letter of Consolation

To my dear and beloved sons and daughters,

The purpose of this letter is to console you for when I will not be with you anymore. A person does not know when his time will be up, but the day will come (may Hashem bless me with a long life) when my place at home will be empty and you will be orphans.

My beloved, I have seen many orphans, most of whom find themselves in darkness without hope. Some are jealous, thinking, "Others have parents, but not me." Others feel that their world has tumbled down. Few are able to strengthen and brace themselves and to eventually elevate themselves after the tragedy in their lives. I therefore came to the conclusion that before one can comfort a mourner it is essential to teach him how to deal with the situation. I hope I succeed in this endeavor and may you understand these words so that they illuminate your lives.

The key to the mystery of life is faith in the true G-d, the Creator of the Universe! It is G-d's power that keeps the world going, even each and every blade of grass derives its sustenance from the Creator and surely each human being. This spirit of life is the essence of everything and the most important part of a person is his spirit and soul.

I trust that I have raised you to have faith in G-d. I now encourage you to strengthen your faith and to realize that this is also the secret to the mystery of death! If life would be over for a dead person, it would be difficult to comfort a mourner. But that is not so! Although the body passes away, the person continues to exist!

Our great teacher (Rav Yeruchem Levovitz of the Mir) wrote: "Death should be understood as one who moves from one city to another. This is the real truth. Your father has not died, may his memory be blessed, for he is alive. He has merely moved. To the understanding person there is even more to say. The deceased is now even closer to you than before for now there are no separations."

One who has faith is able to deal with the concept of death. The truth is that the deceased is *alive!* He is aware of everything and he is close to his relatives at all times!

However, I realize that you will still be bothered by his seeming absence. Children are accustomed to seeing their parents, asking for advice and being helped. Even after they move away from home they rely on and know they can always turn to their parents. Who can fill this void?

But, think it over, my beloved ones. If you really loved me when I was with you, and if your love was not just superficial, you can always picture me in front of your eye. You will know what I would have said and how I would have advised you. As an example, we see what our Sages say about Joseph: He withstood temptation in Egypt because of the vision of his father before his eyes.

Use the vision of your father to give you strength and encouragement. Keep in mind: The essence of a person is the spiritual and that part continues to live!

Another point. All people feel an urge to come closer to good deeds at a time of mourning. Even those who were non-observant come to say *Kaddish*, they put on a *tallis* and *tefillin* and pray. What is the reason for this?

There is a deep reason. Our Sages teach that there are three partners to every human being: his father, mother and the Holy One, Blessed is He. Now a child is used to seeing only his father and mother. The third partner is invisible. However, when the physical partners leave this world, there is an inner feeling in the person that pushes him closer to the third partner ...

One whose faith is strong feels this in a concrete way: "My father and mother (may) have left me — but Hashem is always there."

The truth is: The physical parent was merely a messenger from the Heavenly Father. Now that the physical father's job is over — the child's relationship to his Heavenly Father becomes stronger.

... This then is the most important message to bear in mind, for all people at any age: to strengthen one's faith, to sense Hashem's Providence, to realize how Hashem guides and leads a person daily and provides all your physical and spiritual needs. You will not lack anything if you keep your faith strong!

Through faith one will be consoled ... Normally, a person is surrounded by his family, his teachers, his friends — all of them help him to maintain his life properly. However, when a relative passes away — may Hashem spare us — one of the supports has been removed.

The process of comforting the mourner, is to help replace the missing support, to raise his spirits and to help him continue ...

Now my beloved ones, come closer to each other, help each other, encourage each other; your friendship should be wholesome, faithful, amidst the love of Torah and of those who study Torah. Always be willing to learn and to improve ... Hashem will surely comfort you and help you continue ... Be strong in faith and in Torah, build for yourselves loyal homes with the aim of fulfilling Hashem's commandments. Your actions shall then serve to benefit me as our Sages say: When one's children observe the commandments it is considered as if the father has not passed away. This is my advice and last request of you.

My Beloved Ones: Have faith and your faith will be fulfilled and may your lives be successful forever!

With love,

Your father

[Excerpted from "To Comfort the Living" by Rabbi M. Goldberger]

✺§ Geulah

by Fraida Milka Abramowitz
Rimnitzer Rebbetzin

I wanted to write
to relieve the heaviness
from within
words came not
tears did.
Oh! *Geulah, Geulah*
you're closer than we know.
The voice of a multitude
cries from within me
could it be heard
it would deafen all humanity
and volcano's would bow in shame.
The flame of *Klal Yisroel* can never be extinguished
and so my fire continues to burn.
Klal Yisroel, oh, beloved children
I cry with you and for you
yet rejoice while perceiving
your upcoming glory . . .
Every Jewish soul scattered
links itself with mine,
even the sinful . . .
how drawn I am
to their hidden sparks,
while perceiving a moment of truth
each sinner turns to potential *Tzaddik* . . .
The songs of *Geulah*
The melodies of *Yerushalayim*
The humming of *Moshiach's* footsteps
The descending sounds of *Yerushalayim shel maalah* . . .
Can a billion violin strings ecstatically exploding
compare to the sweetness of my song
its for *Knesses Yisroel,* I am pleading and moaning
Forgive them, it's your chosen children,
who are in the wrong.

Challenged

Maybe this Year

ברוך ה' כי שמע קול תחנוני . . . (תהלים כח:ו)

 young couple begins their new life together with trepidation, full of hope that their lives will harmonize and uphold the golden chain of tradition.

The weeks and months passed swiftly; it was almost a year since their wedding day. It was quite naturally assumed that by about this time they would probably already be parents. After all, isn't it automatic? But soon realization began to sink in. It's not at all an automatic phenomenon, but something controlled by Higher Powers.

For about a year or two after our wedding, we considered ourselves like any other young couple, but suddenly I became aware that perhaps we were a bit different. People unabashedly pitied us, "You know they're already married a number of years and still have no children ... " Gradually I felt the subtle looks and hushed whispers take their toll on me; I became a victim of people's pity.

Suddenly, as if awakening from a dream, I became determined to fight them. Why should anyone pity me, I thought? Does my face portray such bitterness, such anguish? Does the fact that I don't have a child yet make me so different? After all, everything is dependent on Supreme Providence. If Hashem wills it, I can easily become a happy mother. And if it is not destined for me, does my life then have to become a tragedy? It was then that I firmly resolved to let everyone know of my intentions. The way to counter-attack the pity was so simple — להיות בשמחה תמיד — always to be good natured, always with a smile — not just on the surface, but with complete confidence that Hashem is Omnipotent and we can not simply change His will.

At this point we go through certain motions which are permissible to us. We can visit doctors, seek blessings from *rabbanim* and other great men, go to the graves of righteous individuals so that their prayers should arouse pity from Heaven and effect the miracle. But most important, we never cease our own prayers.

Two very important factors which helped me to be joyful constantly were, first: parents, who wisely did not interfere with private lives, did not nag for details. I was aware that my parents were always interested in what was happening, but they always contained their curiosity. They were ready with advice when it was requested and were helpful in general, but they never badgered or nagged. Sometimes the pressure of "What should I say when they ask?" is as disturbing as the problem itself. The various treatments one undergoes (for infertility) are not always easily discussed. And throughout all this my father always reminded me, that in merit of always being joyful and doing good deeds, a person can be helped.

The second important factor was my job. I was involved with the education of children, which not only gave me tremendous spiritual fulfillment, but also filled an obvious void.

People are generally kind and well meaning, and the advice that we received would just about fill a book. It takes great self-control, but one must hear their advice and thank them graciously. Sometimes it's difficult when they attempt to follow up their advice and inquire about results.

At every gathering of women, the topic of children is invariably raised. I always tried to minimize the discomfort of others by contributing to the conversation. At times someone might innocently inquire about my children. Once while having my wig set, one woman innocently asked me, "Are your children sleeping already?" At first I found these situations awkward and painful, for it was difficult to say, "I don't have any children yet." However, eventually I realized that it was much more uncomfortable for the one who innocently asked the question. But if it was such a normal question, why did it illicit such discomfort from me? Is there any reason why a perfect stranger should be aware of my circumstances?

And so the years passed; every year we lived with renewed hope. Maybe this year? Fifteen years of "maybe" passed, fifteen years of visiting *rabbanim*, fifteen years under various treatments and medical procedures. But when things are in the hands of the One Above, help can come in a split second.

I always felt that the many good wishes of the worthy people who prayed for us would eventually be fulfilled. One day my husband was inspired to visit an esteemed *Rebbe* for a blessing, and his words were magic to our ears — "You will be blessed with a son." We had great faith but the worthy Rabbi advised us to see a doctor so that the miracle would appear to be a natural phenomenon. It was ordained for us to see a competent doctor who was the right messenger to accomplish Hashem's mission, and almost immediately thereafter everything evolved into that fruition. After fifteen and a half years we became the overjoyed parents of our first-born son . . . Our friends and relatives rejoiced with us; the *mazel tov* wishes were so genuine.

I sit here now trying to express in writing how I feel. How can I tell you how it feels to be a mother? Can I describe how it feels to see my fondest wishes, my dream come true? It still seems like a sweet dream. Sometimes I thought I would awaken and see that it never happened. Suddenly I understood the verse: בשוב ה' את שיבת ציון היינו כחולמים — "When Hashem will return the exiles of Zion we will think we are dreaming."

❦   ❦   ❦

My precious *yingele* is now three years old. He is a constant source of *simchah* in our home. I chose not to go back to teach when he was a baby — I could not bear the thought of sharing him with any babysitter.

A Fear of the Unknown

שמע בני . . . (משלי א:ח)

s I observe my dear son Moishe putting on *tefillin* for the very first time, my heart is filled with praise and gratitude to *Hakadosh Baruch Hu* for all He has done for us over the past thirteen years. Memories fill my mind. Memories of fear of pain and hardship. I feel choked with emotions. Moishe is *bar mitzvah* like any other yeshivah boy. On second thought he's not really like any other child his age. He has experienced more in his lifetime and as a result he has become deeper and more understanding, indeed, a better person.

Looking back at the last twelve years I find it unbelievable and I bless Hashem who has brought us this far. At age eleven-and-a-half months my healthy baby — whose smiling cheerful face was always shining — suddenly became deathly ill. It was meningitis. The doctor gave no hope. The pediatric neurologist lifted his arms up to the sky and said, "It's out of my hands. Only the One Above can do something for your child. If he does survive he may be brain damaged for life." The weeks following were crucial. My husband and I sat at his cribside and waited. *I lift my eyes to the mountains. Whence comes my help. My help is from Hashem who created heaven and earth.* My husband's voice at the baby's side pleading to Hashem for a cure was heard by the nurses. They stood in awe and only later on commented, "It looks like you people have special pull up there, things are progressing at a faster speed than we expected." Slowly he began to recuperate. His illness and weakness caused him to regress. It took a while until he began standing again and still longer until he moved around. After three-and-one-half weeks of being hospitalized, Moishe was ready to be discharged.

It was the last Chanukah candle when we brought him home. Our hearts were filled with joy. Moishe brought light into our house.

A week after Moishe was discharged from the hospital I gave birth to another son. I felt helpless. How would I be able to care for my other children and give Moishe the specialized attention that was so essential. When I would sigh and express these feelings, my husband would constantly say that surely we can't have complaints to Hashem. He gave us more than we deserve. This is our challenge and Hashem only gives tests to those people who can handle them, and only as much as they can handle. We can and we will, with His help.

Little did we realize that hard times were just beginning.

At eighteen months Moishe was diagnosed as profoundly deaf, a side-effect from a drug called Chloramycitin which had been administered in order to save his life. Moishe was fitted with hearing aids and we began going daily for language and speech development therapy. Trying to teach him lip-reading skills so he could be an oral child rather than use sign language was a tremendous undertaking. It was a long hard year but we slowly saw some fruits of our labor. Although he heard nothing we slowly began to communicate. He began associating the vocabulary taught to him with communicative language.

At age three he continued his therapy and attended a nursery class for the deaf. Moishe's special intuition made him realize that this was not a *yeshivah* like his brothers attended. His strong yearning for warmth and *yiddishkeit* began to develop. We saw that this desire would not be able to be cultivated in this atmosphere.

Moishe's future depended on our next step. With great insecurity and much trepidation and with a prayer on our lips we approached the principal of our neighborhood *yeshivah*. We pleaded that he accept our otherwise perfectly normal, above-average-intelligence child into their kindergarten class. He tried convincing us that we were making a wrong move, all the while convincing himself not to feel guilty that he didn't want to accept Moishe. The second yeshivah hesitantly consented after conferring with the teacher and receiving her approval.

Orientation Day was no picnic for me — facing the staring eyes of children and parents. Questions that aren't asked are even more difficult to respond to. Nobody had the courage to speak to me. I felt their pitying glances. I felt like saying, "If you really care, act normal and then we will feel we can act normal as well." Instead, when the children stared and questioningly pointed their fingers at the strange contraption that had wires going into Moishe's ears, the mothers instinctively pulled them by their hands and motioned them to keep quiet. I had made up my mind. No one was going to feel uncomfortable around us. I would have to be the one to take the first step.

The first day of school was an opportune time. After asking the teacher for permission I gathered the children in a small circle. I told them, "Moishe's ears do not work well. However, Hashem has not forgotten him. Instead Hashem enables Moishe to hear with his eyes." I went on to explain that if they wanted to speak to him they would have to make sure to face him so he could read their lips. I showed them his hearing aids and explained how it worked. They were fascinated. No longer was there a fear of the unknown.

The year went comparatively well. The compassion and understanding exhibited by the teachers were felt by the children. They naturally followed suit. The mothers were invited to see the children's Chanukah performance. I came to *yeshivah* that day with a heavy heart. Here was the first time that Moishe's handicap would publicly make him different. How would he react during the play when he still had almost no expressive language?

Wrapped in my private thoughts I felt a woman tap me on the shoulder. "Hi," she said, "which one is your son?"

I calmly pointed my finger towards Moishe and said, "That one."

I expected to see instant withdrawal. However, to my amazement she exclaimed, "Really! My son doesn't stop talking about his friend Moishe. He says everyone wants to claim him as their friend. He's one of the best-liked kids in the class." Moishe's charming personality and his warm, giving nature was felt by his peers. He was accepted for his own merits. I left the *yeshivah* strongly encouraged.

We continued his therapy sessions four times a week. I was taught to use every second and every opportunity to "pump him with language." Talk until you're blue in the face and then some more. When walking with him and when traveling we would stop and use our surroundings as pointers for conversation. Sun, sky, trees, flowers and more were introduced to Moishe. I would repeat the words thousands of times through the next few months. Finally one day I saw that flicker of recognition in his eyes as he recognized the word on my lips and associated it with its proper object. I prayed to

Hashem Who is Omnipotent to continue to give Moishe the knowledge and wisdom he would need to succeed.

Teaching him about the tangible was difficult but possible. However, my concern was great in regard to how we would teach him about the intangible. Hearing children normally absorb without even realizing that they are learning. Such was not the case with Moishe. How could I possibly teach him about the existence of G-d? On the other hand how could I not enlighten him with something all small children grow to understand? After much thought and no clue as to how we would present this concept, I told his tutor, "Today we will try. Let's ask for Divine guidance and hopefully we will succeed."

To our great surprise we clearly saw the simple faith that this little soul possessed. His eyes opened wide as he drank in every detail. This was the beginning of his special understanding of the Creator. He would encounter many difficulties as he grew up and now he knew to Whom he could turn for encouragement and support.

Our next project was to teach him to recite a *brachah*. Since he could not hear the sounds, every word had to be repeated countless times until he picked up the word and mimicked each sound. Months of hard work brought success. Moishe finally made all the blessings like his other brothers.

We could not stop and rest. There was so much to be done. I remember sighing many times and praying: Will my child ever learn the *aleph-beis*? Will he ever be able to *daven*? Little did I dream that the time would come when he would be learning *gemara*.

One *erev Shabbos*, Moishe approached my husband and insisted on going to *shul*. My husband explained that it was too early and in fact he hadn't even dressed for Shabbos. Moishe explained that he was very well aware that it was quite early; however, he said, "Tatty, I want you to be there before the people and when they come in stand near the door and ask each one individually to *daven* for me tonight. Tell them to ask Hashem to make me hear again." Moishe had no complaints to Hashem. He only had requests for recovery.

It was a long hard road on which we traveled. From teaching him *brachos* until he mastered his first *pasuk* of *chumash*, *mishnayos* and then *gemara*. What we thought was the impossible became possible. To us it is now a reality. In fact, in preparation for his *bar mitzvah*, my husband prepared a *d'var torah* with him and he managed on his own to write it all down. This an accomplishment most *bar mitzvah* boys have not achieved.

Just as Moishe has a great thirst for learning Torah, he has a very strong feeling for Talmudic scholars. His desire to see *gedolim* was always very strong. Many a time he would beg my husband to take him for a blessing to a sage or rebbe who happened to be in New York. He visited Rabbi Moshe Feinstein several times. When he was three years old we took him to Reb Moshe for a blessing. The Rebbetzin opened the door and said, "The *Rosh Hayeshivah* is resting. I'm sorry you can't go in now," and she handed Moishe a lollipop. In the interim Reb Moshe came to the door and asked us to enter. Reb Moshe also offered Moishe a lollipop which he did not accept. Reb Moshe smiled and said, "He has the attribute of being satisfied with small quantities." Yes, Moishe has learned to accept his limitations.

The *brachos* given to him were always reassuring. The one most often given was he will grow up to be a great *talmid chacham*. We found this blessing very interesting, since at the time he had not yet acquired the tools necessary to learn Torah. When he mastered the understanding of his first bit of *gemara*, we expressed deep pleasure and happiness. He merely shrugged his shoulders and answered very matter of factly, "I don't know why you're getting so excited, didn't Reb Moshe say I'll be a *talmid chacham*?" Yes, as Moishe grew so did his trust and faith.

During the summer he attends a summer camp which hosts many Torah sages during the vacation recess from school. Moishe managed as usual to make the acquaintance of one *rosh yeshivah* who was greatly impressed with him. After hearing him learn *gemara* he presented him with a beautiful *siddur* which he personally inscribed. The *rosh yeshivah* told him that everyone should be obligated to see his accomplishments. If he could achieve what he had along with the drawbacks he had to contend with, what will others answer on their judgment day? The *rosh yeshivah* said, "I will take home these thoughts with me as an incentive to myself and my students for the new *yeshivah* term." Before leaving he kissed Moishe on the face, took Moishe's hands into his and said, "Do you see these hands? They have such strength and encouragement. May you be worthy to write many *chiddushei Torah* with them and call the *sefer* which you will write, *Yad Moishe*.

Yes, Hashem has definitely given us a great challenge. All through life it will continue to be one. We ask Hashem to continue with His great kindness and to give us strength and fortitude for the future.

A Letter to Libby

Dear Libby,

I was just a baby when they discovered you couldn't hear. You were two. It was a shock to them and for everyone who knew us. And so began the endless, painful struggle to get you to speak, communicate and in other words — be normal. Our mother tells me now that when I was about two or three, I walked with you through the streets of Williamsburg, naming objects so you could repeat them, "garbage can" I said, and you would repeat "aae an". Only vowels you heard, only vowels you spoke. I suppose I enjoyed teaching you, the older sibling, but they tell me now that you were hurt and bitter by the fact that I could name by voice at age two or three what you struggled with at four and five.

As time went on, it became hard for me to cope with you. You never heard *anything* the first time and it frustrated me to the point of tears and even contempt for you. You always got *all* the attention from the time you were young. Three days a week I was dragged along to *your* therapy on a hot, crowded train. I was always dragged along and then *you* received lavish praise at the slightest progress shown. I guess I was too young to realize that you would have gladly exchanged all that extra love and praise to hear, to understand, to be heard, to be understood.

As time went on, you were speaking, and since we were the only two, we grew close and you were so good to me. I guess I didn't really deserve your true affection (simply because it was too hard to repeat myself everytime). At times I do hate myself for that, and when we got into an occasional fight, you shouted your complaint and then turned away so my retort couldn't be heard. So the anger bottled up and at times I even wished you hadn't been born.

Basically, when I was reaching those teenage years and you were about fourteen, you were a great help with personal problems, school troubles, etc. It was wonderful having a sister just twenty months older, one who was wiser and more experienced, yet not too old to be in a world of her own, excluding me.

But in high school I was your shadow. You, with your hearing deficiency, were a big success. The principals were awed by your strength, the teachers impressed with your coping, your classmates honored to be friends with a success like you. It was so tough for me, and I love our mother and father for understanding my pain, and giving me all the love I thought they never felt for me.

As time went on, I was still "your sister," NOT "me, myself, and I." But you were such a success, I could not help but admire you. You got your ALS permit, your driver's license, you were in dance, in production, spoke easily on the phone, and on and on and on. Everybody knew about you. Phone calls came in from all over — Los Angeles, Texas, Canada, wanting to hear about you, how you did it, loving you. At parties you were introduced and gazed upon, loved, admired, and then "meet my other daughter," a pause, a smile, "Hello," and then right back to you. It was a pain in the neck to have you around sometimes and I was grateful when you were away for Shabbos sometimes so I could be noticed and spoiled a little.

Well, it may not sound like it, but I was happy. I had my own friends and loved life and school. Then this year you were accepted into BJJ and again — WOW! — love and admiration, pleasant surprises ... Now that I know you are leaving for the year, I realize that these are the last few months we will be together, really together, and now I can finally say honestly, with all my heart ...

"I love you, Libby"

Rivky

❁   ❁   ❁

[Rivky has made her mark on the homefront this year, while Libby is away in seminary in Yerushalayim and independent. The family is proud of both girls. Rivky is seventeen years old and graduating high school. Libby is eighteen years old. — Ed.]

Thoughts of a Chronic Visitor

I walked steadily down the quiet corridor nodding a quick, nervous "Good morning!" to everyone in sight. "You're going to be performing a *mitzvah* of tremendous importance — be happy," I told myself, but I was approaching this new experience with great trepidation. I and other volunteers like myself were going to help feed and talk to the ailing, lonely patients of the Chronic Disease Hospital.

"Chronic" is forever.

"Disease" is sickness.

These people would be sick forever . . . There is almost nothing a doctor can do to permanently cure the ailments of these suffering people — nothing short of a miracle, that is. My first thoughts were of dread as I hesitantly stepped into a ward.

I was greeted by a scream of agony. At the far end of the room I saw a woman twisting herself in obvious pain as she tried to raise her slowly deteriorating, pain-racked body off the bed. I winced every time she fell back against her pillows, but I was powerless to help her. It was against the rules to assist a patient off the bed. I turned on my heel and ran out of the room extremely disheartened. I didn't feel much like going into another ward until I was convinced that it would be a "better" one.

I swallowed hard, braced myself and went over to a patient: "May I help you with your breakfast?" I tried to sound as bright and cheery as I could.

"Oh, yes! Please open my egg." I picked it up and clunked it hard on the edge of the tray. It was softboiled, I discovered, my hand dripping egg-yolk.

Eventually I overcame my nervousness; it took about six weeks. I was soon able to walk into the ward with the most critical patients without revealing any emotion.

I had realized that what these people needed was *not* for me to recoil from their sufferings, but to focus my thoughts on their needs and wants.

From the very beginning we caught on to the terrible conditions in some of the wards — that without us, some patients would not get breakfast. The nurses for the most part are either tired, overburdened, or simply indifferent. In addition to the physical needs we attend to, we perform another vital function. Many of these patients have been abandoned or just plain forgotten by their families. By spending some time with these people who have been cut off from any contact with the outside world, we provide them with a sort of link with "reality." We're the substitute daughter, granddaughter, or friend that they look forward to seeing to cheer their day, to give some form to a shapeless, timeless week.

Laura is young and attractive, but is gradually losing muscular control. She spends a full hour every day guiding a volunteer in putting on her make-up. She examines the results in the mirror and enjoys the cosmetic effect.

The dressed-up image covers up a very ugly reality. Laura's husband abandoned her and their year-old son ten years ago, when the debilitating disease first struck her. Her little boy, now eleven, lives with his great aunt and attends a yeshivah. Our daily visits make things look better for Laura, and help her hold out until the morrow.

Mrs. Glatstein is much older than Laura, and she has been hospitalized for many, many years. She suffers enormously but always has a smile and a cheery "Good morning!" waiting for us.

Bedridden, unable to tend to most of her personal needs, we never hear her utter a complaint. Instead: "Thank G-d, I can see, I can hear — Look how lucky I am! Those three beautiful children are my grandchildren. They were just here to visit me last Wednesday. They're the cutest things."

Leaving her bedside, I often feel that she has given me something greater than what I've given her.

We get up one morning each week at 6:00 A.M., and wait for our lift in all kinds of conditions — in the freezing cold, dripping rain, chilling snow and predawn dark. We stumble out of the van still rubbing the sleep from our eyes and rush into the warm hospital building out of the cold, only to be met by that distinct odor.

But in a moment you forget all of that. You forget your tiredness. You forget the cold. You forget how you didn't feel like getting out of bed. You forget it all, when your special patient says simply: "I knew you'd come — I was waiting for you."

[Excerpted from the Jewish Observer
by Feige Beer Kobre]

✺§ Kindness

by Fradel Berger

Is anybody happier
For meeting you today?
Considering himself happy
Because he came your way?
Has anyone been helped
Because you lent a hand
Spared a little time to listen
Tried to understand
Has anyone been made to feel
His help was somewhere near
Has someone somewhere been relieved
of worry and fear?
Have you helped someone rediscover
What is good and true
Seen another side of life
Another point of view?
If the answer is yes
You've earned your night's repose
If no, your day was wasted
Spent in vain and at its close
There can be no satisfaction
Not unless you say
That somebody's tomorrow
Will be better than today

Focus on Life

לא אמות כי אחיה ואספר מעשי קה (תהלים קיח:יז)

ordechai, once a vibrant young intelligent medical student, was also my husband for almost a year. I was ever so fortunate to have married him, learned from him and helped him face his death with complete *emunah*. Mordechai's life was a success, he died with *bitachon*. He never failed any treatment protocol or any test by dying. He won. His soul went to Hashem pure because he always believed in Hashem's goodness no matter what the pain or suffering. Death is not an end, especially since we believe in the World to Come.

Being diagnosed with leukemia myself at the age of sixteen, the height of adolescence, was not easy by any means. It was then that my *emunah* was put to a real test. At that point I realized the worst thing that could happen would be I could die and the best thing would be to go into remission. After living almost eleven years with CML (Chronic Myelogenous Leukemia), I can add the worst thing would not be to die, but to die *without* complete belief in Hashem's ways and goodness. Eleven years is a long time to think about life and death and to grow and develop. At twenty-seven, in some ways I have lived an entire lifetime. I not only survived adolescence, chemotherapy, college and the deaths of many close friends, but the death of my husband as well. Yet, I was fortunate that Hashem brought us together through an incredible mesh of circumstances which may at first appear terrible, but were necessary for us to meet.

July 13th, 1977, is a day I'll never forget. It was the sharp turnabout of my youth, a new beginning for an incredible future and instant adulthood.

My cancer was diagnosed totally by chance. I was to go to the dentist to have my impacted wisdom teeth extracted under anesthesia in the hospital. I had all the lab tests done the day before the surgery and that night the dentist called. My white blood count was too high. They had to cancel surgery. He said, "It's probably just an infection; go to the doctor tomorrow." At the time, I was feeling fine and this made me a bit nervous because I had no fever, no symptoms.

The next morning, my mother and I went to the family doctor and he confirmed the high white count. Upon his examination he found an enlarged spleen. He mentioned that it may have to be removed. When he also said the possibility of leukemia existed, I got worried.

Later that day I had a bone marrow aspiration. They did a total blood workup. I was the kind of child who asked a lot of questions. I still do! I had to know everything. Fortunately, not much was hidden from me then. My mother and aunt were present, but I was alone in the room after the doctor came in and told me I had leukemia. I thought, "Oh my goodness." I didn't cry. I didn't quite realize the full implication of what I had.

Once the diagnosis of CML was made, the tests had to confirm whether or not the bone marrow possessed a certain marker, the Philadelphia chromosome. If this marker is present the statistics for life span are three-to-five years. Without it there is a very poor prognosis. I possessed this chromosomal abnormality. My parents were relieved, my prognosis was at least three-to-five years.

In the beginning I thought I would take pills daily and be fine. What I didn't realize was that the chronic phase could eventually turn into a blast crisis, where the cells wildly divide out of control. CML is a rare form of leukemia. Once in remission, a person can lead a normal life practically symptom free. However, to this date, CML is a fatal illness, unless a person is fortunate to receive a bone marrow transplant from a suitable donor. With time, research may bring new treatments and I continue to live with hope, knowing that *every day is a gift from Hashem.*

That night after my diagnosis, my family and I were emotionally and physically exhausted. I was alone in the house. I finally broke down and cried in the shower. I cried not so much because I worried about dying, but because everything was so overwhelming. I felt normal, I looked normal and I had been told that day that I had leukemia. My blood was not normal, it was bewildering to me. My tears blended with the warm water. Then I began to feel lucky, fortunate, here I was an artist with my hands, my sight. No amputations were necessary. I wasn't being admitted to the hospital. The doctor just gave me a few pills to take nightly. No one could really tell that I was sick. Leukemia is a disease well hidden except when under strong chemotherapy. I realized that there were cases much worse than mine. I felt as if I had some time to sort out my choices, my future.

My future had a direction until that day. I was already counting the days until going to Israel for a year of intensive studying at a women's college. Israel was put on the back burner and tomorrow had to be dealt with right away.

My parents seemed much more upset than I, and I tried to reassure them at the dinner table that night when they pulled long faces. I suppose they were concerned whether or not I would really make it. I am their only child.

One of my greatest fears centered around rejection from others. That evening I told my best friend I had leukemia, fully expecting her to tell me goodbye forever. I was pleasantly surprised when she told me she cared for me and would stand by me. This certainly helped me form a much more positive attitude, especially at an age when appearances and peer opinion means quite a great deal.

The love, care and concern that others demonstrated added to my feelings of being supported by those around me — especially my parents. While I was in high school, I knew I had a strong belief in Hashem. Praying was an uplifting experience. As a child, I enjoyed going to *shul*. The influence and atmosphere there helped develop my conscientiousness. The seeds were planted by my parents and they nourished my religious learning. Suddenly the words in the *siddur* became even more meaningful to me. I never felt like blaming Hashem. He gives me life daily. I knew I had to take responsibility or try to make changes. So when I got sick, I felt grateful that Hashem was with me, on my side. I began to realize this disease is a matter of life and death. I prayed for life, I wanted to live. I still very much want to live. Each day is a reward. *Life is a reward.*

My closest friend, Chana, had moved to New York and I called her to tell her about the leukemia. Her parents are both doctors and strongly recommended a major cancer hospital in New York. They suggested that we check out their treatment protocols for CML. Due to their concern, and persistence, my parents and I considered this option. We were referred to Dr. A. Conventional treatment for CML is taking several chemotherapy pills daily. I wanted more. I wanted to try a treatment that might provide a cure or at least what I thought was a chance at one. Dr. A. was very blunt, realistic and concerned. We heard about hair loss, chemotherapy, surgery, radiation, and life-threatening infections due to a lowered immune system after chemo. This was when it truly hit me that this diagnosis could be fatal. The aggressive chemo regimen was designed to bring down the white cell count, and reverse the Philadelphia chromosome to normal thereby hoping for a "cure".

At this time I developed a different attitude. I began thinking, well, the worst thing that could happen would be to die. So it freed me to think of all the other possibilities about living. Then I learned about true *emunah*. I thought, if I'm meant to live, I will. I was leaving everything in Hashem's hands. I was going to do *my* best and hoped Hashem would send a cure through the doctors.

From July through September, I was taking my chemotherapy pills and responding well. My white count was going down. Since my spleen was very enlarged, radiation had to be given to shrink the spleen before removal as the treatment protocol dictated. This was done as a prophylactic surgery, to prevent the spleen from harboring huge amounts of white cells.

I had the feeling I wanted to do something more with my time. I needed to get a lot of things done, I had a feeling of time pressure even though I was only sixteen. What I wanted was to volunteer in the very hospital where I was receiving radiation and blood counts.

The most special volunteers were those who gave of their time to see patients. When I heard of other people living with CML, I wanted to get in touch with them. To see another face, another human being, with the exact disease would be a tremendous comfort. My hopes soared at seeing Mr. D. He survived a splenectomy and chemotherapy. This meeting gave me the reassurance and courage to go ahead with the rest of the hospital's treatment protocol.

In deciding to volunteer, I wanted to share some of the hope I had received. Maybe someone seeing me would feel the strength to cope, go on and meet life's challenges. If this one man gave me so much, didn't I owe it to myself and others to pass on that self-determination and optimism.

Starting as a recreation volunteer seemed just perfect. I loved the experience. This was something I needed and felt good about. Despite having cancer, I wasn't helpless. I was still able to help and visit other patients. I felt fortunate to be alive and able to share my talents in art and my love of people. *Bikur cholim* became my *mitzvah*. This is still probably the *mitzvah* which I try to do the most and receive the most from in return. On Rosh Hashanah and Yom Kippur, I suppose I bargain with Hashem to an extent. I ask of Him, "Please keep me alive so I can continue to visit those who are sick." This *mitzvah* is *so* important. It can make all the difference in a person's attitude and outcome during a crisis or serious illness. Having leukemia has helped me learn my strength and find continued purpose in life.

On my birthday, my radiation treatments ended. I returned to my home town for *Yom Tov* and came back to New York to have my spleen removed at the end of September. I can remember the fear of having surgery. Being put to sleep had a finality to it. The fear of never waking up filled my thoughts. Praying helped and I accepted it was Hashem's decision to give me life or death.

My recovery was uneventful and quick. I begged the doctors to let me go home. After six days, I was discharged and allowed to go south for a couple of days. In October, I finally had my wisdom teeth removed. This time local anesthesia was given. I firmly decided I did not want to be put to sleep again. A few days after I recovered, inpatient chemotherapy was begun. The next step was to wait ...

Those on the protocol who did not respond well nor show any reversal of the Philadelphia chromosome were put on conventional therapy. When I considered the possibility of not responding, I thought, "If it was meant to be, it will be." To contemplate enduring harsh chemo and ... not see any response would be a setback psychologically; yet knowing that no matter what the next few weeks brought, I had to have faith I would make it. I felt strong at the time. I asked Hashem for continued strength.

My bone marrow results came back. The doctors entered the room excitedly and said, "Well, we have some very good news to tell you." My mother and I listened carefully to the doctors words. "She turned 100% Philadelphia-chromosome negative." This had never happened before. Only one treatment had totally reversed it.

We had a family conference with the doctors. The doctors wanted to continue with potent chemo treatments to prevent reversal and hopefully maintain a "true marrow remission." From previous clinical experience, the doctors realized that in most patients the chromosomal abnormality returned only months later. The doctors were pushing for a "cure". Their goal was to permanently eradicate the Philadelphia chromosome.

After much intensive thinking and talking with my parents, I agreed to continue treatment. One step at a time. The thought of going through six or seven more rounds of chemo experimentally was too overwhelming. One round at a time seemed manageable.

With the second round of chemo, I realized what it was like to be sick, really sick. I felt nauseous and threw up. Throwing up became a way of life for me while on chemo. In essence, the good moments became the means of survival. The good days were the ones to reassure and accomplish the most I could. On those days, I went to the recreation department and worked on various art projects. Just because I had cancer didn't mean I couldn't use my hands, my brain and creativity. I knew well enough what I couldn't do while on chemo; I needed to focus on *what I could do* and accomplish small goals one step at a time.

About that time, people I had seen and gotten to know passed away. This upset me greatly. My identification with them was strong and I told myself, "This doesn't have to be me." Every case is different, every patient responds differently. I couldn't believe that at seventeen, I was worrying about death and dying. I couldn't believe I might one day be one of them. I was not ready for death. I asked Hashem daily to let me live. Worst of all, my friend Mr. D. had developed lung cancer which traveled to his brain and he too died. This crushed my hopes temporarily. I was strongly affected. I reflected upon our brief friendship and all that he had given me. His death was a sign that I had to continue volunteering, helping people see that *others do live*. Survival meant reaching out to others around me, not closing people off. It was an emotional risk I had to take and continually do so.

While my rounds of chemo continued, there was a real feeling of Hashem being with me, very close to me. I woke up every morning and the literal meaning of *Modeh Ani* was always a profound discovery. It was great! That joy was intense the whole time I was on chemo, not just while in the hospital. After I finished the treatment protocol, the feelings of gratitude were still there, but not with the same intensity.

The experience was such that it would be hard to live like that every day. Life is too easy to take for granted. I am acutely aware that

I'm alive and doing well. I developed the theory that I had before, "take it day by day" — one day at a time. My goals had been crushed when I was diagnosed. I learned not to make long term plans, but goals with steps toward immediate reachability. Goals that provide immediate chances for attainment. Every person's time frame is different. For me, the future was hazy, yet goals that took a year to reach would provide me with hope and structure during a time with an uncertain future.

Knowing that my hair would probably fall out, I had already cut it short in preparation. By December, my mother and I went to buy a wig. Soon afterwards I began to wear it regularly along with scarves and berets. I used to have long straight brown hair back then and seeing it short was strange. Even stranger was trying on clothes in stores and watching my hair stick to the sweater I just pulled over my head. I couldn't pull the strands of hair off the sweater. There were too many. The only solution was to buy the sweater. I liked it anyhow! At seventeen though, wearing a wig and hoping it didn't look "wiggy" wasn't easy. I tried styling it, brushing it, shaking it and even yelling at it to get the look I wanted. Eventually, I found scarves and berets more colorful and comfortable.

❦   ❦   ❦

Round after round of chemo, I kept hoping the end of treatment would be closer. The end of getting poked and prodded. Sometimes that end didn't seem to be in focus. I hated when the I.V. needle would infiltrate and chemo had to be halted until an I.V. nurse would restick me in a new vein. At moments like that, one more minute of treatment seemed unbearable.

Eventually an end to the constant chemo and hospitalizations seemed to be in sight. My last hospitalization was a few weeks before Pesach. I had looked forward to the moment of being with my father and friends at home for a long time. My father, a businessman, always had the difficult position of waiting for a phone call or a visit. This desire to finally return home drove me and gave me a constant goal of finally finishing chemo to resume some sort of normalcy in my life again.

Once in my home town, receiving chemo on a cyclic basis allowed for days of freedom with no treatment or nausea. It also helped me think about where to go from there. Living in New York, life moved from moment to moment. I had to be ready to go to the hospital any time for chemo, platelet infusions or infections. Now at home, I had time to think about what normal daily living was like once again.

Less than two weeks after my return, I started considering summer courses at the nearby state college as well as finding a part time job. I needed structure and a sense of normalcy in my life. My friends were finishing finals and had plans for college that fall. Those were the same plans I wanted for myself.

The college accepted me and a job welcomed me as a new part-time employee. This was a tremendous boost to my ego. I saw *I could function in life again*, not just deal with cancer, chemo and the fear of dying. Still insecure, I told my boss I would need off once in every ten days to receive chemo. He was understanding about my situation and worked with me to develop a schedule that suited both our needs. That first paycheck was a delight. I had been doing well from tips, but having a real check to cash put me on cloud nine. Charity was sure to receive a good sum. I was proud, my parents were proud of me and most of all, with Hashem's help, *I knew I could do it.*

Not used to writing papers nor tests for almost a year, school was a little difficult. My concentration was not the same. I only took two courses. There was an excitement in my struggle, a self-determination that I could do this. I had to. Juggling school in the mornings, changing into my work uniform after class and catching the bus to work were all a challenge of normal teenagers.

I prepared to undergo a procedure which would involve storing my Philadelphia-chromosome-negative bone marrow in case I ever needed it for an autologous bone marrow transplant. Since the New York protocol eradicaed most of PH negative marrow, freezing my present marrow would be the next step. I am an only child with no siblings as potential matched donors. My mother and I flew to Seattle for a few days. The surgery was quick but I returned home very sore.

The fall meant beginning Stern College. The thought of going to New York alone was not too frightening. I had a year of "preparation" you might say. The first few weeks were the most difficult in terms of adjustment.

That first day, I wore a wig because my hair had not fully grown back. Not knowing who my roommates would be caused me much anxiety. I wasn't afraid of getting along with them, but I was unsure of how to tell them I have leukemia. This would be something I couldn't and didn't want to hide. I began telling one of my roomates about my hospital volunteer experience. I then jumped to asking her if she would like to volunteer with me. By later that day, I told her the truth. Despite my difficulty in expressing this to three girls, I think they had a harder time absorbing the shock.

One night before going to sleep, I hung my wig on the bathroom door hook. I put on my scarf and left the bathroom. One of my roommates walked in, closed the door and let out such a shriek! She didn't know what to think, was it an animal, fur or what on the door. The surprise of seeing a wig on a hook was a bit much. Sooner or later these occurrences were typical and we all laughed together.

My roommates were terrific. They grew to accept and learn about my illness. Whenever the earlier fear of rejection crept up they reassured me and encouraged me to take care of myself, tell them the doctors reports and get some sleep (something I did very little in college). Four nights during a cycle of chemo taking my thirteen-and-a-half pills was a true night long ordeal. Pills in general were never easy for me to swallow. I tried applesauce, which I *never* eat anymore, jello, ice cream, you name it. However, my roommates came to the rescue with this song. "Rachel, Rachel, take your pills; Rachel, Rachel, don't get ill." Whatever fears my roommates had were not often expressed. We all reached out and were able to cope and connect to each other like any other college roomates.

Some of the more difficult moments emotionally occured when other students stopped me in the halls, stairways and in the dorm to ask if I was married. It became evident that they noticed my wig immediately and naturally connected it with wearing a *sheitel*. If anyone elsewhere noticed they never commented. Now, these expert *sheitel* spotters assumed I was married. When I answered, "no" the surprised look on their faces and glance upward at my wig were enough to make a lasting imprint.

❀   ❀   ❀

About the time my hair was growing back sufficiently to remove the wig, I was volunteering once again at my hospital, this time as a Patient-to-Patient volunteer. I met several other CML patients undergoing the same treatment protocol as myself.

Right after Rosh Hashanah, my doctor asked me to call a new patient with CML. He said, "Mordechai, a twenty-one-year-old Jewish, *frum* medical student, is considering the hospital's treatment protocol." Sometimes, doctors get to play matchmaker, too.

Mordechai and I spoke about our diagnoses and the hospital's protocol. We planned to meet on October 29th, 1978.

That date I'll never forget. The purpose of our meeting was to discuss the experimental protocol I had gone through the previous year. Mordechai figured that seeing someone who had gone through treatment already would be a boost and proof of survival.

During dinner, Mordechai mostly listened to me tell my story. He was rather quiet, but sat absorbed, wanting to hear more. I know he marveled at the fact that someone could go through chemo, still look good and carry on a reasonably normal life. This gave him the hope he was looking for, the hope of continuing medical school and the hope for a future.

Mordechai spoke of his fears and hopes. Not the type to complain, or express anger, Mordechai, with time, began to open up slowly, conscious of not wanting to burden me. Required to have a blood test done for his entrance to medical school, he kept postponing it until after his college graduation. He finally went for the examination and had the blood work done. Annoyed with the results, he was told to take the test over again, the lab was in error. His white blood cell count was very high.

The next morning, Mordechai and his father saw a hematologist. CML was the diagnosis. Mordechai was very aware of what was transpiring. When he broke the news to his mother, he said, "I've got good news and bad news. The good news is it's not acute; the bad news is it's leukemia."

A bone marrow aspiration determined that Mordechai, too, had the Philadelphia chromosome. They explored the possibility of immunotherapy and bone marrow transplant. The doctors were realistic and stated the three-to-five year prognosis of CML. One of the doctors told them, "Look, I have heart disease, and will probably die of heart disease. Mordechai has leukemia, and he will probably die of leukemia." There were no guarantees. His fate was *in the hands of Hashem.* Mordechai believed this strongly.

At first Mordechai felt that there would be no point in starting medical school, he would never finish it. It was difficult for him to imagine that he was really sick. He had no physical symptoms. This aspect of CML is truly difficult to deal with, especially when treatment makes one feel worse than he ever felt before. Mordechai realized he had goals to accomplish and knew he needed to at least *try* and reach his goals. Life had to be lived one day at a time. It was the *quality* of life not the quantity that was essential. Mordechai's attitude was a positive one. He had normal and understandable moments of upset and despair too. Yet, he firmly believed this illness, for whatever reason, was Hashem's will and he prayed for strength and for life with all his heart.

Mordechai and I had a great deal in common besides having CML. That factor brought us together. Despite the pain of a devastating illness, Hashem saw it in His kindness for us to find happiness and comfort through one another even in our darkest moments. We both shared in our *emunah* and *bitachon*. We acknowledged the miracle of Hashem bringing us together through our doctor. Mordechai had a lot to offer and teach me. Yes, we identified with each other, and we were able to reach out for help and support, but most of all our self-determination and a real zest for life along with Hashem's help, kept us going from day to day.

The day-to-day ups and downs were very much a part of living. Mordechai also experienced a total reversal of his PHL-positive-chromosome marrow. We shared in that moment of joy. One of Mordechai's friends had a tee-shirt made with words "Think Negative" emblazoned across the front. This "in joke" was taken one step further when Mordechai, myself and another dear CML patient we had befriended all wore our light blue shirts with this same message to outpatient clinic one morning. The doctors had a good laugh and posed for a unique picture; other patients stared in disbelief; and yet others questioned us on our outlook towards life! Philadelphia-chromosome negative was the way we had been told to think and that was just what we were doing successfully.

Soon after this, Mordechai, also an only child, traveled to Seattle to store his PH-negative marrow. Little did we know that this marrow would be used one day in the future for an autologous bone marrow transplant.

Mordechai revealed the feelings of amazement and shock when his hair began falling out in great clumps. He said, "This is not normal!" In order to solve the problem, Mordechai shaved his head. He would not have to deal with the trauma slowly. Hair loss then wouldn't be a mess on his sheets, pillow and clothes. I used to call him "egg head" affectionately. Seeing him with just a *kippa* on his bald head looked rather odd, yet Mordechai came up with all kinds of reasons and jokes for his baldness. It certainly made finding him in a crowd much easier.

As the months went by, treatment went well. We were both in school and we became serious in our relationship. Many thoughts crossed our minds. Could we, would we ever get married? What about children, the future? How long would our remissions last? Should we continue our goals, schooling and all attempts at leading as normal of a life as possible? The fear of relapse hung low over our heads.

We felt well, were *very* active, yet the time clock ticked onward. Time . . . tick-tock, tick-tock. As I write the seconds go by. Is time my friend or enemy? Is there ever enough time . . . for anything? Twenty-four hours, 1,440 minutes, 86,400 seconds all compose one day. What do I do with that day, that time, that second? How much can I do? A great deal, I tell myself, if I only put my mind to it. Each moment is a gift. I shouldn't waste it, but I do. Usually, that is okay too. It's never a waste — just a thought, a reflection, a moment of silence. Time goes by. I can't hold back the hands of the clock, nor stop the sun in mid-sky like Joshua. I can let my watch tick itself out, forget to replace the batteries, but time goes on. So does life. Never forget that. One must live. We owe it to ourselves, to those around us and to Hashem who gives us that time daily. Time is in my favor.

I remember one cold night Mordechai and I went into Citibank with his trusty card and we sat on a ledge talking. We discussed moments of upset, argument and feelings of being overwhelmed by our situation. We both ended up crying. Crying was okay. It did not last forever. It had a beginning, and an end. There are times for crying. That closeness in crying brought us through many difficult moments. We gave *us* permission to cry and accept Hashem's Will for what we saw as good or perceived to be bad. This took much work on both our parts to achieve and yet we were determined fighters with *bitachon* to guide us.

There is pain in caring, reaching out and especially in losing someone you love. That risk *must* be taken. We took it. In April of 1980, Erev Pesach, we became engaged. That day was one of several best days of my life. We were on top of the world and nothing could bring us down. Pesach with Mordechai in my parent's home was wonderful.

Reality set in, we had to wait fourteen months to marry due to insurance problems. We both had to be certain of our medical coverage. A religious ceremony only was not opted for and we waited for a religious and civil marriage together. This was not our ideal choice. Dr. A. even advised against this decision because of constant time pressure. One never knows what will be. And yet, we waited a difficult year, but a year filled with most memorable events. A year of mostly good news, accomplishments and good health.

Despite a very hectic and demanding schedule, Mordechai always found time to help someone physically or emotionally. The hours of classes and studying are draining for any medical student. Early morning, he was one of the first at the dorm *minyan*. He knocked on doors and made phone calls. Colleagues felt if Mordechai could attend *minyan*, then they certainly had an obligation to be there on time for prayers. He helped to keep the library in order, managed to swim laps after classes, and most regularly participated in his rav's *Gemara* class. He even became a Patient-to-Patient volunteer at the hospital when time permitted.

❦   ❦   ❦

Time went by, month by month, day by day. We had been preparing for a lovely wedding down south. I had my dress, the invitations were sent out, everything was arranged and art school was coming to an end for May 1981. We were in good health. My fear increased as the days to our wedding got closer. The fear of relapse, the fear of not making it. Was it still fated to be? I hoped and prayed. Mordechai and I spoke of this fear, especially late at night while on the phone. He was under a great deal of pressure from medical school, the wedding and upcoming medical boards that second-year students take upon completion of that year. I was ready to go home several weeks before the wedding. It was the end of May, we were happy, excited and in good health.

Until ... the world appeared to come crashing down on our shoulders one day right before Shabbos. Mordechai strongly felt something was awry with his blood counts. He was used to checking them regularly at his school's lab. All we could do was pray and wait until Monday.

Monday, I never dreamed Mordechai would or could relapse first. The bone marrow results indicated he was entering blast crisis. His marrow was producing very immature white cells rapidly, out of control. There were no physical symptoms outwardly to even suggest Mordechai's relapse, just a look at a blood slide told it all, changed our future plans.

We came home from the doctors and cried. All of us together,

Mordechai, his parents and me. Shock set in. I knew what was happening, but I couldn't stop the process. Every moment cells were wildly dividing, more blasts, crowding out normal cells in the marrow and blood. Some people die shortly after the onset of blast crisis. Mordechai and I were not even married yet. What about our wedding, our dreams, our future?

His rav told us to say *Tehillim*, especially the psalm one higher in number than Mordechai's age. Mordechai was only twenty-three at the time. Psalm 24 begins לדוד מזמור לה' הארץ ומלואה — "Of David a psalm, Hashem's is the earth and its fullness ... " The words of the psalm were comforting. Ultimately, Hashem knows what is best. I believed that. מי הוא זה מלך הכבוד, ה' צבאות, הוא מלך הכבוד סלה — *Who then is the King of Glory? Hashem, Master of Legions, He is the King of Glory, selah!*

The clock moved forward. Mordechai wanted to move up the wedding date and marry as soon as possible. He felt time pressure and didn't know what the future would bring. But he *did know* he wanted to marry me.

By Thursday of the same week, we decided to marry one week later in New York, instead of down south. Mordechai had been studying for the medical boards. They too were to be held that very next Thursday. He was going to do both.

In need of a place to marry, we did some heavy phone calling and rearranging of plans. We went to one rabbi who saw us in his study. He asked me "Do you, Rachel, still want to go through with this marriage?" Shocked at the question, I took a moment to answer. I knew my answer was *yes*, yet the question baffled me. Why would I *not* want to go through with the wedding? I couldn't understand the thought. After knowing Mordechai and longing to marry by now, how or why would I want to cop out at this point? We had grown together, suffered together, coped together, wouldn't I want to see the process through. I didn't know what tomorrow would bring, but I *knew* I wanted to marry Mordechai! You don't turn your back on someone when he is sick. I realized I could be a young widow, but *life was my focus*. Mordechai needed me and I needed him too. I wanted to spend my life with him, however long or short.

The decision to change the wedding was difficult, because it meant things were not normal and probably would not be for a while. We were living in crisis. We planned a moderate wedding in two days to include a hall, photographer, dinner, flowers, and especially our family and friends. Many previous arrangements were cancelled and others kept, but in New York instead. I already had my dress. I flew to my parents for that week.

It was a difficult week. Talking on the phone to Mordechai was a strain at times. The morning of the wedding, my parents, aunt and I flew to New York. We almost got bumped from the flight. I held my long white gown in my hands and told the airline, "No way would I miss this flight!" We went to Mordechai's parents' house. He was at school taking the medical boards. Unbelievable!

Thursday evening, June 11th, 1981, only a couple of days after Shavuos, Mordechai and I were married. My bridesmaids and his ushers were there, they detoured their plans to New York The wedding was beautiful, of course. The most special people in our lives attended.

Mordechai and I enjoyed the wedding. Tears flowed at the *chupah*. No one knew what the next day would bring. Under the *chupah*, I prayed for Mordechai's life and the complete recovery of other sick people I knew. I asked Hashem for at least one married day with Mordechai, then one week, then one month. I allowed myself to think ahead and asked Hashem for at least one year together. And the very least, *I had the moment to cherish.*

Dancing, singing, clapping and festive music were all part of that intensive evening. Mordechai didn't dance as much as he wanted to, he looked a little pale. Our friends made up for that and danced up a storm with the floor and chandelier shaking in unison.

Towards the end of the wedding, our doctor approached us and said Mordechai would have to start outpatient chemo the next day. He could not wait any longer. Dr. A. was kind in waiting until late that evening to inform us of his decision. We couldn't worry about tomorrow, tonight had to be lived. Our *simchah* had to be a true *simchah* with a full heart.

A long evening passed. I said an emotional goodbye to my parents. I kissed them, told them I loved them and waved goodbye. Mordechai and I drove off as husband and wife.

Early the next morning, Mordechai and I, newlyweds, appeared at the hospital's outpatient department. We were beaming. The sour thought of chemo was sweetened by the bliss of marriage. "Congratulations" rang out from those doctors, nurses, social workers and patients who knew us as the hospital's "couple." Chemo did not seem quite as bad on the heels of a wedding. *Hashem sends joy when we need it most*.

We had several *sheva brachos* that week. They were lovely. Just what we needed during a time of crisis. Support systems all around. Family, friends, everyone cared. We were fortunate. Fortunate to have our parents, friends — and most of all — each other to lean on during those ups and downs. The next few weeks brought other *simchos*. Some of my friends got married and we attended those weddings with hearts full of joy.

The summer passed and it appeared Mordechai was responding to chemo, at least partially. Now that we were married, I could stand by his side during spinal taps, and offer words of comfort or look at him in silence. I understood the pain, I felt it with him, so much that I had to distance myself emotionally at times. I thought, "Wait a minute, I can't feel every pain, every ache, with Mordechai; I can't do this any longer." I was of no help to him if I couldn't separate, just a little. I needed the space to be strong for him and to push my own fears away, just a little. The identification was overwhelming at moments. Mordechai lay before me enduring what *I too* might have to undergo one day. I couldn't think about myself. I had to be well. I prayed to be well. I couldn't imagine not being well at a time like this.

From then on, it was increasingly difficult for Mordechai. He continued to receive outpatient chemo, but never achieved a full remission despite two tries. Our first three months of marriage were filled with its share of disappointments. At times communication was distant. Mordechai became sick from the chemo, he was tired and in pain. Mostly he felt a silent pain, a pain he did not talk about, but a pain that showed. Fortunately, our strong relationship endured the pain, the mood swings, the moments when tension filled the air, the crisis and the day to day living. Mordechai always mentioned, "The quality of time, not the quantity makes moments special." Good moments *were* special.

Since Mordechai did not have a complete remission, other options had to be considered. One choice, involved using Mordechai's previously stored bone marrow for an autologous transplant. He had the marrow frozen in Seattle, Washington. Since chemo was not producing a total remission, the best chance for transplant was now, the end of August, 1981. The transplant meant killing Mordechai's diseased bone marrow with total body irradiation and potent doses of chemo and replacing it with the stored marrow. Only seven other

CML patients underwent this process in blast crisis and none survived. The odds of remission statistically were zero with chemo only, and zero with a transplant. Which zero does one pick? We knew this is a fatal illness. We just wanted to buy time, maybe just a little time. Hashem would be the judge of that. Our faith guided us once again.

Mordechai, a person of action, not passivity, decided to consult different rabbis. We had to believe that we would get through this hurdle. There was no other way. I couldn't believe anything would happen to Mordechai in Seattle. Denial. I was very scared at the prospect of being so far away from New York and my family. Truthfully I didn't know if I would return with Mordechai alive.

My twenty-first birthday present was our leaving for Seattle. Mordechai, his father and I packed our many bags in preparation of a three-month stay. His mother joined us later that week.

The transplant center in Seattle set us up with an apartment near the hospital, less than a fifteen-minute walk. When I saw the apartment I thought of our departure hours earlier. Mordechai had sat in his brown recliner chair facing the many *seforim* he had on the bookshelves. He just looked at them. I'm sure his fears were great. He hoped to sit in that seat again, learning *gemara* or studying medicine. He had kissed the *mezuzah* with tears in his eyes and put his right foot forward. And now, we were in Seattle, so far from home and friends. Time was of the utmost.

The Jewish community was absolutely wonderful. We received assistance and food from people we didn't know and who didn't know us. All they knew was that a Jewish family was in need. They were there for us throughout our *entire* stay.

Things began to progress very quickly. Two potent doses of chemo and 225 rads of radiation for seven days straight prepared Mordechai for the transplant. The blast cells were reducing in number. His blood counts lowered. Mordechai took a sterile bath and entered his laminar air flow room. Now a plastic wall separated us, unless I gowned up and entered the sterile environment. I could talk through the plastic, see through it and even hold his hand through the plastic gloves extended into the room. The air blower circulated air out of his room. Imagine a germ-free situation behind a plastic curtain. A powerful image. One germ could burst that bubble, infect Mordechai, bring on an early death. He had no immune system to fight off infection like normal people. On sterile paper I wrote *Shivisi*

Hashem Lenegdi Samid and hung it on his wall. That same piece of paper hangs in my apartment as a constant source of inspiration. *Hashem is everywhere*. Even in a laminar air flow room.

As *selichos* before Rosh Hashanah approached, so too did the day of his actual transplant. At *selichos* I reflected upon the year. I knew I had a chance to repent and pray for a future year of life and good health filled with Torah and *mitzvos*. I thought about the quality of my life, my goals and my values. I have my path and *mitzvos* to do and no matter what, my path is set out for me. *I have a purpose here.* "Devotion to Hashem and self-perfection ..." I wrote in my diary. "Self perfection, not material self perfection but inner perfection that deals with one's heart and doing *mitzvos* even though there are so many we do not understand. Our devotion to Hashem comes through the love of Hashem by doing His *mitzvos*." And with those thoughts I faced Mordechai's transplant.

September 21st, Day zero. Mordechai's parents were at his side while the cold marrow was infused into his Hickman line to find its way miraculously to the marrow bed where it could reproduce normal healthy cells. This marrow still contained the leukemia, however, that previously stored marrow was marrow in chronic phase, PH-negative remission. *A chance at life.*

Seeing some other patients do well increased our sense of hope. I kept thanking Hashem for Mordechai's life, each day I could be with him, even from the other side of a plastic curtain. I wondered what life as a normal married couple would be like! What is "normal"? We were supra-normal. Only Mordechai could have told what the transplant experience meant to him. I can not describe the loneliness and pain of being in reverse isolation for over thirty days. That meant no touch from a hand, only through a plastic sterile glove. Everyone who entered his small sterile room had to don a gown, gloves, boots, hat and a mask. Everything in the room had to be sterilized, from the ceiling to the floor and in between.

Rosh Hashanah passed, the rabbi from the nearby *shul* came to blow *shofar* for Mordechai. I *davened* for both of us. I remember lighting my first set of holiday candles as a married woman and reciting the blessing of *shehecheyanu*. Mordechai's health was always at the top of my prayers. Before Yom Kippur, Mordechai's graft appeared to be taking. The bone marrow results looked good. Cells were developing. Yom Kippur was a long day of fasting and prayer. During the short break, I ran to visit Mordechai. And during *neilah*, I stood facing the Ark, almost crying. Then I heard the beautiful long blast of the *shofar*, a symbol of hope and awakening. Hopefully the gates of Heaven were open to our prayers. I felt good.

Mordechai came back to the apartment. I prepared a *Bruchim Haboim* sign for our front door, already equipped with a *mezuzah* on loan from the Jewish community. His cells were reproducing and he had "polys", white cells with which to fight infection. This was a great day of accomplishment. With Hashem's help, Mordechai made it through one of the most critical stages. That night we celebrated.

Shabbos was beautiful. He sang *Sholom Aleichem* and *Aishes Chayil*. I wanted to cry. His parents were with us. We were together. *Kiddush* rang through my ears with a depth of words. Mordechai had his heart in every word. He had experienced a true *yitzioh* — going out. He was in the apartment now, a human being once again, not just a patient.

Support from all around continued to pour in, from New York especially. Our *shul* had sent a check to cover some of the hidden expenses not reimbursed by insurance companies. When that check arrived, Mordechai lit up, knowing that *Hashem sends help when we need it most*.

Burdens. There were many. The emotional burden of the transplant and being so far away from home seemed the heaviest. My deepest moments of depression were probably when Mordechai was in the hospital. Now that he was out, hope seemed renewed. I infrequently continued having blood counts, to monitor my own health situation. Luckily, Mordechai's parents were with us to ease some of the constant burden. They helped to cook, clean, shop, and simply be there for Mordechai and myself as well. Despite tension caused by living in close quarters, we coped daily, some days better than others.

Life centered around Mordechai's recovery and the hope of returning to New York. Days were busy, yet not structured enough for me. Goals were difficult to make. Plans changed daily, depending on Mordechai's health status. I felt the need to do things for myself whether it be a haircut, shopping or a long distance phone call to my parents or a friend. These spurts of energy enabled me to pass that enthusiasm on to Mordechai, otherwise I would drain easily. Writing in my diary became my extra outlet. And so I wrote. Each day, pages became filled with words, expressions and hopes for the future. Now as I write, I look back at this diary and recall the emotions. I see the purple handwriting, the date, and the abundance of information I captured.

By day fifty-nine, post-transplant excitement rose. There was talk of going home early, finally leaving Seattle. This set us on a new track, one focused with thoughts of returning to our own home. It seemed like a dream come true. Mordechai had relatively few complications during the transplant. He had fevers, needed transfusions, but never required hospitalization after his return. I had mixed feelings. I wanted to know for sure Mordechai was physically ready to leave. There were no guarantees. He was not out of danger yet, the road ahead was a long one. Many precautions had to be taken. On another level, there were things about Seattle I would miss.

Flight arrangements had to be made, packing began and now we were involved in a flurry of activity. An end to our long ordeal seemed in sight. I decided to see my parents before returning to New York. All I needed was a short visit, a chance to focus on myself and be pampered. I could always depend on them to be there for me.

❀   ❀   ❀

November 29th, we said our goodbyes to everyone and to each other. Mordechai's marrow was clear according to the doctors. His Hickman line was pulled. There was no evidence of blast crisis. Day sixty-nine, I flew home to my parents.

Mordechai surprised his friends back in New York by returning early. He had kept his arrival a secret. He stayed with his parents. Our apartment was still sublet. Life seemed wonderful. We were grateful.

Thursday night I received a phone call from Mordechai. He sounded apprehensive, cautiously choosing his words. I detected the anxiety in his voice. He stated, "Rachel, my counts are going up."

I said, "Terrific."

He interrupted, "No, they are getting too high, too quickly."

Now I understood the concern in his voice. He was worried. We hoped this was a sign of something other than what we feared most. I hung up the phone, tried to shake my own apprehension before telling my parents everything seemed all right, but that I wanted to go back to New York a day earlier, on Sunday. That night I cried hard into my pillow. Something deep inside told me that Monday was going to be a difficult day. Again, it appeared as if our world was crashing down. Shabbos I prayed in *shul*. It was impossible to relax until I saw Mordechai.

Monday, we didn't know where to turn. The bone marrow aspiration confirmed blast crisis. Relapse. The transplant did not hold. His old cells were not totally destroyed. Just after we thought we did everything possible, our hopes were crushed. What *do* you do after a bone marrow transplant? How do you treat someone without a strong immune system? The doctors did not want to wipe out the graft. How much chemo *can* you give? Not many people came back from this type of transplant alive.

Step one. Lower Mordechai's blood count.

Step two. Cope! The events that followed seemed like a blur. The clock ticked onward. Time was racing. We were racing against the clock, or so it felt. Concentrate on living. Get through each day. Don't worry about tomorrow. Life continued from moment to moment. I think we existed.

The chemo was working. His counts fell. Mordechai needed a lot of rest. He wanted me to register for classes again, to finish art school. In the house, he was able to take care of himself. He could not travel in crowds, nor take public transportation. He wore a mask outdoors to help guard against infection. We did a great deal of soul searching and talking. We couldn't sit back and wait, my staying home would have meant that to Mordechai. Some sort of normalcy and routine had to take place.

I learned to live with frequent hospitalizations, attending classes, completing artwork, doing housework (that got neglected the most) and trying to keep my own sanity.

For short periods things were stable. Mordechai was cautious about his health care. His weight was good. He did everything possible and more to ensure proper hygiene and nutrition.

Mordechai also nourished his spiritual health by learning *parshas hashavua* and *gemara*. Friends continuously called and supported his actions. These were our good moments. We communicated better during those times.

While enjoying a Shabbos meal the candles illuminated Mordechai's face. He looked a bit jaundiced. This was cause for concern. Monday the tests indicated a strong possibility of hepatitis related to the many blood and platelet transfusions he had received. The next day, we were flying to my parents for Pesach. Packed and waiting in the airport during the pre-Pesach blizzard of April, 1982,

Mordechai called the hospital to find out the definite report. Hepatitis confirmed. Someone near the front airline desk overheard. Suddenly we were told we can not fly. The airline feared it was contagious. Our apartment was not equipped for Pesach. My parents were expecting us and I feared spending the holiday in an airport because of the weather. Have faith I thought. Eventually our doctor phoned the airline and allayed their concerns. The weather cleared and our flight departed. That Pesach Mordechai donned a mask, drank grape juice and ate from paper plates. We were fortunate he did not need hospitalization. *Each day is a miracle filled with miracles.*

One day Mordechai had to be hospitalized because an infection on his thigh was not healing. The doctors reinserted a Hickman Broviac line. Receiving chemo and blood products would be easier. This was done on the day of his good friend's wedding. Yehoshua had originally asked Mordechai to sing under the *chupah*. Mordechai was in no shape to attend, much less sing at a wedding. However, he waited for this *simcha*, it gave him a goal, a purpose. Living from *simcha* to *simcha* became our focus. Mordechai determined not to miss his chance, obtained a day pass from the hospital, went home, dressed and with face and neck swollen attended the wedding smiling even though he was in pain. I don't know how many pain killers he took that evening. He did not sing under the *chupah*. Instead his heart sang with joy for his friend. After the *chupah*, he returned to his hospital room to become a patient once again.

Living from *simcha* to *simcha*. Even our doctor, Dr. A. helped us achieve this. He emphasized, "You made it through Pesach. Let's go for Shavuos." Life centered around the holidays.

Complications set in for Mordechai, he had a fever that could not be shaken. The doctors requested permission to try an experimental chemo. They never pushed us before, yet this time they asked us to strongly consider the new drug, DMDR. After talking and much thought, we agreed.

Mordechai rarely used the words "I'm scared." The one powerful time he did was a week before his death. Mordechai needed me by his side. This hit home hard. Things were going downhill. His health deteriorated. The new drug was given days before Shavuos. Kidney failure. Dialysis was not an option. His parents remained by his side as I prepared for Shavuous.

Mordechai was slipping in and out of consciousness. Death was only a matter of time. Shavuos began. Mordechai tried to be in control up to the point of becoming comatose. He always requested to know what drugs he received, how much, and what the nurse was doing. Now his parents and I were in control, watching every move. Mordechai had taken responsibility to settle matters when possible. We had discussed death on several occasions, but Mordechai stressed the *quality* of time. We knew death would come in its own time. And so we dwelled on life ...

Millions of thoughts flooded my mind that first Shavuos night. Mordechai lay on the bed, covered with a white sheet up to his dusky colored face. I prayed. And I waited. The private nurse sat in her chair. I slumped in my chair looking for a comfortable position. Mordechai was in a coma. I believed strongly he could hear what was said. Therefore, I was careful not to discuss his slow decline anywhere near him.

Tick-tock, my watch echoed in my ear. I dozed for moments, but did not sleep. How could I sleep, Mordechai was dying. I do not think that thought actually set in until morning. I fooled myself at believing that Mordechai was just sleeping a long heavy sleep.

Dr. A. entered and said what was to be his last goodbye. The private nurse comforted me. The nurse called his parents. It was only a matter of time. Hashem decides our ultimate time. I put my anger aside and sat next to Mordechai. It was early Friday morning, Shavuos.

Panic began. My insides were trembling. Sitting next to Mordechai I said *Tehillim*. I gazed at Mordechai's face, now swollen and his eyelids a puffed blue color. Thank G-d he still had hair. He could die with some dignity. This was my husband, my best friend, my companion. "Mordechai is dying now. I can't believe this is happening now. I'm really here, by his side."

Mordechai's parents arrived. I felt less alone. I would not leave Mordechai's room. I didn't want him to die without me by his side. I felt that I had to be there, right next to him.

Friday turned into Shabbos. Beforehand, my parents arrived at the hospital from the apartment. From previous reading, I had learned some laws in regard to the dying. Procedures had to be *halachically* correct.

The hospital bed next to Mordechai's was empty. I lay down, afraid to sleep lest I sleep too long. I was emotionally and physically exhausted. Wait. Mordechai hung on for life. His heart beat still strong.

Friday night Bob, a good friend with CML visited, offered his words of comfort as well as a listening ear. Somehow he encouraged me to leave the room for a short while. We spoke. I cried and told him I wanted to tell Mordechai so many things, but I needed privacy. He promptly asked everyone in the room to leave, something I could never have done. And they left. I don't know how long Mordechai and I were alone, but I asked for his forgiveness. I told him not to worry, Hashem was taking good care of him. I suppose on some level I was letting him know he could die, I knew the time was close.

I felt like a crazy person in that room alone with him. I poured my heart out until I felt ready to open the door for everyone to re-enter. I can't thank my friend, now gone himself, enough for that intervention. I was able to express the words I wanted to say to Mordechai without guilt or reservation. I had to know I did my best. I prepared to say goodbye.

My mother encouraged me to say *Shema* with Mordechai. Tears rolled down my cheeks as I said each word slowly to him. I believe he heard me. His soul was preparing for its return to Hashem, our Creator.

The night was long. Shabbos did not feel like Shabbos. Shavuos did not feel like Shavuos. And all I was aware of at the time was Mordechai's labored breathing. The scene must have been difficult for my parents as well. They probably envisioned me in that bed one day. I wondered what my own death would be like. Would I be alert or comatose? Would I be in pain or at peace? Mordechai did not appear in pain. He felt the pain all those months beforehand up to this point.

5:25 a.m., Shabbos, May 29th, 1982. Mordechai's soul returned to Hashem in hopefully as pure a state as he entered the world.

The seventh day of Sivan, the second day of Shavuos, Shabbos, the seventh day of the week. Mordechai was born on Shabbos and died on Shabbos. He was born on the seventh day of Tammuz and now died on the seventh day of Sivan, not far from his twenty-fifth birthday. Two plus five equal seven. The mystical number seven appeared again and again. Dovid Hamelech died on Shavuos. These thoughts comforted me. Mordechai and I were almost married one year. Hashem saw that Shabbos Shavuos was the proper time for his soul to return to its Creator.

The doctor pronounced Mordechai dead. What a cold world. I couldn't cry. I had cried so much already. I said goodbye. I removed the oxygen mask to feel possibly one more breath. His chest did not rise, my hand did not feel warmth from life. Only his body lay before me. The essence of Mordechai was gone. His soul departed. Never having seen a dead person before, I felt strange, eerie. Yet, he seemed at peace. The family began to leave the room.

Knowing I would never lay eyes on Mordechai again, I left the room. I tiptoed out, almost careful not to wake Mordechai. One's mind plays funny tricks when in shock.

Since it was Shabbos, my parents and I were forced to remain in the hospital. I knew the clinic area was empty, quiet and had couches. We went there. With no more for me to do, exhaustion and shock set in, so I slept. I had stayed awake forty eight hours. My job was done. I had stayed by Mordechai's side all along. The next day would be a long one, the funeral. My parents were uncomfortable with my sleeping. Here they had just lost their son-in-law, and saw their own daughter with CML sleeping on a hospital couch. My mother woke me.

Immediately after Shabbos ended, I called the funeral home and Mordechai's rav. All I remember was going home without Mordechai and with my parents. As I entered, it struck me that Mordechai was never to come home again. My apartment seemed comforting though. It was home. Mordechai's presence was everywhere. My parents and I made phone calls. I must have repeated the words, "Mordechai was *niftar*," at least twenty times. News travels quickly. My parents prepared the apartment for *shivah*.

We went to the funeral home. The man there reminded me I could never see Mordechai again. I obviously knew this. I found his words awkward. We brought the stark white *kittel* and Mordechai's *tallis*. The man removed the silver collar and asked if I wished to keep it. Mordechai was married in this *kittel* and wore his *tallis* regularly during his married life. Now stripped of its decoration, he would be clothed in it for burial. All Jews are buried equal.

Sleep. One sixtieth of death. I slept a few hours. The funeral parlor was packed. So many people crowded inside and others stood outside on the street. The service was short. People cried. I stood gazing at the cover over the casket. Only a simple pine box lay underneath. This is what ultimately happens to man. A woman took a blade to my shirt and I tore *kriyah*. The sound of the rip penetrated my heart. Would this broken heart ever heal? I wondered. I watched. I listened. I walked. I followed. And I said *Tehillim* in the car. I moved mechanically. At the grave, the many friends Mordechai had accumulated walked the coffin to the grave, slowly, pausing every several steps. They lowered it gently into the freshly dug ground, with love and respect. Dirt was placed on the grave and I heard the loud echoing thuds. The repetitive sound reinforced the reality. As the coffin became covered with soil, I thought, "I'll never see Mordechai again ... until *Moshiach* comes and the dead are resurrected." Sadness filled the air. We would all miss Mordechai. The loss *was* great.

Shivah began. A quorum prayed every day. A Torah was kept in the closet. People began learning *mishnayos* in Mordechai's memory. Hundreds of people paid their respects. Stories of Mordechai and the strength he exemplified were exchanged. People I never knew came to the *shivah*. People who had only heard of him visited. Phone calls arrived from as far away as Israel. Letters were delivered filled with expressions of sadness and words of comfort. המקום ינחם אתכם בתוך שאר אבילי ציון וירושלים had true meaning now. I never wanted to understand those words. Now I do. The family comforted one another.

At the end of *shloshim*, a *seudah* was made in Mordechai's memory. Friends and strangers studied Torah in his name. His medical school dedicated the Judaica Library in his memory. My parents' community sent charity funds to Israel. Through the generosity of many, a Torah and its cover was purchased for and presented to Mordechai's *shul*. The support of others continued. Mordechai's memory lives on. He died with a *shem tov* — a good name. People remembered him for his deeds, for the special moments he gave to others, for the time he spent helping those in need and for the *emunah* he demonstrated up until his death. No, Mordechai *did not* fail. He won. *Bitachon* and *emunah* carried him through life, through misery, challenges, pain and through joy. This is what Mordechai left me and those who knew him. He imbued strength, strength to cope, survive and continue living. He taught me there is *no* limit to Hashem's kindness and mercy. There are *no* boundaries on faith and power.

❦   ❦   ❦

Imagine, six years since his death I have survived. Yes I am alive. I cope. I remember with pain and joy the precious memories of what we shared together. I have also continued to live my life without

Mordechai's physical presence, but his impact has changed my life forever. Shortly after his death, I continued art school with dreams of graduation. I pursued my art studies and volunteering right in the same hospital where we were patients. I returned to very room where he died. There, a patient struggled to live. Hope renewed. I *must* survive. With Hashem's help, *I have* thus far.

Dreams come true. Upon graduating art school, I was determined to continue dreaming. A master's degree became my focus. Again family and friends supported me through my struggles. Mordechai's parents are surrogate parents to me. They treat me as a daughter. They listen, advise and laugh with me. The first year was the hardest, yet we endured.

Living was not easy. Many days I left school, racing to reach my room to unburden tears of pain in the comfort of my pillow. Time begins to heal, whether we want it to or not. In the beginning process of my mourning, my attitude was one of deprivation. You don't take money or power to the grave, only your good deeds or sins. The materialistic became immaterial. I probably took this to an extreme. Eventually after years, I leveled out by integrating various attitudes developed over my mourning process.

Dream. Fulfillment. At my graduation for a master's degree my parents and I knew with a full heart, this day indeed was great. Once again, I was a survivor. The family celebrated. I thanked Hashem for the honor and pleasure of reaching new goals, new heights in accomplishment. I was able now to continue helping others with my talents. I tasted success once again

Before Mordechai's death we discussed what I might do upon his demise. Morbid as it may seem, it helped him to know *I would cope* and it helped me find a focus. His dream was moving to Eretz Yisrael. I adopted that dream. When he died, several months later, burning desire sent me on my way. I returned year after year loving the land more each time.

Every so often, the loss and sadness of losing Mordechai holds me back, keeps me from caring enough to marry again. Mordechai stated openly in a conversation with me that I *should* marry one day. He gave me "permission". This permission left no room for guilt. The rest is up to *me*. Will I allow myself? Time will tell and in the meanwhile, I make the best out of my time as possible.

Life is transient; Hashem, Eternal. Man must return to dust, but before his time on earth terminates, he will be judged on what he did with his life. What is the essence of life? Soul, vitality, backbone, strength, humor, spirit, spark, breath, quality, drive and so on. Each person must find *his* own answer for himself. Within that, a purpose exists. That purpose creates a will to live, a reason, a desire. I hope I never lose sight of that purpose. Each person is unique. At times I thought I would be unable to really "live" again after Mordechai's death. Hashem renews my life daily, therefore I *must* go on. How unfair to Mordechai or myself if I do not accomplish what it is that I, Rachel, must do in my remaining time. Focus on life.

❁   ❁   ❁

[Rachel is managing a hectic schedule as usual. P.S. *She is also enjoying living!* It is now eleven years since her diagnosis, *kein yirbu.* — Ed.]

❧ Yesterday, Today and Tomorrow

by Fradel Berger

Yesterday is dead, tomorrow is unborn,
So there is nothing to fear and nothing to mourn.
For all that is past and all that has been,
Can never return to be lived once again.
And what lies ahead and what things will be,
Are in Hashem's hands so it is not up to me.
To live in the future that is Hashem's great unknown,
For the past and present Hashem claims for His own.
All I need to do is to live for today,
And trust Hashem to show me the truth and the way.
For it is only the memory of things that have been,
And expecting tomorrow to bring trouble again.
That fills my today which should be blessed,
With uncertain fears and borrowed distress.
For all I need to live for is this one minute,
For life is here and now do your repentance
      and good deeds in it.

Jewish Way to Suffering

Remembering Fradel Berger

בקראי עֲנֵנִי אֱלֹקֵי צִדְקִי, בַּצָּר הִרְחַבְתָּ לִּי,
חָנֵּנִי וּשְׁמַע תְּפִלָּתִי (תהלים ד:ב)

For some time we had been aware of the threat that was hanging over her and we knew that she too was fully aware of it. We could notice with awe and admiration — hardly trusting our perception — that the clouds on her horizon did not deter her in her ways of active participation in all that happened around her, including the sorrows and suffering of the needy. Praising every new day given to her within what she realized was a limited span of time, she marched on as it were with a song in her heart, and continued to do what she was wont to do: to use every ounce of her blessed and singular charm to comfort, to encourage, to give hope and practical help in an unprecedented way to those who were afflicted by misfortune.

Who was like Fradel Berger, a messenger of practical down-to-earth help who went personally into the houses of the sick, of the chronically ill, of the bedridden, of the invalids? In her own kitchen she cooked meals and packed large hampers with the best that the larder would contain and in a minicab took it all to the bedridden, actually often waiting until the meal had been eaten to make sure. She invited the lonely, who were, alas, somehow excluded from the friendship of general society, to her table again and again. She invited the handicapped to her festive home and embellished her hospitality with the charm of her musical talent and the exuberance of her joyful nature. This, no doubt, is something that remains indelibly inscribed in the memory of many. She took her young daughters with her to the houses of the poor to let them see where true values often are hidden and make them understand the flimsiness of affluence, the vanity of luxuries and the shabbiness that is often camouflaged by a facade.

She never ever forgot the dark days when as a young girl she lived in squalor and danger in Nazi Europe, when a piece of bread was an enviable treasure and sleeping on the floor a bliss for which to give thanks to Hashem. She wanted to pay back to Hashem thanks for His mercy in sparing her and she did it on the quiet — only the nearest being aware of it. She had the gift to detect the needs of the needy, the loneliness of those who shun company and she also had the alertness to do something tangible about it. She had the smile and the grace, the bearing and gallantry of nobility and she used it to bring sunshine to those who had forgotten what sunshine is. She used it to delight the hearts of the old to make them feel young again by her melodious presentations and her girlish, catching cheer. The young lady with the accordion who gilded their wrinkled age, was a mother and grandmother of blossoming families. She shared the riches of her heart and good fortune unstintingly with them all.

Fradel Berger belonged to many and each was convinced that she was the one to own her special friendship. With her blend of beauty of heart and humility, she radiated exemplary qualities all interwoven with her outstanding *emunah*. She faced the vicissitudes of life — and the last one was her illness — with a strength, deeply embedded in her inheritance of her noble ancestry. Her *emunah* was so overwhelming that it made us ignore all shadows around her while she was still with us.

Now the sky has darkened for all of us, for the teeming circle of those who had gathered around her magnetic personality and for the countless who had benefited by the rays of her goodness. The place that she occupied, how can it ever be filled?

Yet she would not have liked our horizon to be darkened by her departure. She would want the trail of sunshine of her *emunah* to accompany us. Although she lived with us, alas, too short a time, she left us a supreme example of the positive way of finding G-d's mercy in everything. This was her hallmark and it is our duty to hold on to it.

It was this trait that motivated her to write and complete the pamphlet "The Jewish Way to Suffering" * in order to enlighten and guide her fellow Jews through the trying stage of facing a serious illness.

This was her final act of *chesed*. It kept her going through her last difficult phases of life ... the knowledge that she will leave behind a booklet that would help others accept Hashem's will with the *emunah* and *bitachon* as she herself did. This pamphlet was completed before she succumbed to her illness. She conveyed her approval with a smile of recognition. She departed from the world at the age of fifty-three, Shavuos 1984. She left a most valuable legacy. May she be a מליצה ישרה for her family and their children. Her sensitivity and appreciation for the beauty and values of Hashem's glorious world are evident in the poetry featured throughout Times of Challenge.

Dr. Judith Grunfeld

* [The version of this work that appears on the following pages has been slightly abridged. — Ed.]

The Jewish Way to Suffering

On Death and On Dying

I am not a professional writer, nor an expert on the subject of death or dying, even though I have attended many sick people during my lifetime, nor do I claim to possess any profound knowledge about these matters. It was my own serious illness that prompted me to write this booklet in the hope that it would help other sufferers in similar situations.

When I first learned of my illness I was naturally deeply shocked and distressed. These anxieties were intensified when I found that I could not share these fears with anyone, as I did not want to distress those I love. I was, of course, not yet aware of the whole range of negative responses circulating inside me. In short, I was faced with the tragic fact of a very serious illness for the first time in my life and, as the experience was a new one, I was bewildered and at a complete loss to understand how to handle the situation. My family was also going through a difficult time and none of us dared to speak about it.

On the positive side, the stress caused by my suffering forced me to find out more about my illness and its accompanying problems. I began reading books written by doctors and nurses, as well as by some terminally ill people themselves. I found tremendous comfort in them for I no longer felt alone. There were people who understood exactly how I felt from their long years of experience with the dying. Then I took to reciting *Tehillim* every day and found it very comforting. I derived great strength and faith from my regular readings.

I also tried to read as much as possible about our Torah's view on the purpose of man and the Torah's approach to death. Once I had gained a deeper understanding, I felt more at ease and my mind was at peace.

It is this newly found tranquility and fresh hope which I am trying to convey in the belief that it will assist others.

What are my feelings as I write these sad paragraphs? Firstly, I am happy that I have survived long enough to write. Secondly, I am convinced that even if only one person benefits from it, the effort will have been worthwhile. If the patient and his family get 'in tune' with each other's needs, and come to accept the inevitable fact together, they can help to spare the hopelessly sick — and even more so, the family to be left behind — much unnecessary agony and suffering.

The past decade has seen much literature published on the subject of death and dying. Many of these books have helped to break the taboo with which our society conceals the certainty and finality of death. They have brought to light many valuable insights on the practical management of dying patients. Yet none of these publications have been written for Torah-true Jews.

In a comfortable and quiet life one tends to become more and more easy going, and the fulfillment of one's real purpose in life is more and more liable to be postponed. We tell ourselves that 'There is always tomorrow' and 'Other people die, but I still have time in front of me.' A serious illness suddenly brings home the message that it is now our turn and tomorrow may be much nearer than we thought. Death teaches the living the fleeting nature of time. Dying makes life suddenly appear more real.

My slow physical deterioration reaffirmed the belief that there is something else within me which I hardly knew existed, a hidden strength, a strong faith in Hashem, as well as hope for the future. I have gradually come to terms with my own circumstances, though everyone must find his own way to solve his problems. Suddenly I no longer felt alone. A new understanding of my serious condition helped me to see the futility of keeping it secret from my family. Suddenly I felt free to talk and to share my grief with them. What a great relief this was for them and for me! With the veil of secrecy lifted, we could now approach my problem realistically as a loving family with prayer and hope. As their own inner strength grew we felt a closeness we had never experienced before, as though we were walking together.

It is heartbreaking to note that we give prominence and due thought to preparation for birth and marriage but not for death. We recognize that it is a vital part of education to teach our children how to live. We seem unconcerned that no one ever speaks of dying. Education for death is after all a very necessary preparation for a full and wholesome life. Indeed there seems to be no event in life for which we prepare so scantily as for death. What is the miserable man or woman to do? The medical profession is only involved with a very small proportion of a patient's terminal care, mainly on the physical level. A dedicated physician, conducting regular visits, will increase them though the period of illness may be a prolonged one. The rabbis in our community do not usually talk to the dying unless they happen to be intimate friends or close relatives. But who shows concern for the woman facing death? What of patients who have no family to support and comfort them? Is it right to leave this vital and crucial part of one's life to the bleak walls of the hospital and its overburdened nurses? We must remember that our lives have dramatically changed over the past few decades. We saw the breakup of family and old community ties, when people knew each other so well, and were involved in sharing and caring for one another's problems. In our vast urban Jewish communities with their increased geographical mobility, life has become a most precious commodity. Against this background what provision is offered to a dying person who, above all, needs someone's time and sympathy to relieve his suffering? A point has been reached when such a serious matter ought to be discussed openly and realistically with a view to alleviating the situation.

This has been written to provide a simple and straightforward guide, hopefully a realistic one, in order to prepare us for our departure from this world. It takes the form of a series of talks with the dying, and deals with the importance of facing up to the fact of death, the various fears associated with it and how best they can be overcome.

I tried to discuss some of the psychological and emotional strains and stresses through which we pass when we feel we may be nearing the end. I tried to give some information on how to put our affairs, both material and spiritual, in order, and how to make adequate provisions for those we leave behind. Each talk has a specific theme which I indicated in the heading. The material is meant to be used with discretion and adjusted where necessary. I have assumed that the patient knows his or her condition. Where he or she does not, it is hoped that the talks will still be helpful. This is a very difficult and complicated subject to write about, and I tried my best to convey some of the problems of suffering as I have experienced them. It is hoped that at least some of the subjects mentioned will be of help to those who are concerned in this most delicate task. The talks are written primarily from the point of view of a sufferer, with the aim of helping others in a similar position. I feel that this task has been left far too long to professionals. Is it not time the community as a whole fulfilled its responsibility to the dying?

It is my humble and sincere prayer that what has been written here will serve to direct and guide those whose privilege it is to help and support the dying in whatever capacity.

In many ways this is a book for every man, for all of us have to die. This thought should prompt each one of us to repent, to be better prepared and ready, so that when our time comes to set out on life's last and longest journey we may face the great unknown with courage and faith. 'He will swallow up death for ever. And the Lord G-d wipe away tears from off all faces' (*Isaiah* 25:8).

When we look back in time and recall old people, we realize that death has always been distasteful to man and probably always will be. From a psychiatrist's point of view this is very understandable. It can perhaps best be explained by our basic awareness that in our subconscious, death is never possible in regard to ourselves. It is inconceivable for our subconscious to imagine an actual ending of our own life here on earth, other than by being killed.

The more progress we make in science, the more we seem to fear and deny the reality of death. How is this possible? One of the most important reasons is that dying is more gruesome, lonely, mechanical and dehumanized today than in the past. At times it has been difficult to determine technically when the time of death occurred. The patient is often taken out of his familiar environment and rushed into a hospital, which is a very frightening experience. When a patient is severely ill he is often treated like a person who has no right to an opinion. It should be remembered that the sick person, too, has wishes and opinions and the right to be heard.

When our patient has reached the emergency room, he will be surrounded by an army of people, nurses, orderlies, technicians, x-ray departments, etc., and slowly but surely he will be treated like a thing. He is no longer a sick person; decisions are made for him. He may cry out for rest, peace and dignity, but he will get infusions, transfusions, etc. He may want one single person to stop for one single minute so that he can ask one single question, but he will get a dozen people around the clock, all busily occupied with his heart rate, pulse, etc., but not with him as a human being. He may wish to fight it all, but it is going to be a useless fight. All this is done in the fight for his life, and if they manage to save his life they can consider the patient afterwards. This is very much in contrast to the olden days when dying was seen as the natural end to one's life and accepted with a much stronger faith. People died in their own homes, surrounded by their families and in their accustomed environment.

Another aspect that is often taken into account is what kind of fatal illness the patient has. Cancer is often viewed as a lingering, pain-producing illness, while heart trouble might strike suddenly and painlessly, causing a swift death. I think there is a great deal of difference between the fate of a loved one who dies slowly and has time available for grief and soul-searching, as in my own case, compared with that of one who is taken suddenly from family and friends. I think it is easier to talk to a cancer patient about death and dying then to a cardiac patient who arouses our fears of hastening his end by our calls to repentance.

From my reading on the subject of death and dying, it is evident that the terminally ill patient has very special needs, which can be fulfilled if we take time to sit and listen. Work with the dying patient requires a certain maturity and willingness to share some of his concerns. The door-opening interview is a meeting of two people who communicate without fear and anxiety. This could be either the doctor, a friend, a rabbi or a therapist who should let the patient know that he will stand by for as long as he is needed.

Confronting patients after the diagnosis of a malignancy is always very difficult. Some doctors are sensitive to their patients' needs and can quite successfully present the problem without taking all hope away from him. I personally feel this question should never give rise to a real conflict. The question should not be 'Should I tell?' but rather 'How do I share this with my patient?' If a doctor can speak freely with his patient about his malignancy, without equating it necessarily with impending death, he will do the patient a great service. He should always leave the door open for hope, namely new drugs, treatments, prospects of new techniques, and new research. The main thing is that he communicates to his patient the view that all is not lost; that he is not going to give him up; that it is a battle they are going to fight together — patient, family, doctor — irrespective of the end. Such a patient will not fear isolation, deceit, or rejection, but will continue to have confidence in the honesty of the physician and know that if there is anything that can be done, they will do it together. The family also greatly depends on both verbal and non-verbal reassurance from the doctor.

Patients react very differently to bad news depending on their personality, make-up and the style and manner which they were used to in the past. Patients who have previously faced stressful situations openly will do similarly in the present situation. It is therefore helpful to get acquainted with a new patient.

The patient may find comfort in the words of King David, *Psalm 23*. 'Though I walk in the valley of the shadow of death I shall fear no evil, for You are with me ... Surely goodness and mercy shall follow me all the days of my life and I shall dwell in the House of the L-rd forever.'

⋰§ Facing The Facts

I understand the doctor has been explaining the results of the x-rays and your operation. He has intimated that your illness is rather a serious one.

Although such news is distressing, one must not abandon hope because there are times when a doctor's diagnosis or words are so mesmerizing and powerful that we believe all he says, and that as Torah-Jews we must understand that Hashem's cure transcends all x-ray results and medical opinion, as we have seen in countless cases where doctors have given a patient up, and the patient has fully recovered. Miracles happen all the time and we must never give up hope. As the *Gemara* says: Even when a sharp sword is at your neck you must not abandon hope.

When we are ill and have to face up to the crisis of a serious illness, what we need apart from faith is to share our feelings and anxieties and hopes with the family or friends and of course with doctors or co-sufferers. Sharing your sufferings with others, bringing them out in the open, helps you to adjust and accept the situation.

So now that we've met, let's sit down and discuss this calmly and unemotionally. We meet sickness best when we sense that we are accepted and understood, and that we are not alone when we face the future. It may also be reassuring to remember that Hashem is the 'Healer of all flesh Who does wonders,' as we say in our daily morning prayers.

You may probably have been suspicious about your illness for some little time. You may have felt over the past few weeks that you have not been improving as much as you had hoped. Now the doctor has told you the truth, so that you can at least adjust to the situation. I am sure you would agree it is much better to know the truth than to be tossed to and fro in uncertainty.

I was saddened by the tendency to deny the fact of serious illness and to shut it out of our minds which only aggravates our plights. It puts up a painful barrier between us and those we love, and casts a dark and secretive cloud over the family. "This dear one is too ill, let's pretend it is not so." But sickness is as normal as health, and comes to all of us sooner or later. We may shrink from it, and want to be sheltered from it, we may decide to play games of make-believe, but to escape the fact of the illness we never can.

You may be thinking that such ideas as these only tend to depress you and make you feel gloomy and morbid. But preparation for an illness with its possible consequences need not depress you at all. Indeed often the opposite is true. In many ways your life can now be more full, more fruitful than before. This can become for you a time of deeper awareness of spiritual realities. It can bring out the best in you. It is a time of receiving and giving, of doing true repentance, of repairing old cracks dividing individuals. It is a time to do kindness and good deeds as much as your condition allows. Not only will this help you both in this world and the next, but it also takes your mind off your present problems by concentrating on others. For those who had no time before, now is the time to do so; a kind word to everyone, a phone call to the lonely, a visit to the sick, and a kind letter for someone suffering. No, it is not those who think about their illness and prepare for the possible consequences who are most afraid of it. It is rather those who have determined to put such thoughts on one side who are most frightened and depressed when their time comes. What you and I have to remember is that we have a lease, not a freehold, on this earthly life of ours. Now this does not mean that you have to dwell on death all the time in a morbid sort of way, but rather as preparation for a long journey as the following story which I took from an old Jewish song will illustrate:

A court jester was once called to the bedside of the king to listen to his troubles. The jester's mirth, however, failed for once; his jokes drew no smile from the king's pallid face. 'Master,' said the jester, 'why so sad?' 'Because,' replied the King, 'I have to leave my home and my people and go on a journey.' 'Is it a long journey?' asked the jester. 'It is indeed the longest journey any man can take.' 'When are you going?' inquired the clown. 'I think it will be quite soon now.' 'But what of your majesty's preparations?' asked the jester. 'I see no clothing laid out, no boxes in the hall, no horses in the courtyard.' 'Alas,' was the reply, 'I have had so much else to occupy me, that I have made no preparations for departure.' 'Then take my cap and bells,' said the bold jester, 'I thought I was the court fool, but I see that here lies a greater fool than I, since he is going on the longest journey man ever took, and yet calls me here to beguile his precious moments with jest and tales instead of preparing for his travels.'

It is not only the sick person who has to prepare himself for his last journey, but everyone of us. In *Pirkei Avos* we read that you should repent one day before your death. Since nobody knows the day of his or her death, one should repent every day.

In this initial talk we have at least been able to be honest with each other. We have seen how essential it is to prepare for death, whenever it may come. I am pleased we were able to discuss some of the difficult things which were obviously on your mind and which have been difficult to bring out into the open. Perhaps you would like to think about them further and we can have another talk. Meanwhile may Hashem fill you with joy and peace and hope. Remember that you must prepare yourself now for your entry into the World to Come by means of repentance and good deeds. Rabbi Jacob tells us (*Pirkei Avos* 4:21) that this world is like an entrance hall in front of the World to Come. Prepare yourself in the entrance hall, so that you may enter the palace.

✺§ Your Thoughts

When you were first told the full truth about the seriousness of your illness and its likely outcome, you were, like me, very shocked.

You just could not believe it and asked yourself, what have I done to deserve this? Surely the diagnosis can't be true, you protested. As the days have gone by, you have had a chance to reflect and to talk things over. You seem to be working through some of these very natural and normal reactions. I felt that the shock of it had brought me closer to Hashem, Who has eased my suffering.

A doctor has explained to me, and I read it in some books, how some of our reactions of denial, anger and depression affect us. It is only by talking about them openly and trying to understand how they work that we are able to face them and eventually overcome them. One of the most common reactions to being told bad news is that of denial. We simply don't want to hear this news, so we forget or suppress it. We want to pretend, not only to our family and friends, but even to ourselves, that we are not as seriously ill as we are. The doctor may have explained our condition as plainly as he could, but we don't accept it. And, furthermore, because we have not 'heard' it, we say, doctors don't tell you a thing! No one explains anything properly. We have blocked and shut it out. These are some of the unconscious mechanisms which we constantly use in our everyday lives, even when we are fit and well. The purpose of denial is to enable us to cope with the threat of any impending danger or potential calamity. From time to time you will probably find yourself denying the facts of your illness or its diagnosis and prognosis, in spite of what the doctor has told you. These periods of denial are often most necessary, particularly if they can serve to strengthen hope and prevent despair. So, your response of denial is quite a healthy and normal response to shock. It enables you to look at a small piece of your problem at a time, and once you have faced up to it, you will be able to act more realistically. Partial denial, I was told, can therefore be beneficial.

When denial becomes prolonged you are likely to find yourself in difficulties, as it can interfere and inhibit your relationships with those around you, and postpone further treatment. Try to increase your optimism, and you will find that you can develop a healthy attitude. Feelings of hope and confidence are very necessary to you at the present time. "Seek the L-rd and you shall find Him, if you seek Him with all your heart and with all your soul. When you are in tribulation, and all these things come upon you, if you'll turn to Hashem and obey His voice, He will help you." I have experienced this myself. When my heart ached, I took a long walk and prayed to Him. I was amazed at the instant relief I felt on returning home, which further strengthened my faith in Him. Talk to a friend about your fears and you will be better able to work through these phases of denial. I hope these talks with me will enable you to do just that.

When the first stage of shock and denial cannot be maintained any longer, it is often replaced by feelings of anger, rage, envy and resentment, although one is not always aware of this. In contrast to the stage of denial, this stage of anger is very difficult for family and staff to cope with. The reason for this, as far as I can see, is the fact that anger is displayed freely in all directions. The doctors are just no good, they don't know the right treatment to give, the nurses are even more often a target of anger. Whatever they do is wrong. The visiting family is received without cheerfulness, which makes the encounter a painful event. They may respond with guilt and grief, or try to avoid future visits, which increases the patient's anger.

I found the attitude of the doctor towards his patient at such times very important, as it greatly influences the response of the patient towards his illness. If a doctor can speak freely with his patient about the diagnosis of a malignancy, while at the same time leaving the door open for hope, he will do the patient a great service. The main thing is that he communicates to the patient the feeling that all is not lost; they are facing a battle which the patient, the family and the doctor are going to fight together whatever the outcome may be. Such a patient will not fear rejection and isolation, but will continue to have confidence in the honesty of his physician.

All these different reactions of shock, denial and anger are natural. You will find that your attitudes and moods are quite likely to vary from day to day, even from minute to minute. What you are able to bear today you want to shun tomorrow! Courage and despair, optimism and pessimism all seem to alternate and interact. I am afraid there are no easy answers to the problems and difficulties we've been talking about. Suffering is a very real problem, and what we have to do is to try to discover Hashem's pattern in it all, rather than see it as totally meaningless and wasteful. As I mentioned in our previous talk, this is a wonderful opportunity for you to do as much good as you can. Then Hashem in His immense loving kindness will respond and help you as He helps all those who approach Him sincerely.

We have to try to glimpse, through the darkness of suffering, the light of Divine purpose. Even when stricken by suffering Job exclaimed: 'I know that my Father lives and cares.' All our ancestors knew Hashem cared, and He always helped them in their despair. Our best weapon in trouble is faith — *Ani maamin b'emunah sheleimah.*

This does not mean that you have to submit meekly to your suffering, as this is only passive and negative. What you have to do is try to accept it as your share of tragedy in this life; such an attitude is active and positive. It is not suffering in itself which ennobles, but rather the way we face up to it and bear it. At first I found it very difficult to see my troubles in this light. When finally through my suffering I came to this realization, I felt a great sense of relief. I became fully aware of the immense kindness of Hashem above, Who helped me take a positive approach and gave me energy and courage to face my future. Whenever you are worried, remember: *Shivisi Hashem Lenegdi Samid* — Hashem is with me always and I fear not.

◦§ Your Fears

The third stage, the stage of 'bargaining,' is equally helpful to the patient, though only for brief periods of time, as I was told by my own doctor. If we have been unable to face the sad facts in the first period, and have been angry at people in the second phase, perhaps we can succeed in entering into some sort of agreement with Hashem, which may postpone the inevitable happening. If Hashem has decided to take me from this earth, He may help me if I promise to be good and if I ask nicely. We are all familiar with this reaction from our observation of children who first demand, then ask us for a favor. When we refuse they may at first be angry and stamp their feet, or lock themselves in their bedroom and express their anger. But they will soon have second thoughts, and try a new approach. 'If I am good all week and help in the house may I then go to my friends?' The seriously ill patient uses similar maneuvers. He bargains with Hashem for an extension of his life. 'Give me life,' I bargained, 'and I will change and become much better.' Such bargaining is really an attempt to postpone the inevitable in exchange for a price. May Hashem give us the chance to keep all our promises to Him.

When the seriously ill patient can no longer deny his illness, because he is forced to undergo more surgery or treatment, or becomes thinner and weaker, his anger and numbness, or stoicism, will be replaced by a sense of great loss and deep depression, mixed with fear and guilt. All these are normal and healthy reactions in an unhealthy situation. Bringing fears out into the open, so that we can discuss them, should be a great relief. It is the worst thing possible for us to pretend that they are not there. Though I am sometimes afraid, I put my trust in You.

You have, I know, been thinking of what you will have to face in the future. One of the difficulties is that dying is strange and unknown to us, for we have never done it before. No one has ever come back to tell us what actually happens when death occurs, and what lies on the other side. This fear of the unknown is real and besets all of us at one time or another; there is no easy answer to it. One's thoughts should constantly be directed to Hashem, says Rabbeinu Yonah, for a man does not know his time.

But you feel sick, maybe you are in pain. You worry about your family and dependents, and you are cut off from your daily work and contacts from people. As your sickness progresses you worry about becoming more dependent on others. You probably worry about how your family manages without you. One of the ways in which you can ensure they are being cared for and looked after is to make every provision for their welfare, as discussed with family and friends.

The dread of pain has been worrying you, too, I am sure. Physical pain can make you anxious and frightened but you will find that the more fearful you become, the greater will be your sensitivity to pain. Fortunately, much can be done today to relieve the pain and physical discomfort. Pain can now be regularly controlled, and this means you can be kept pain free and alert, instead of drugged as used to be the case before all these new drugs were introduced.

When we are ill we have a fear of the Day of Judgment, and thoughts of punishment torment us. Also instinctively we associate the thought of our illness with feelings of guilt, and there can be a general dissatisfaction with what we have made with our lives. As our illness continues, our sense of guilt seems to grow in intensity. There is a tendency for us to look back on the past and recall opportunities which have been neglected and good deeds that have been missed. Now is the time to repent. You can help your family a lot by showing courage and faith in Hashem. Just as King David declared when in distress, 'Your rod and Your staff shall comfort me' (*Psalm* 23).

ᴥᔆ Hope

So far we have discussed the different stages that people go through when they are faced with tragic news. I have read about psychiatric terms such as defense mechanisms and coping mechanisms. Now that I have experienced them myself I know these feelings are true. These different responses will last for varying lengths of time and will replace each other, or at times continue side by side. The one thing, I am told, that persists in all these stages (in most cases) is hope, and it is this glimpse of hope which sustains people through days, weeks, and months of suffering. An eminent doctor said he found that almost all his patients maintained some hope of a cure, a new drug, or a last minute success in some research project. This helps many terminally ill patients to keep up their spirits through necessary denial. This does not mean that doctors have to tell them lies; doctors should express a hope that something unforeseen may well happen, so that we will live longer than expected. The conflicting opinions with regard to possible improvement generally arise from two main sources. The first and most painful one is an impression of hopelessness, conveyed by the staff or the family, when the patient needs hope. A second source of anguish often comes from the family's inability to accept a patient's final stage; they desperately cling to hope, when the patient is ready to die. Many doctors feel that every patient should be given the most effective treatment available and should not be 'given up.' A patient who is beyond medical help needs more care than others. And when a seriously sick person is cared for with kindness and deep understanding, he will keep his glimmer of hope and continue to regard his doctor as a friend, who will help him to the end.

Hope is the most effective antidote to fear. Whenever you are oppressed by fear and doubt, try to keep a close watch on your thoughts. If you dwell on depressing things, you'll only intensify your anxieties. Think sound, healthy and wholesome thoughts whenever you can. The more you worry, the more tense you will become. It is all rather a vicious circle. If only you can learn to relax and let go you will find that you will become calmer and will gradually lose the tension which fear induces. Try to throw your worries to Hashem and He will help and strengthen you. Whether in celebrations or in misfortune and grief, the Almighty stealthily reveals His Presence and from the grey mist of depression the Creator breaks through in all His glory and places His hands on the solitary. Thus we acknowledge Him in our blessings as the Healer of all flesh Who does wonders.

Try always to be thankful for all the great goodness Hashem has granted you in the past. I am sure, however hard you try, you cannot count them. I know you suffer physical and mental pain, and you wish your life could go on as before. When you feel sad, do you give a thought to the millions of our people who died without proper burial, without family and without friends around them? Even today there are many who meet with sudden death, without the time or opportunity to prepare for their last journey. Hard as it is for us to accept our imminent death, at least there is a consolation in the fact that we have been given the opportunity to get ready for our 'return' and, hopefully, Hashem will help us to purify ourselves properly. But what's the use, you may tell me, in all this, when you know you are approaching death? Have you given a thought to the millions of people who, while living, are dead? They drift along aimlessly, without a purpose and without any joy or hope. They wish to die, but are condemned to lives in which every day and every hour is filled with mental anguish. You should thank Hashem for all past happiness, as there is a credit side, as well as a debit side, to life's balance-sheet. We are very exceptional people indeed if our blessings don't outnumber our troubles. Whenever you are despondent, it is good to take a walk among Hashem's gifts since being grateful to Him is a remedy for self-pity and low spirits.

There are so many gifts to be recalled — many years of good health, perhaps the blessings of friendship, acts of kindness and sympathy and great miracles as well as family affection and the skills of doctors and nurses. Finally, may I try to help you over the fear of the unknown, which is very real to all of us? When you think back, there have been many experiences throughout our lives when we have been faced with fears when our lives were in danger and we dreaded the unknown, especially during the war. All these experiences were at the time rather threatening. When we look back upon them, we see that we were able to pass through them. Hashem has helped us to survive them. What was so frightening proved to be lifegiving and challenging. So, too, with this final fear of the great unknown — our last adventure. Hope must never leave us. Hope is not the belief in a Divine dispenser of barbiturates and tranquilizers. We need a tough and sturdy faith, to provide the optimism with which we can live in hope. Sensitive people should realize that Hashem cares for us always.

'He is with me and I shall not be afraid.' (*Adon Olam*)

⋑ The Family

It is only natural that you are concerned about the members of your family who are visiting you every day. No one can help the seriously ill person in a really meaningful way without including or considering his family. When we are ill, our relatives often need help in dealing with the situation and coping with their own feelings. I know that you are thinking about them at this time, and perhaps wondering how they are managing at home without you. It is important that you still feel part of their lives and share in their many emotions.

Family members often suffer if they can't express their anxieties and fears, and there is genuine and mutual relief when things can be discussed openly. Family members don't need to be guarded in what they say or in what you have to tell them. Pretense can easily lead to tension and deceit. Openness is a treasured experience; you can share not only sadness but also joy. You can look back on good and happy memories, rather than look forward to some dreaded future.

You will notice that your relations, who witness suffering and pain, sometimes have feelings of guilt. They feel so helpless and inadequate; you have probably heard them say more than once, "We only wish there would be something more we could do." You will do a great deal for them if you relieve them of these frustrations. You can explain that it is all in Hashem's hands and they can best help by staying quietly and calmly by your bedside. Frenzied activity and fuss only serve to make matters worse, as well as outward activity and busyness which are of course sometimes necessary. There is also an inward activity, and it is this that reflects hope and healing, sympathy and love.

If only you and your family can think deeply and love deeply together, there will be no need for words. You don't always feel like talking, just being quietly together with your family is relaxing and reassuring. The members of your family, as I said before, experience feelings of guilt and unresolved tension, which make it sometimes difficult for them to communicate freely with you. They, too, need a listener, for they often feel lonely and isolated themselves. In one sense they are patients too, with anxieties to be expressed and needs to be fulfilled. They should be reassured by the doctor and made to understand that, because you are at present very ill, you may from time to time be rather sleepy and drowsy as a result of the different medicines and drugs. You need to sleep or just keep quiet and still. The doctor will also understand how keenly you must feel your present loss of independence, and it is only natural that you sometimes express this in terms of gratitude mingled with bouts of irritability, as I have often observed with sick people whom I have visited in the past. In constant pain there is a tendency to give way to anxiety and resentment. Pain causes anxiety and anxiety seems to aggravate pain. Where there is a good relationship between you and those around you such fears can, however, be kept to a minimum. Severe pain can also create feelings of apartness from others; relationships seem distant and you may feel the threat of being unloved or abandoned. Here again, loving reassurance by your family will help you to realize that you are loved and you do belong, and they will see you through. Because of their love and understanding you will be more able to come to terms with your illness. What a relief and strength it is when someone loves you and cares for you. To share anything — joys and sorrows, hopes fears — gives a keener edge and a deeper meaning to all that happens. You feel more deeply, you live more richly. I am sure that many of your friends are remembering you in their prayers in *shul* or at home. We always feel strengthened by the prayers of others when we are weak and ill. *Hamispallel be'ad chavero neeneh techilah.* Whoever prays for his friend will be answered first by Hashem. What a great consolation it is to know that you are supported by others in their thoughts. It is reassuring to know that repentance, prayer and charity can annul severe decrees.

You should be able to relax and be upheld by your nearest and dearest, who are sharing your suffering with you. In turn, you can help your family to face up to your illness by sharing some of your own thoughts and feelings with them. This will encourage them to speak openly about their own fears and anxieties, and should they have any feelings of guilt these will be appeased by your frank talks together. They may be thinking they should have sent for the doctor earlier. They may be feeling they should have done more to help you, when you were fit and well. Indeed, they are experiencing similar feelings to those you have yourself. Perhaps at the beginning they couldn't come to terms with the severity of your illness. They probably thought the diagnosis was wrong and the doctor mistaken. They too were probably shocked, angry and depressed when they heard the news. In fact, families often share these responses with their sick member. Sharing all these concerns can prove most helpful. When secrets are kept between people who are normally open and frank, artificial barriers are set up and conversation inevitably becomes meaningless. Do try to be 'in tune' with your family and face up to the facts together. Where there are strong emotional strains they only result in considerable anxiety for all concerned.

At the same time, it must be understood that not every family is able to converse openly about such things as death and dying. For those that can't, reciting *Tehillim* is most beneficial and can be a great comfort to all. Some people just find it hard to discuss painful matters openly, nevertheless they do care.

I think it is unfair to expect the constant presence of any family member. They too need to recharge their batteries outside the sickroom sometimes, so that they can function more efficiently.

During these crucial days or weeks, a neutral outsider who is not emotionally overinvolved can be of great help in supporting you and the family. The closer your relationship with your family and friends, the more essential it is that their visits to your bedside be frequent, but not too prolonged, for little good is done by the long hours of vigil at the bedside. This can be so tiring and exhausting for all concerned. Short, frequent visits are preferable.

It is during times of severe illness and distress, such as you are going through now, that relationships with friends can be strengthened and perhaps wounds healed. After all, no family is perfect. Now comes an opportunity for you to take stock and repair, if possible, the old rifts; if not completely healed, at least they can be eased.

It may be helpful to say our night prayers with greater concentration and understanding; especially comforting for many is the thought that the Guardian of Israel does not sleep nor slumber, and 'I hope for Your salvation G-d,' as well as 'Guard me, G-d for I trust in You.' Sincere prayer can bring relief and reassurance.

I find it remarkable that the word faith in Hebrew is *emunah*. The same word has also another meaning: steady. What is *bitachon* if not steadiness? When gloom descends and sorrow falls steady again, *BITACHON IS OUR GUIDE*.

৵৽ The Children

What about the children? How are they going to react when you finally go home? Children's attitudes to the dying are extremely difficult to discover, for we adults know very little about unpleasant and sad things from them. What can I say about your situation? I think it would be extremely difficult to exclude your children or grandchildren from some awareness of the severity of your illness. They need not know all the facts, but they should be allowed to share in the family's concern.

The idea that what children don't actually hear or see they won't know is a complete myth. Again, the belief that children are 'too young to understand' is a sentiment which is often expressed to explain two very common, but contradictory, approaches to life-and-death situations. We either think that young children are unable to take in anything unpleasant, and therefore should not be offered any feasible explanations, or they are too sensitive and vulnerable for the true facts of life to be revealed to them. Often such attitudes are reflections of our own inner needs rather than a realistic appreciation of the true feelings of children. It is only when we adults try to master our own conflicting feelings in the face of adversity, that we become able to adopt helpful attitudes towards our young children.

Instead of true answers to their many questions we tend to offer children half-truths, hastily concocted, hoping they will drop the subject. It is not what you all say as a family, but how you say it. Your children will be strengthened by the realization that sickness and death can be talked about quite openly and without fear. It will be wise to make clear to them that whatever happens, there will be someone there to look after them, care for them and love them. Children are particularly sensitive to a highly emotional climate and have fairly shrewd awareness of things in general, even if they don't entirely understand them. They overhear things that are being said or whispered, and become suspicious and anxious when they sense a difference in the family routine. Any noticeable change in the household can cause them much distress and insecurity.

If they are not given some sort of explanation which fits in with what they overheard or sensed, their imagination is apt to run wild. They are aware that something is happening, but are not quite sure what. It is always better to tell them about the likely prospects, no matter how distressing. Otherwise they will search for their own explanation, for no child lives in an emotional vacuum. Obviously such explanations must be determined by the age of your children and grandchildren, and your understanding of their feelings. You will find that they can face up to the truth better than to deceit.

Explaining the situation need not be at all formal. Take things as they come — the more honesty the better. Illness is a family crisis; it is generally felt by doctors and nurses that children should be allowed to share in it and shown they have a part to play in it. As parents, we can face up to questions from our children about the beginning of life far more easily than queries about the end of life, though many parents find great difficulties in explaining the facts of life to their children. The explanation must be in words children understand, and expressed openly, clearly and honestly. However, there may be moments when the family or you become particularly distraught or upset; at such times the presence of young children should be avoided if possible. The way in which your present circumstances are presented to your children or grandchildren will be of great importance for their future attitude to death and dying. Children are usually resilient and able to cope, as long as they are being told the truth and are being loved and cared for.

Unless there are very special circumstances, do not send children off to relations to care for them. They will feel far more secure at home. Staying with others, even favorite uncles or aunts, may only heighten their sense of isolation and exclusion. They might also grow up to regard sickness as something secretive and fearful. They may feel resentful that their mother is spending less and less time with them. Their anxiety is lessened if they know what's happening around them. They may feel sorrow, anger and anxiety about the future; all this may have an affect on their behavior. Reactions will, of course, depend on the age of the child. Very young children seem to ignore the unpleasant and real meaning of dying and death is grasped only by degrees. When they are aware of the situation, they may feel deep anxiety about separation. It should be stressed again that children cannot accept deception, and questions should therefore be answered on the level of their understanding, according to your personal judgment. What you and your family know, you can express honestly and consistently. Follow it up with as much support and guidance as possible . . .

You'll appreciate that there is no neat, clear-cut classification describing the reactions of young children to dying and death. Each child is unique and no two children will behave in identical patterns. You'll know your children and grandchildren far better than anyone else; each one will be an individual in his own right and must be given every opportunity to express himself in his own way.

It must be remembered that young children are often taken aback when they first see their parents cry — particularly if their father cries. They should be shown that crying is a natural and normal expression of feeling. Preparing children to talk freely of death and dying is very sensible on the part of the parents. If such instruction forms part of the normal upbringing of children, then they are better equipped to deal with death when it occurs, as it inevitably must sometime in the family circle. It is important that when death is explained to children, it should be done in terms that are not only valid from the point of view of our faith, but also emotionally satisfying to them. Unfortunately, the expressions commonly used by some parents are not as helpful and satisfying as might be hoped; indeed they are often harmful. 'Hashem is taking Booba away from us,' or 'Hashem wants to take her to heaven.' Even when the family has strong religious views, the terms in which they express death to children can represent Hashem in a cruel and distorted way. A child may then become angry with the Holy One for taking his grandmother or favorite relative away. What young children need is not a theory or an explanation of death, but rather a sense of reassurance and feeling of security when they feel deprived of a loved relative.

The questions they want to ask are in the main simple: 'What happens when people die? Are their eyes open or closed? Why are they put in a deep hole in the ground? Will I die one day? Does everyone have to die?' ...

It is generally held that it is not very helpful to talk to the very young about the will of Hashem in cases of death as it may arouse anger and rebellion; comparing death with sleeping is not a good idea because it may cause the child when going to bed to fear that he or she will never wake up again.

They should be told simply about the World to Come where there will be no more pain or death, and where those who have died will go on living in a different world and in a different form. As a family you will have to explain this in simple yet straightforward language in order to help children. If great care is taken, then whatever their ages may be they will derive a deeper understanding of death and a stronger trust in life hereafter ...

⋙ Grief and Suffering

When you think that you may have to leave those you love and those who have formed part of your life for many years, it is only natural for you to feel keenly the painful pangs of grief. First, we grieve for ourselves, our sense of loss at the thought of being separated from our loved ones. Second, there is fear for our family and fear of the unknown.

Grief is the price we have to pay for love, and both you and your family will be experiencing somewhat similar emotions. It will be helpful therefore, if your anguish or grief can be shared. I know that not all families will feel up to doing this. But if it is at all possible for you, you'll find that in this sharing much of your fear, anxiety, bitterness and loneliness will be lessened and your deepest thoughts given full expression. You can't avoid the pain of parting, but you can at least work through it together. Grief is an intense emotion; if you bottle it up, it will only lead to trouble later on, for it brings with it a flood of negative feelings.

It is quite natural to feel lonely and bewildered at this time. Your whole life-pattern is being disrupted and broken, and there will be a loss of heart and strength, loss of the role you once played in the home and the community. All of this is very difficult to bear. You may often feel bitter and angry and become critical of everything and everybody. There will be moments of bitter depression and you may find yourself thinking thoughts you seldom have thought in more normal circumstances. It becomes difficult to concentrate, and your mind may be full of distressing thoughts.

Closely related to depression are feelings of guilt, perhaps the most painful companion of death. When an illness is diagnosed as a potentially fatal one, the family members — as we have already discussed in our earlier talks — often feel they are to be blamed for it. "If I had sent him to a doctor earlier," and "I should have tried harder" are frequent statements made by members of the seriously ill patient's family. Needless to say, a friend of the family, a family doctor or a rabbi can be a great help to such a relative by relieving her of her unrealistic reproach and by reassuring her that she probably did everything possible to obtain help.

'Don't feel guilty, because you are not guilty,' is not enough. By listening to such guilt feelings more carefully, one can often elicit a more realistic reason for their guilt. A high percentage of widows and widowers and various family members seen in clinics or by private physicians present themselves with somatic symptoms, as a result of failure to work through their grief and guilt. If they had been helped before the death of their partner to bridge the gulf between themselves and the dying, one half of the battle would have been won. It is understandable that people are reluctant to talk freely about death and dying, especially if it has come close to their own doorstep. Some people find communicating difficult only at the start. It becomes easier with time and practice. Often they find a much deeper sense of closeness and understanding which only suffering can bring.

The Book of Job tells the story of a righteous and universally revered man, who is suddenly overwhelmed by deep misfortune. He loses all he has, his children meet violent deaths, and he himself is in the grip of a malignant disease. He is shunned and overwhelmed by his misery, and at first vehemently demands an explanation. Gradually he realizes that Hashem gives mortals an opportunity for the purification of heart and spirit in preparation for meeting Hashem. He bears it all with humble resignation.

I can almost hear you say that Job was a saintly man, who could endure a lot. But we do not have those high standards of faith. While this is true, we still have to try and accept our lot lovingly, as an ancient Talmudic Sage said: Offer a blessing in adversity, as you do in good fortune, for adversity can bring us personal refinement. Though it brings us low, it gives us depths; though it pains us, it brings us closer to Hashem. Crisis sensitizes a person; it permits him to feel the real sensibilities, not the luxuries of life. He looks upwards, raising his sights to Hashem, while he is lying flat on his back.

Our life is a gift which comes from Hashem. We accept life from Him with its joys and sorrows and, in our daily prayers, we offer to give it back to Him. I know that I place my life in His hands and I will not be abandoned. Hashem will do what He feels is right. In time it will become clear that His way is the best.

When you are ill and feel weak, you may in your bitterness ask, 'Why me? What have I done to deserve such suffering?' The *Chofetz Chaim* once gave this example which illustrates our lack of understanding of Hashem's plans. A visiting Jew came to spend a Shabbos in a small town. He felt that the *aliyos* — 'call-ups' — to the Torah were wrongly distributed, and promptly demanded an explanation for them from the sexton, who answered, 'You are a stranger in this place. Today you are here, tomorrow you've gone. But I, who reside here permanently, have a better understanding.'

The same is true with us. We feel grieved, because we suffer, and it is sometimes difficult for us to see the Divine pattern. But we must remember that we are also strangers in this world in which we only spend a short time. We cannot understand our Master's plans.

As you lie there, feeling weaker and weaker, feelings of guilt plague you. You begin to feel a deep sense of regret for all the sins you have committed and for all the *mitzvos* you have omitted. You remember so well when, in the past you met with death in the family, how strongly you became aware of the futility of life. You promised yourself to repent and ignore all trivialities, as King Solomon so rightly explained *hakol havel*. Everything is futile. But after the few days of sadness had passed, your life and thoughts returned to their former routine. The concept of death became more and more removed from your thoughts, until you gradually talked yourself into believing that death is only something that happens to other people. Now your serious illness has made you face the sad realities; suddenly your sins loom up larger than life. Don't hold back; express your sorrows naturally as you experience them. But what you must try hard to do, if possible, is to resist the brooding grief which is full of self-pity, for this is the grieving for those who have abandoned all hope. There is a world of difference between self-pity, when thoughts are centered on self, and genuine grief, when hopes and thoughts are centered on Hashem. Little help is promised to the former, for it is only the latter who will be comforted by our Creator. 'If you will seek Hashem, your G-d, you shall find Him, if you seek Him with all your heart and soul. When you are in trouble and all these things come upon you, if you turn to Hashem, your G-d, and are obedient to His voice,' He will help you.

I am sure you will derive much support and comfort from your family and friends. Their warm encouragement will strengthen your will to live. If you are prepared to face up to things properly, openly and honestly, then you have taken the first step towards overcoming them. Sorrow tends to become more and more painful when it remains a secret. You will find much inner comfort if you can become master of your circumstances, rather than allowing yourself to be mastered by them. If you can say while in pain, 'I trust Hashem,' you will derive a deep sense of growth and of wholeness. 'Guard me G-d, for I trust in You.'

Pain is an intensely subjective experience, which some people are able to tolerate better than others. It is a common observation that if one's mind is occupied in some activity, pain is less distressing. The same is true if one is emotionally and spiritually at rest and free from worry. Suffering does sometimes bring out remarkable qualities in people in whom one would least expect it. We must keep our lines of communication open with Hashem. As one grows weaker, shorter of breath, and uncomfortable, living becomes more and more of an effort. It is hard not to grow selfish when the simplest matters become difficult. Against this background all but the most righteous will become moody and irritable, making unkind and hurtful remarks to those they love most. Does he or she really understand what you as a patient are actually going through? Possibly not, but remember that your loved one is suffering as acutely as you are, though in a different way, and following a path as lonely and desolate as your own. It is hard to watch the suffering of those you love.

For him who trusts in Hashem in his moments of anguish, says

Rabbeinu Yonah: Darkness will be the cause of light, as it is written: 'Though I have fallen, I shall rise. Though I sit in darkness, Hashem is a light unto me.' The spirit of man will sustain his infirmity, but who can bear a broken spirit? When the body is sick, the spirit assists and supports the body with its sympathy and provides consolation, acceptance, and endurance. But when the spirit is sick and broken with sorrow and care, who will console, support and sustain it? Worry and bitterness of heart is worse than bodily illness; for the spirit supports the body in its illness, but when the spirit is sick and broken by its suffering, the body will not support it.

Whether in celebration or in misfortune and grief, stealthily Hashem reveals His presence, and from the grey mist of depression, the Creator breaks through in all His glory and places His hands on the solitary shoulders of man, and whispers softly to him, 'Be consoled, man, you are not alone.'

In *Tehillim* we read, 'Hope to Hashem and observe His ways; He will raise you to inherit the land; He will cut off the wicked, you will see.

G-d forbid, it may happen to a Jew in misfortune that he feels lonely and abandoned. He paces back and forth and goes from room to room endlessly, in the dim hope of finding someone, yet all the rooms are empty. At such a moment, the man confronts despair and dark desperation. Now he should become aware of the comforting Almighty telling him, 'You are not alone, Hashem is ever with you.' *Ashrei hagever* — Happy the man who trusts in Him.

Rabbeinu Yonah advises us that people in trouble should perform *mitzvos* which protect them from affliction, such as the *mitzvah* of charity, which also rescues from death. A person who has no money with which to do charity should speak well of the poor man and ask others to treat him well, since one who causes others to give to charity has even greater merit than the charitable themselves. Let him also engage in the *mitzvah* of performing acts of kindness: He should assist his neighbors through his personal exertions, as our Sages have said: 'Performing acts of kindness is even more praiseworthy than charity, for charity is given with one's wealth, whereas kindnesses are performed both by a personal effort and by means of wealth. Charity is given only to the poor, but kindness may be bestowed upon rich and poor alike.'

Prayer takes the place of sacrifice, because true prayer involves spiritual torment. This idea is beautifuly described in *Tanya*, by the first Rebbe of Lubavitch, and also in *Shaarei Teshuvah*. How humble a man must feel during prayer, and how many tears does he shed over his remoteness from the Creator of the universe! How difficult it is to draw near to Hashem! Through prayer, especially when offered on Yom Kippur, a man can undergo the spiritual torment which he is obliged to endure in order to effect a reconciliation between him and his Creator. In *Tehillim* we find: 'Let my prayer come before You like incense, and may the lifting up of my hands be seen as an evening-offering.' Prayer is service of the heart, and it can help even the seriously ill patient to come near to his Creator and obtain Divine comfort in his suffering.

⊸§ Teshuvah

One of the deepest fears confronting every devout Jew in serious illness is the fact that he has sinned. He is terrified of being charged with these sins on his Judgment Day. He realizes only too clearly how strongly he has allowed himself to be influenced by the evil inclination and its 'attractions'.

'Repent one day before your death,' says Rabbi Eliezer (*Pirkei Avos*). However, by nature man is drawn to sin. He allows himself to be enslaved by impulses and drives which master him and in the end bring about his own destruction. They demand a price which he cannot pay, stifle the spark of life in him and darken the light of his soul.

Hashem forgives the truly penitent as He knows that we are only flesh and blood, and the evil inclination forever influences them. Though they (sins) be red like crimson, they shall be as bleached wool. 'I will heal their sinfulness,' is the Divine assurance. 'I will love them freely,' is Hashem's promise. 'Return unto Me,' is Hashem's plea. And 'I will return unto you,' is the Divine pledge. This is not easy. It is much easier to sin than to repent! Countless *sefarim*, some with English translation, are available on repentance. They are helpful and important, I need not elaborate on them. But for the sake of convenience I will briefly mention Maimonides' three phases, the three stages in the process of repentance.

The first, and the most difficult, he calls recognition of the sin; it is not easy for any individual to recognize and admit his errors. The second stage is regret. This stage is not too difficult, for regret means relief from torture and guilt. The third stage is determination to sin no more. When he reaches this stage he is fully recovered.

How does the process of repentance take place? To whom shall one confess his sins? Every man can approach Hashem as shown by the true story of Menashe, son of Hezekiah, King of Judah. King Menashe filled Hashem's Temple with idols. He brought corruption to the land and was guilty of every crime, including the murder of the prophet Isaiah. All the hosts of Heaven were determined not to permit his prayers for forgiveness to reach Hashem. What did Hashem do? He built a private tunnel to permit the prayers of Menashe to reach him. This shows us that man needs no intermediary. We all have a direct line to Hashem, and He never fails to respond to our call.

The decision to depart from sin is easily followed by the decision to pursue righteousness. Repentance requires assertion, rectitude then follows naturally.

In *Sha'arei Teshuvah* we are told that Hashem sends suffering to man for his own good, in order that man should repent. As we read in *Tehillim*, 'See my affliction and my travail and forgive all my sins.' Hashem heals the soul's sickness through bodily ailments, as it is said, 'Heal my soul for I have sinned against you.' When a man receives Hashem's chastisement and improves his ways and deeds, he should rejoice in his afflictions, says Rabbeinu Yonah. They serve a lofty purpose, for through suffering he finds favor in Hashem's eyes as we have already discussed earlier.

Our Sages said 'If I had not fallen I would not have risen. If I had not sat in darkness, there would be no light for me.' Through suffering we offer sacrifices to Hashem; we give something up for Him. Thus our Patriarch Abraham offered his soul to the Almighty. He also took a ram and offered it as a burnt-offering, instead of his son. Every kind of giving contains an element of sacrifice. Since the destruction of the Temple we cannot fulfill our sacrificial obligations as before, suffering then takes the place of burnt-offerings.

We all have our ups and downs, extreme opposites, sunrise and sunset, joy and sorrow, triumph and tragedy. We cannot accept the sweet and reject the bitter if we are to find a measure of serenity and composure. We can face sorrow with defeat and rebellion, scorn and cynicism. But our cup of bitterness overflows not only because of what we have lost, but also because of what is left to us. Instead, by mobilizing our faith, courage and willingness to accept what cannot be changed, we can avoid defeat.

If the sinner is beset by hardship and trouble and willingly accepts his punishment, this will protect him against the many afflictions which might befall him. Maimonides stated that it is a positive commandment to know that there is a Primary Being, who created all that exists.

In the *Gates of Repentance*, Rabbeinu Yonah states that at the time of repentance sins are forgiven and previous righteous deeds are remembered. He also tells us that when troubles come upon man, he should commune with his heart and acknowledge that these are the results of his sins. He should 'return' to Hashem Who will be compassionate to Him.

In the area of human relations we find that when people in distress humble themselves before another person and ask for forgiveness, they will often be frowned upon by the others, who may ask him: '*Why* are you coming to me now that you are in distress?' It is among the loving kindnesses of Hashem, says Rabbeinu Yonah, that He accepts repentance resulting from affliction. He generously loves the sinner who returns to Him, for whom Hashem loves He chastises, as a father chastises his son (in whom he delights).

Rabbi Eliezer says, 'Repent one day before your death.' His disciples asked him whether a man knows on which day he will die. To this he replied: 'Let him repent today, for he might die tomorrow.' A man must perform *mitzvos* every day. Our Sages have said: If a man performs one *mitzvah* close to his death, it is considered as if he had fulfilled the whole Torah.

Our Sages have said: From all your sins you shall be purified before Hashem. Yom Kippur atones for transgressions between man and Hashem, but for transgressions between man and his neighbors Yom Kippur does not atone, until he conciliates his neighbors. One who antagonizes his friend must appease Him, for this is one of the more severe transgressions. Yom Kippur possesses a special power of purification, not present on any other day of the year. The essence of Yom Kippur does not only serve to erase transgressions, but also to purify the sinner's soul.

The Torah repeats: 'And He will return to gather you from all the nations whither Hashem, your G-d, has scattered you.' We are assured that 'if any of yours be driven out to the most distant part of heaven, from there Hashem, your G-d, will gather you, and from there He will fetch you. Hashem, your G-d, will bring you into the land which your fathers possessed and you should possess it, and He will benefit you and make you more numerous than your fathers.' For the way is cleared for him who comes to be purified and he is extended a helping hand.

Perhaps this idea can best be summed up in the prayer *Elokai Neshamah* 'The soul You gave me is pure.' Sin afflicted me and it became defiled. Heal my soul, and cure my sinfulness. Turn my heart unto You, Merciful G-d, turn me round. 'Let us return, O G-d to You, and we shall truly return. Renew our days as before!' (*Psalms*).

⊷§ Summing It Up

We have discussed most of the practical, physical and psychological aspects of our situation. Now let us consider the deeper meaning of life, the Torah way, in order to gain a more profound understanding and come to terms with our serious condition.

Let us first answer the basic question: What is man? *Tehillim* answers in the following way: L-rd, 'What is man that You regard him, or the son of man that You take account of him?... Man is like a breath, his days are like a passing shadow. You sweep men away... They are like a dream; like grass which is renewed in the morning. In the morning it flourishes and grows, but in the evening it fades and withers. The years of our life are seventy, or even by reason of special strength eighty; yet their pride is but toil and trouble. They are soon gone and we fly away... So, teach us to treasure our days that we may get wise in heart... Observe the good man, and behold the upright, for there is immortality for the man of peace... Surely Hashem will ransom my soul from the grave: He will gladly accept me. The Hashem redeems the soul of His servants. None of those who take refuge in Him will be condemned... The dust returns to the earth as it was, but the spirit returns to Hashem Who gave it.'

What is expressed here is despair at the brevity of man's life. He asks, what can be the significance of a life that withers so quickly? But faith informs us that it is Hashem who guides and will care for us.

The next question we must ask ourselves is: What is death? Is it merely the cessation of the biological function of living? Is it but a tragedy to end all other tragedies? Is it simply the disappearance of the soul, the end of consciousness, the disintegration of the body? Is it an end beyond which there is only a black void? Or is there significance, some deep and abiding meaning to death? With all of modern man's sophistication, his brilliant technological achievements, the immense progress of his science and the discovery of new ideas, he has not come one iota closer to grasping the meaning of death than did his ancestors.

In practice we must realize that what death means to the individual depends very much on what life means to him.

If life is a stage and we the poor players in purposeless entertainment, then death is only the heavy curtain that falls on the final act. The comedy is finished and life itself has no more meaning, so death has no significance.

If life is only the arithmetic progression of coincidences, the world a haphazard place without design or purpose, then death is only a useless game of chance.

If life is only nature, mindlessly spinning its complicated web, and man a high-level beast whose values are those of the jungle, aimed only at the satisfaction of animal appetites, then death is simply a reduction to nothingness, and our existence on this earth a cosmic trap.

If life is altogether absurd, with man bound and chained by circumstances, where he is never able to achieve real freedom from sin, and only dread and anguish prevail, then death is the welcome release from the chains of despair. The puppet returned to its box, the string is severed, and he is gone.

But if life is the creation of a benevolent Creator, the infusion of the Divine breath; if man is not only higher than the animal but also a "little lower than the angels"; if he has a soul, as well as a body; if his concern is not only for himself and his needs, but also for the demands made on him by Hashem and His Law; if he tempers his passions with the moral commands of Hashem, then death is a return to the Creator, the time of death set by the Creator, and life after death the only way to achieve complete perfection. For the Jew, life assumes a deeper significance if he is convinced that some day his body will be replaced, just as his soul will unite with the eternal Hashem.

For a truly religious Jew, death has a profound meaning, because he has lived his life according to the laws of the Torah. Death has meaning if life has meaning. If a man is not able to live, will he be able to die? Frightening though it may be, death is the threshold to a new world — the World to Come . . .

I know you may feel that it is very difficult, especially in your present state of health, to perceive all this. Maimonides said that man cannot have a clear picture of the After-life, and compares the earthbound creature to a blind man who cannot learn to appreciate colors merely by being given verbal instruction. Flesh and blood cannot have any precise conception of the pure spiritual bliss of the world beyond. The concept of an After-life is fundamental to the Jewish religion. The denial of an After-life means a denial of our faith. The Mishnah (*Sanhedrin* 10:1) expressly excludes all those who deny it from being rewarded the World to Come. Maimonides considers belief in Mashiach and the resurrection of the dead as two of the thirteen basic truths which every Jew is commanded to hold. These two concepts have entered our *siddur* in the prayers *Yigdal* and *Ani-Maamin*. Centuries later hundreds and thousands of Jews packed in cattle trucks on their way to the crematoria sang the *Ani-Maamin*, the affirmation of the coming of Mashiach.

Concepts such as *Gehinom* and *Gan Eden* are too complicated for discussion here.

The belief in the resurrection of the dead appears at first sight to be incredible. But when seen from Hashem's view, why should rebirth be more miraculous than birth? The complex network of tubes and glands, bones and organs, their incredibly precise functioning and unbelievably intricate human brain that guides them is surely a miracle of the first magnitude. Curiously, the miraculous object that is man takes this for granted. In his preoccupation with daily living he ignores the miracle of his own existence. The idea of rebirth may appear strange because we have never experienced a similar occur-

rence. Perhaps it is because we can be active in creating life, but cannot participate with Hashem in the re-creation of life.

Our Sages simplified this concept by comparing man to a tree that was once alive with blossoms and fruit, while now it is cold and bare in the winter. Its leaves have turned brown and fallen, its fruit rots on the ground. But in spring the warm rain comes and the sun shines. Buds sprout, green leaves appear and colorful fruit bursts from the blossoms. With the coming of spring Hashem re-creates nature. This is one of the reasons why the body and all its limbs are required to be buried in the earth and not cremated, for this expresses our faith in the future rebirth. Recreation affirms that the body is of value, because it came from Hashem and will be revived by Him.

Sometimes it may appear to you that life is unfair, because we see all too often the fact of '*tzaddik vera lo, rasha vetov lo*', the righteous who suffer and wicked who prosper. The answer our Torah gives us is that in life after death Hashem balances the scales, and rewards or punishes those who truly deserve it.

Having told you that death is natural, I don't expect you to overlook or to underestimate its ugliness and bitterness. The real bitterness is found in moral evil — sin, which mars and spoils our true nature, created as we are in the image and likeness of Hashem. Although death is the natural and expected end of life, this in no way implies that we all have to be enthusiastic about it, especially those who die young. Few people really want to die. The majority of us want to go on living, because there is so much delight in the life Hashem gave us here, in ourselves and in those we love. What should be remembered is that it is not enthusiasm so much as readiness which is all important. Death is natural, because it is the inevitable end of life. In death each of us has to render back to Hashem all that we have and all that we are. About many other experiences of life we can say that we know what they are like; I've been through it myself and I can speak from experience. But if you ask a doctor what exactly is death, he will find it difficult to answer, for nobody knows exactly what it is like. Doctors have theories about it — they have witnessed the effects of it — but they cannot understand it.

Death can never be seen as a total end if seen as the final offering of our life to Hashem. It is an inexplicable mystery.

◁§ Home Or Hospital?

I hear there is talk about your going home from the hospital? You are going to discuss this with your family and make up your mind within the next few days.

There is so much to be said for being at home, provided adequate care is available. If you know that you will be comfortable and have peace of mind, then home is the place. I am sure the hospital has left the final choice with you and your family, for this is as it should be. If you make up your mind to return to your home, you should be sure that the proper domiciliary support services are available in your area. This is very important, for you must feel confident that you will have as skilled and efficient care in your home as you have been having in hospital.

Among your main needs will be a feeling of confidence and security, the control of your physical symptoms, and an assurance of companionship; granted these, both you and your family can find a great sense of satisfaction and experience a feeling of achievement in being able to manage at home, with the support and cooperation of the various community resources.

I am sure you will derive much emotional support from being constantly with loved ones; from being in your own home. Surrounded by all that is familiar — the furniture, the view, the garden, the neighbors and the natural surroundings. You will gain much, too, from the tender loving care of your loved ones. You feel so much more part of the family rather than part of the highly organized clinical environment of the hospital world.

If you should find it difficult to decide and cannot make the final decision yourself, then let someone who knows you very well — a relative, one of your friends, your hospital or family doctor — help you to make up your mind one way or another. Probably your best guide will be your general practitioner, after satisfying himself that home care is appropriate. Whoever helps you, there must be firm agreement between your family and yourself, assessing as fully as you all can, the amount of work required and how best the various members of the family can adjust to the circumstances. Should your family be anxious about having you home, fearing they might be inadequate or unable to cope, the doctor or the nurse will be only too pleased to explain what will be needed, and how best they can deal with various aspects of your illness. Much, of course, depends on the nursing support available.

Unfortunately there is not always the liaison there should be between the hospital and the community, depending of course where you live, as some are much better served than others ...

It may be helpful to you if I mention some of the persons who should be involved in caring for you at home, and explain what their function is. Your home doctor should of course be in constant touch with the hospital authorities. If he is one of a group-practice or if there is a health clinic in your area, the health visitor, social worker and community nurse will be attached to his team. The health visitor will advise on your home care and act as liaison between the hospital and the general practitioner. She should be involved in preparatory plans for your homecoming, and have already visited your family and discussed the necessary preparations with them. There will also be the community or district nurses who will be responsible for your nursing care. If necessary, they will administer your pain-relieving drugs and whatever treatment the doctor prescribes for you. They will also be able to provide special equipment you may need, e.g., backrest, a rubber ring to sit on if an ordinary armchair is uncomfortable, rubber mats, drawsheets, commodes, bedpans or urinals. You may need a feeding-cup or a wool sheepskin. The sheepskin can be machine or hand washed and spin dried. Shaped woolen pads are also available for your heels and elbows. Should you be incontinent, special incontinence pads and sheets can be provided. In some areas there may be soiled laundry services available. The nurse can also show your family how best they can look after you and give them some useful and practical hints — keeping a special eye on pressure areas; how best to lift you up should you slip down in bed; and seeing to the care of your mouth, if necessary. She can perhaps arrange for your family or relatives to have a short break from the sickroom. She can also give them advice on any special diets and how best they can be prepared for you.

Should there be any financial difficulties or emotional problems, the social worker will be a most valuable member of the caring team. It might be possible to arrange for night-nurses, if only on a part-time basis. The night-sitter service can relieve the members of your family, should it be necessary for them to sit up with you at night. They can give you the special nourishment, adjust your pillows or your airring and provide you with sedatives, should they have been prescribed by your doctor.

As I already mentioned before, these services are all right in theory, but I found that in practice they don't work very well. That is why I suggest that every possible arrangement should be made so that you receive the best care available, not relying too heavily on the local authority provisions.

In cases where there is no immediate family, the rabbi will be visiting you regularly. As well as reciting *Tehillim* he can also bring some moral support to the members of the family. He may also arrange, especially in cases where there is no family, for community members to do the shopping, help and arrange for meals to be brought in, without intrusion into your family life or personal privacy. The companionship of friends will serve to break the monotony of a long day or restless night ...

If you decide to return home, don't let the family spoil you. Let them see that you can still be a vital part of their family, sharing in its interest and involved in its decisions. You may even be able to participate in the everyday running of the home, in helping with the household chores, and in keeping the children amused, for example. Dependent upon how you feel, you can do some occupational therapy, perhaps paint, sew or do some embroidery. In all these various ways you can be yourself while at home and continue to be an important member of the household and its management.

Whenever the need should arise, always remember that you can return to the hospital, even if only for a short period of time. What we really need are some special units, acting as halfway houses between hospital and home; there are so very few of them. Fortunately, there are now more hospices being set up in various centers, throughout the country ... Some important advantages of specialized units are that they are small, they create much local interest and concern and the standard of nursing care is usually very high, being carried out with a deep sense of vocation and dedication. All these services I have mentioned can help to improve the quality of life, for all who are involved in your care will be serving as a community to help express the fact that life goes on — ordinary continuing life — life of which sicknesses and death are only one part!

◄§ Your Material Affairs

You may recall that in a previous talk we were reminding ourselves to prepare for death. A sense of completion can only be achieved when we have put our affairs in order and made adequate provision for those we leave behind. As true Torah Jews we should, as far as possible, make sure that both our worldly affairs and our spiritual life are in proper order, so that we are never totally unprepared for death when it comes. Everyone should make a will and ideally it should have been done while we enjoyed good health. Many people are frightened to make a will as long as they are well, because they are superstitious and believe that by arranging their affairs they help to bring about death more quickly. Much mental strain and quarrels could be avoided if only people would prepare properly. If, however, you are one of the people who have delayed, you can now go about remedying the omission.

A will is quite legal if drawn up simply on a piece of paper and signed and witnessed. A printed form can be purchased at a stationer's. It is, however, always safer to have legal help which will eliminate all risk of misunderstanding and errors. It is well worth the cost of a lawyer's fee to have everything drawn up in a correct legal manner. [A rabbi should also be consulted to ensure that the will meets halachic standards.] You will, of course, have to make up your mind how you want your property to be divided. It will be helpful to draw up a list of those people whom you would see as beneficiaries. There may be specific items of particular sentimental value, belongings you wish to leave to certain members after your death, or you may wish to allocate a sum of money to each of them. There may be certain charities you have supported throughout the years and now there is an opportunity for you to bequeath them part of your estate. It is necessary for your family or executors to know where your will and safe are kept and the deeds of your house. It is also necessary for them to know where your keys are kept and how you wish your personal belongings, papers, clothing and personal things of sentimental value to be disposed and distributed.

You will derive much satisfaction in making sure your practical affairs are now in order and that provisions have been made for your family and friends, just like our Patriarch Jacob.

⋐§ Grief

Judaism, with its long history of dealing with the soul of man, has wisely devised graduated periods during which the mourner may express his grief, and release with calculated regularity the built up tensions caused by bereavement. The Jewish religion provides a beautifully structured approach to mourning.

The insight of the Torah, together with his accumulated religious experience of centuries, has taught the Jew how best to manage the grief situation. Psychiatry has revealed how essential it is to express rather than repress grief, to talk about one's loss with friends and companions, to move step by step from inactivity to activity. The Jewish rules of mourning remind us that the ancient teachers of Judaism often had great insight into human nature and its needs. Traditional Judaism had the wisdom to devise many regulations to help the mourner recover from grief, which resemble the counsel of contemporary psychologists, although Judaism did not possess the tools for scientific experiment and systematic study of the mind. The Jewish tradition has thus provided for a gradual release from grief. It has ordained five successive periods of mourning, each with its own laws, governing the expression of grief and the process of return to normal society. They fit in perfectly with the normal cycle of bereavement.

The first period, *Aninus*, is that between death and burial, during which time shock and despair are most intense. At this time, not only social obligations but even major religious requirements are canceled, in recognition of the mourner's troubled mind. At this stage of the grief — experience shows those who stand by may not know what to say. The important thing is not to say something, but just to be there, to share the experience.

The second stage consists of the first three days following burial, devoted to weeping and lamentation. During this time visiting the mourner is usually discouraged, for it is too early to comfort the mourner when the wound is so fresh. During this second stage of grief the mourner may feel numb, as if under a partial anaesthetic. Things seem unreal. There is a loss of feeling. We walk around in a daze unable to think clearly. It is generally doubtful whether it is wise to administer heavy sedatives to those in grief. Often we would understand more and feel better later if we were given less medication. Heavier sedation than necessary is an injustice to the bereaved, since it interferes with the process of recovery from grief.

Next comes the last four days of the *shivah*, the seven days following burial. During this time the mourner emerges from the stage of intense grief to a new state of mind, in which he is prepared to talk about his loss, and accept comfort from family and friends. The inner numbness caused by the death now begins to thaw. In this stage there is usually a conflict between reality and fantasy. Frequently in this situation people say: It seems as if he had just gone away and will come back.

A boy of seven and a boy of nine were playing with their father just a month after their mother died. In their play the father hurt the younger boy and he cried 'Mommy! Mommy! Make Daddy stop.' In the silence that followed, they all realized that Mommy was not there. The boy's mind was still moving between fantasy and reality.

During this period there may be some guilt feeling. The grieving person may say, 'If only I had tried a different doctor! If only we had taken him to another hospital, then it would not have happened.' We should come to understand that these are futile negative thoughts. We do not have to feel guilty, since everything is decreed by Hashem Who decides every step in our life, as it is said: 'We do not hurt a finger, without this being prompted from Above.'

The fourth stage is the *sheloshim*, the thirty days following burial (which includes *shivah*). The mourner is encouraged to leave the house after the *shivah* and gradually to rejoin society, though he cannot yet resume his full normal social life. There is generally a loss of feeling and a certain degree of apathy. The bereaved cling to the daily routine of prescribed activities, but these activities do not proceed in the automatic fashion characteristic of normal work, but require much greater effort. The bereaved person is surprised to find how large a part of his customary activity was done in relation to the deceased and has now lost its significance. Especially the habits of social interaction — meeting friends, making conversation, joint activities no longer appeal to him or her.

The fifth and last stage is the twelve-month period, the year of *avelus* for parents (which includes the *sheloshim*), during which things return to normal and business once again becomes routine. But the inner feelings of the mourner are still sore because of the rupture of his relationship with the parent. The pursuit of entertainment and amusement is curtailed. At the close of this last stage, the twelve-month period, one should be in a position to resume normal life.

There is no norm for mourning and no norm for adaptation, nor can there be a definite time limit for either. The time generally allocated to the various phases and to the whole process of mourning in books on the subject is too short to suit the needs of many mourners. One year may be an ample period of time for the completion of the mourning process, though there are many who after the loss of their partners, suffered episodes of depression and despair for well over two years. Yet later they made exceptionally good adaptations to a new life. Even then, periods of despair and grief may recur on family occasions such as birthdays, anniversaries or illness. These recurrences should not be regarded as pathological. The only valid criteria for pathological grief is when the mourner is unable to cope with his life. Physicians are familiar with means for alleviating pain and aiding the healing power of the wound. There has been great uncertainty in our time as to how far and in what way help can be given. Support from family, friends, and neighbors is of course most effective. Medical or psychotherapeutic help will be required only in exceptional cases; but in view of the loneliness and isolation of individuals in many places, every mourner requires extra sympathy and support from the people around him.

The mourning process, like the process of physical healing, involves the healing of a wound. One of the big obstacles to overcoming grief seems to be the fact that many patients try to avoid the expression of grief, which is very important. They do not feel like sharing it with others. This does not mean that they should become hysterical or lose control, but that shedding tears and showing grief is a normal and often necessary part of the healing process. Emotions ought not to be dammed up inside, or there will be a building up of tension, causing many additional problems.

Many people, after experiencing profound grief, come to reaffirm life. Then their lives are absorbed by a new family or a new community experience, or a new charitable involvement. Their days are filled with good deeds which is the best antidote to grief and depression. Sharing other people's problems is the best way of overcoming one's own.

When death strikes our homes it brings to an end a physical life. But the spirit is mightier than the grave. The thoughts and emotions, the ideals and attitudes remain, and their influence survives in the minds of those left behind.

We must acknowledge that Hashem knows our innermost secrets, that He rewards and punishes us, that He knows what is best for us and that all His actions are for the eventual benefit of the whole of mankind. It is only by virtue of the acceptance of death as the just end of life that life on earth can be lived to the full. When we recognize that only the Creator of the universe understands the design of His creation, we can make successful, fresh adjustments. Thus we recite in the words of the *kaddish*: "Magnified and sanctified be His great Name in the world which He created according to His will." How can our limited intellect understand His exalted greatness? If tragedy strikes, if our families are beset by difficult circumstances, we must keep our strong faith and believe that the Judge of the whole world has acted justly. It is this strong faith, and this alone, that will enable the mourner to resume a full life.

❊　❊　❊

We cannot see what lies outside
Our little patch of light,
We cannot grasp the thing beyond
Our hearing and our sight.
We can't discern the shining souls
Of those we call the dead,
Walking on the road with us
A few short steps ahead.

One must go and one be left,
Ask why should it be?
We cannot hope to understand
So deep a mystery.
Life and death march hand in hand,
The Almighty is our Boss
We cannot have the joys
And escape the pain and loss.

Mourn not beloved ones
Whom Hashem has called away.
In his own good time
We'll meet again someday.
Going on in front of us
Beyond our range of view
They walk in glory and towards
Horizons bright and new.

There is One who knows our troubles,
One who understands,
That is our loved Hashem
You can leave things in His hands.
He will strengthen and will heal you
If to Him you turn
In the wilderness of sorrow
There is so much to learn.
Sharing other people's losses
And the friends you find
Help to fill the aching blank
Your loved one left behind.

❧ Life!

by Fradel Berger

I value it
Treasure it
Reverence it
Glory in it
This precious force called LIFE!
This sweet sweet life
Full of lovely things
Thoughts with wings
Love and friends
Gold where the rainbow ends
Birds in flight
Serenading the light
The restless sea
Music, poetry
A cozy home
Joyous laughter
Flowers children
Smiles following after
Meadows and streams
Trees
Observing their seasons
For Hashem's wise reasons
Roses bright and fair
Perfuming the air
Purim's joys
Chanuka's toys
The sun at dawn
Like heavenly fire
Rising higher and higher
Weddings *Simchos* oh what pleasures
Torah from *Cheder* what treasures
Grumble not should I
At life's darker side
When events collide
Disharmony pain
Misfortune's chain
From Hashem's reign